DATE DUE

DEMCO 38-296

Shadowed Ground

Kenneth E. Foote

Shadowed
Ground

∾

AMERICA'S

LANDSCAPES *of*

VIOLENCE

and TRAGEDY

University of Texas Press / Austin

A version of Chapter 8 was previously published as "Stigmata of National Identity: Exploring the Cosmography of America's Civil Religion," in *Person, Place and Thing: Interpretive and Empirical Essays in Cultural Geography*, ed. Shue Tuck Wong (Baton Rouge: Louisiana State University, Department of Geography and Anthropology, *Geoscience and Man* 31, 1992), 379–402.

Requests for permission to reproduce material from this work should be sent to Permissions, University of Texas Press, Box 7819, Austin, TX 78713-7819.

♾ The paper used in this publication meets the minimum requirements of American National Standard for Library Sciences—Permanence of Paper for Printed Library Material, ANSI Z39.48-1984.

Library of Congress Cataloging-in-Publication Data

Foote, Kenneth E., 1955–
    Shadowed ground : America's landscapes of violence
and tragedy / Kenneth E. Foote. — 1st ed.
        p.   cm.
    Includes bibliographical references and index.
    ISBN 0-292-72499-3 (cloth : alk. paper). —
ISBN 0-292-72500-0 (pbk. : alk. paper)
    1. Historic sites—Social aspects—United States.
2. Violence—United States—History.   3. Disasters—
United States—History.   4. United States—History,
Local.   I. Title.
E159.F68   1997
973—dc20   96-41081

To my parents,
Doris and Harold Foote

Contents

Shadowed Ground

A Landscape of
Violence and Tragedy

This book began in Salem, Massachusetts. Many years and miles have passed since my first visit, but it was in Salem where I first began to think about how tragedy and violence have shaped the American landscape. The idea came to me almost by accident. I had driven north from Boston to visit some of Salem's eighteenth-century homes, the town's legacy of the era of the Yankee trader. At the time I was only vaguely aware of Salem's more distant colonial past and the witchcraft trials of the seventeenth century. For some reason, however, it was the witchcraft episode that caught my attention that day. I suppose I had expected to find it noted distinctly among the historical markers and plaques that usually grace towns like Salem. I was puzzled to discover that very few mention the events of 1692. Most of the town's efforts toward historical self-aggrandizement center on the area's maritime history and its glory years in the eighteenth and nineteenth centuries. There is the Witch Museum, housed in a former church, but it is less a museum than a small auditorium for a sound-and-light show that tells the story of the witchcraft trials in a series of vivid tableaux.

At some point during the day, I realized that I had come across no indication of the places where the accused witches were executed. One of the victims—the unfortunate Giles Corey—had been crushed to death, and the general location of his pressing, near the site of the colonial jail,

Figure 1-1. Gallows Hill in Salem, Massachusetts. All but one of the victims of the witchcraft scare of 1692 were hanged here, but the exact location of the executions is unknown.

was noted. The other nineteen victims were hanged, however. On asking about the location of their execution, I was directed toward a low rise of ground to the south of town called Gallows Hill. In the seventeenth century it lay just outside Salem Town. Today it is dotted with modest homes, except where building is impossible along its craggy slopes (Figure 1-1). Somewhere on this hill nineteen victims of the witchcraft scare were executed, but no one knows exactly where.

Perhaps I was surprised because other, far less significant events are commonly marked in detail and often with great flourish throughout the United States. I am speaking not solely of the ubiquitous roadside markers but also of the thousands of substantial monuments and memorials that pay tribute to the nation's formative events, heroes, and martyrs—Plymouth Rock, the Statue of Liberty, the Washington Monument, and the Lincoln Memorial. There was nothing of this sort in Salem to mark the witchcraft episode. No official record was kept of the site of the executions, although many of the court and colonial records have survived, and inferences about the location are based on the sketchiest of word-of-mouth descriptions passed from generation to generation.[1]

I found it remarkable that the location of such an important event in the history of Salem and the nation not only was unmarked but had been forgotten entirely. Shame certainly played a part. The witchcraft scare lasted less than a year, from January to September 1692, and the proceedings were almost immediately called into question by the colony's legal and religious officials. Particular exception was taken to the use of spectral—that is, supernatural—evidence in court. Furthermore the young girls who had made most of the accusations began to recant their testimony shortly after the executions. People recognized quickly that something had gone significantly wrong, so much so that the Salem episode effectively ended the prosecution of witchcraft in the colonies. Historians looking back on the events of 1692 now argue that the scare was a direct product of other tensions in the community and that the divide that separated the "witches" from their accusers was not supernatural but rather social.[2]

Given the sense of shame cast over the community by the trials and executions, there could have been little desire to call attention to the site of the executions. The saying "out of sight, out of mind" might aptly describe what took place. Geographer David Lowenthal, reflecting on the meanings people ascribe to place and landscape, has observed that "features recalled with pride are apt to be safeguarded against erosion and vandalism; those that reflect shame may be ignored or expunged from the landscape."[3] With this idea in mind, I began to visit other sites of tragedy and violence in the United States and around the world. Indeed, soon after my first trip to Salem, I found myself in Berlin before the reunification of Germany. There I came across similar places—Nazi sites like the Gestapo headquarters and Reichs chancellery—that have lain vacant since just after World War II and seem to be scarred permanently by shame.

I quickly realized that recognizing issues of shame and pride was only a first step in understanding what had happened to these places. I found that many acts of violence are not expunged from landscape but rather transformed into monuments and memorials. In Germany and other nations that lived under the Nazi reign of terror, the remains of concentration camps have been safeguarded against erosion and vandalism and shaped into powerful reminders of the Holocaust, although often hotly contested ones (Figure 1-2).[4] Furthermore vio-

Figure 1-2. Remains of the rail siding that led into the Auschwitz concentration camp. Many Holocaust sites have been transformed into lasting memorials to the victims of Nazi terror. Other sites, such as the Gestapo headquarters in Berlin, remain so stigmatized by their association with the Nazis that they have lain vacant for over fifty years. Photograph by Lisa Nungesser.

lence and tragedy have the power to transform landscape and alter its meaning over long periods of time. I now maintain that Salem has never completely resolved how to view the witchcraft scare within its longer history. The question has always been whether to ignore the episode as a brief, shameful anomaly, to recognize it as a valid part of Salem's history, or to honor it as a turning point in American religion. These problems of interpretation moved into the foreground of debate in Salem in the 1980s with the approach of the witchcraft tercentenary in 1992. Three hundred years after the fact, the question of how to mark the anniversary might have been a minor concern. On the contrary, heated public debate arose over the proper course of action. A proposal to erect a public monument to the victims of the witchcraft episode met with resistance. Opponents argued that it was best to let the tercentenary pass unremarked. Why, they asked, should

Salem wish to continue to draw public attention to such a shameful event? Over these objections, a memorial was unveiled in 1992 paying tribute to the victims of the witchcraft hysteria. The site of the executions remained unmarked, but by erecting a public memorial, Salem was perhaps, after three hundred years, coming to terms with its past.

The more I thought about Salem and other similar sites, the more I became convinced that I had to look beyond the question of why some tragedies inspire memorials, whereas others are ignored or effaced. This was a first step, but I also had to consider the larger issue of how people view violence and tragedy over long periods of time and develop a sense of their past. I realized that I had to look beyond the immediate aftermath of violence to consider how people, in the long term, wanted to remember each event. The key seemed to lie in understanding how people interpreted the events retrospectively as unavoidable accidents, heroic battles, instances of martyrdom, or senseless acts of violence. I noticed repeatedly that sites were transformed to reflect these retrospective assessments. Drawing again on Lowenthal, I recognized that "the tangible past is altered mainly to make history conform with memory. Memory not only conserves the past but adjusts recall to current needs. Instead of remembering exactly what was, we make the past intelligible in the light of present circumstances."[5] This issue lies at the heart of understanding how these places change. The sites have been inscribed with messages that speak to the way individuals, groups, and entire societies wish to interpret their past. When "read" carefully, these places also yield insight into how societies come to terms with violence and tragedy. The role of violence in American society is a fiercely contested issue, and it seemed reasonable to me, as a geographer, to look to the landscape for evidence about attitudes toward violence.

As a geographer I could not help but notice that the sites themselves seemed to play an active role in their own interpretation. What I mean is that the evidence of violence left behind often pressures people, almost involuntarily, to begin debate over meaning. The sites, stained by the blood of violence and covered by the ashes of tragedy, force people to face squarely the meaning of an event. The barbed wire and brick crematoria of the concentration camps cannot be ignored; they demand interpretation. A bare stretch of ground in Berlin, once the Reichssicherheitshauptamt, the headquarters of the Nazi state security, or Gestapo, compels the visitor to reflect on genocide in the twentieth century. In case after case I found that the question of what to do with the site actually precipitates debate and forces competing interpretations into the open. Set in motion is a complex iterative process in which place spurs debate, debate leads to interpretation, and interpretation reshapes place over and over again.

In selecting examples for study, I began first to consider some of the great tragedies of the past. Every society in every period has borne witness to war, disaster, violence, and tragedy. If I had wanted to study a single period, the twentieth century would have provided more than enough examples. This century alone has produced killing fields unparalleled in history, places scarred by tragedy whose names come to mind all too easily: Verdun, the Somme, Guernica, Auschwitz, Dresden, Hiroshima, the Soviet gulags, My Lai, and many more. But attitudes toward violence and tragedy are closely aligned with cultural values. However rich the examples worldwide, the cultural specificity of response to violence and tragedy cautioned against ready comparison of events drawn from vastly different cultures and widely separated periods.

I decided instead to focus on a single nation, the United States. From the hardships of early settlement up to the present day, few periods of its history have been free from tragedy and turmoil. The first "lost" colony on Roanoke Island was an indication of things to come, and over time Americans became intimately acquainted with tragedy and violence. Conflict between the Europeans and Native Americans began early, as did frictions among the European groups competing for territory and influence in the New World. The fears and uncertainties of the seventeenth century were a prelude to those of the eighteenth, a century that culminated in the violent struggle for independence. From nationhood onward the United States experienced wave on wave of war, civil strife, natural calamity, accident, assassination, and crime. The sites of some of the major events, such as the well-marked battlefields of the Revolutionary and Civil Wars, are known to many and attract thousands of visitors every year. There are many other sites that have been touched by tragedy and are not nearly so well known. As the United States moved through the upheavals of industrialization and urbanization and faced the pressures of massive immigration and internal migration, it experienced repeated bursts of violence: the Fetterman Massacre and massacres at Sand Creek, the Little Bighorn, Wounded Knee, and Rock Springs; the strikes and riots of Haymarket, Pullman, Homestead, Ludlow, and Lattimer Mines; and even the urban and campus protests of the 1960s and 1970s. Interspersed among these peaks of violence are hundreds of accidental tragedies and natural disasters.

In this book I consider events from all these categories, from sites that reflect the turmoil of America's economic, social, and political development to places touched by natural disasters and accidents. I by no means survey *all* sites, but I do consider the scenes of some of the nation's worst instances of tragedy and violence, including those associated most closely with the national "past," such as the Revolutionary and Civil Wars. Also included are mass murders, political assassinations, violent labor and race riots, transportation accidents, fires, floods, and explosions. I think that the comparison of such a wide variety of sites can make comparisons difficult, but taken together, all such places offer insights into how society deals with violence and adversity, how people create, sustain, and break emotional attachments to place and landscape, and how Americans view and interpret the past.

The Impress of Tragedy and Violence on Landscape

With so much written about violence and tragedy in American society and history, I find it remarkable that, apart from material on battlefields, little has been written about the fate of the sites themselves. This is unfortunate not just because these places often have interesting histories. Rather, the stories of these sites offer insight into how people grapple with the meaning of tragedy and reveal much about attitudes toward violence. I would never claim that any single site tells the whole story, but patterns do emerge among the many places I have visited and studied. The changes I observed seemed to fall along a continuum that I have divided into four categories: sanctification, designation, rectification, and obliteration. All four outcomes can result in major modifications of the landscape, but of very different sorts.

Sanctification and obliteration occupy the extremes of the continuum. Sanctification occurs when events are seen to hold some lasting positive meaning that people wish to remember—a lesson in heroism or perhaps a sacrifice for community. A memorial or monument is the result. Obliteration results from particularly shameful events people would prefer to forget—for example, a mass murder or gangster killing.

As a consequence all evidence is destroyed or effaced. Designation and rectification fall between these extremes. Designation, or the marking of a site, simply denotes that something "important" has happened there. Rectification involves removing the signs of violence and tragedy and returning a site to use, implying no lasting positive or negative meaning. A brief overview of these outcomes will help to explain the factors that shape the impress of violence and tragedy on landscape.

SANCTIFICATION

Sanctification involves the creation of what geographers term a "sacred" place—a site set apart from its surroundings and dedicated to the memory of an event, person, or group. Sanctification almost always involves the construction of a durable marker, either some sort of monument or memorial or a garden, park, or building that is intended to be maintained in perpetuity. As I employ the term, sanctification always requires the site's ritual dedication to the memory of an event itself or to a martyr, hero, or group of victims. I use the term *sacred* to refer to sites that are publicly consecrated or widely venerated rather than those owned or maintained by a particular religious group. Formal consecration is a prerequisite of sanctification. That is, there must be a ceremony that includes an explicit statement of the site's significance and an explanation of why the event should be remembered. Sanctification demonstrates most clearly the relationship of landscape and memory. These places are transformed into monuments that serve as reminders or warnings, the function indicated by the Latin root of the word *monument*. The site is transformed into a symbol intended to remind future generations of a virtue or sacrifice or to warn them of events to be avoided.

The sanctification of the Gettysburg National Military Cemetery (Figure 1-3) is a good example of this process. The Battle of Gettysburg in July 1863 claimed the lives of thousands of soldiers, not all of whom could be identified or transported home for burial. A cemetery was created on the battlefield, and Abraham Lincoln attended the consecration to deliver his Gettysburg Address at the close of the ceremony.

> Four score and seven years ago, our fathers brought forth upon this continent a new nation, conceived in liberty and dedicated to the proposition that all men are created equal.

Now we are engaged in a great civil war, testing whether that nation—or any nation, so conceived and so dedicated—can long endure.

We are met on a great battle-field of that war. We are met to dedicate a portion of it as the final resting-place of those who have given their lives that that nation might live.

It is altogether fitting and proper that we should do this.

But, in a larger sense, we cannot dedicate, we cannot consecrate, we cannot hallow, this ground. The brave men, living and dead, who struggled here, have consecrated it, far above our power to add or to detract.

The world will very little note nor long remember what we say here; but it can never forget what they did here.

It is for us, the living, rather, to be dedicated, here, to the unfinished work that they have thus far so nobly carried on. It is rather for us to be here dedicated to the great task remaining before us; that from these honored dead we take increased devotion to that cause for which they here gave the last full measure of devotion; that we here highly resolve that these dead shall not have died in vain; that the nation shall, under God, have a new birth of freedom, and that government of people, by the people, for the people, shall not perish from the earth.[6]

Few sites are consecrated with such eloquence, but all are interpreted in the same fashion, in words that capture the essence of the sacrifice and explain why the event is worthy of remembrance. Sanctified places can often be recognized by their distinctive appearance in the landscape. First, they are often clearly bounded from the surrounding environment and marked with great specificity as to what happened where. Second, sanctified sites are usually carefully maintained for long periods of time—decades, generations, and centuries. Third, sanctification typically involves a change of ownership, often a transfer from private to public stewardship. Fourth, sanctified sites frequently attract continued ritual commemoration, such as annual memorial services or pilgrimage. Fifth, sanctified sites often attract additional and sometimes even unrelated monuments and memorials through a process of accretion. That is, once sanctified, these sites seem to act as foci for other commemorative efforts. All these characteristics serve to define these sacred sites as *fields of care*, portions of the

Figure 1-3. The National Cemetery at Gettysburg, Pennsylvania. President Lincoln attended the dedication of the cemetery in November 1863 four months after the battle. His Gettysburg Address is a concise statement of reasons for the cemetery's sanctification.

landscape that are set apart and tended with special attention. Such sites arise in a variety of situations.

The Heroic Struggle

Sanctified places arise from battles, such as Gettysburg, that mark the traumas of nationhood and from events that have given shape to national identity. Although the commemoration of such sites often stems from a need to honor fallen heroes and innocent victims, I will argue that some tragedies attract added attention because they seem to illustrate ethical or moral lessons that transcend the toll of lives. In essence the victims died for a cause, and the cause, rather than the victims, spurs sanctification. In the aftermath of tragedies, great tensions can arise over interpretation—whether the events are to be viewed in a positive or negative light and whether they illustrate some high moral principle or lesson in human conduct. The "victor" usually gains the first say, although not necessarily the final word. The Civil War prison camp at Andersonville, Georgia, was the worst of its kind. By reason of the conditions there, its commandant was executed for a war crime after the Civil War, the only soldier to suffer this fate. Originally viewed as emblematic of Southern atrocities and marked accordingly, Andersonville has through the years been reinterpreted as a monument to American prisoners of war of all conflicts and eras.

In the case of wartime tragedy, the cause of the conflict usually serves to define the principle that is commemorated. The cause may be so clear that there is little debate over the need for sanctification, and consecration may begin before the war is concluded. This occurred at several Civil War battlefields, such as Gettysburg. In the case of an unpopular war, such as Vietnam, acrimonious disputes may ensue, since the cause of sacrifice may be interpreted in several ways. Attempts at sanctification may proceed slowly, if at all, often at first on the private initiative of just a few individuals who are convinced of the event's significance.

Many events other than war generate struggles over meaning. Some of the best examples involve the assertion of rights by minority groups. After riots or massacres, the minority group will assert that the tragedy illustrates principles worth remembering, only to find itself opposed by a more powerful or larger group wishing to ignore the event. The conflict over meaning—and sanctification—becomes a political struggle among social, religious, and ethnic factions. The struggle for control and interpretation of the site may continue for decades. The Haymarket Riot of 1886 engendered such a struggle in Chicago between business and labor. The riot produced martyrs for both sides. The business community claimed as martyrs the police who died in the mêlée, calling them "Protectors of Chicago," even though the police officers helped to precipitate the riot and may have shot some of their fellow officers in the chaos that followed. Eight anarchists were tried and four executed in one of the great miscarriages of justice in U.S. history. These victims became martyrs to the cause of labor. The business community claimed the site of the bombing to erect a policemen's monument and prevented labor from memorializing its martyrs within the city limits (Figure 1-4). The memorial to the

Figure 1-4. The 1962 anniversary of the Haymarket Riot in Chicago. The monument was raised on the site of the 1886 riot and dedicated to the police—"The Protectors of Chicago"—by Chicago's business community. The protesters and labor organizers were not allowed to build a monument on this site or anywhere else in Chicago. This monument was the subject of continuing vandalism, however, and the statue was moved to a protected indoor location at the police academy in the 1970s. Photograph ICHi-19831 courtesy of the Chicago Historical Society.

Figure 1-5. The monument raised at Waldheim Cemetery in Forest Park, Illinois, to the Haymarket martyrs—the labor organizers who were falsely accused and executed for the Haymarket Riot of 1886. Their burial at Waldheim Cemetery was one of the largest funerals in Chicago's history. They are buried here, outside the Chicago city limits.

labor martyrs was placed at their grave in Waldheim Cemetery, across the city line in Forest Park (Figure 1-5). Labor was unable to assert a claim to the site of the riot, but it did not let the business community's plans go unmolested. The policemen's monument attracted vandalism for decades and eventually had to be moved indoors to the police academy after being destroyed twice. All that remains at the site is the defaced pedestal of the police monument.

The labor movement is rich in examples of this sort. Struggles to sanctify the sites of some of the worst massacres of the late nineteenth and early twentieth centuries succeeded only gradually as the cause of labor gained widespread recognition. Similar battles have been fought over the interpretation of sites associated with the suppression of Native American populations, particularly the sites of the Wounded Knee Massacre and the Battle of the Little Bighorn, and both are still in debate.[7] The civil rights movement has also succeeded in marking a limited number of sites associated with its struggle, often in the face of great opposition. Even events such as the internment of Japanese American citizens during World War II and violent attacks on ethnic groups such as Chinese immigrants have raised difficult issues of commemoration and sanctification. These struggles are the subject of Chapter 9, along with other events whose meaning is still in contention. In addition events such as the shootings at Kent State University and Jackson State University in 1970 illustrate political competition over the meaning of contested places.

Martyrs and Heroes

In the United States death by violence or accident rarely inspires sanctification, unless the individuals are great leaders, heroes, or martyrs. Regardless of whether greatness is judged by reputation, position, or accomplishment, there arises a sense that the achievements of these individuals demand commemoration. The general principle is apparent in the fact that, of the four United States presidents who have been assassinated, the sites of the assassinations of three of these are marked, and the fourth, Garfield's, was marked for about twenty-five years. Furthermore, prominent monuments have been erected to each of the four in the cities where they were attacked. The Lincoln monument is the western terminus of the Mall in Washington, whereas the Garfield monument is at the other end, at the foot of the capitol grounds; both are within walking distance of the assassination sites. The McKinley monument was erected in Buffalo's Niagara Square, the symbolic heart of the city, and the Kennedy cenotaph lies in a similarly significant site in Dallas, two blocks from Dealey Plaza in the Dallas County Historical Plaza.

Other political leaders can gain the same level of attention, and nowadays commemoration is almost routine. Similar attention can focus on other prominent individuals, however, including celebrities. John Lennon's death at the entrance to his New York City residence led to the creation of a small memorial garden—Strawberry Fields— immediately opposite the site in Central Park. As I mention in Chapter 2, whether an individual deserves commemoration is often the subject of heated debate. Tension arises between defenders and detractors of the person's reputation. Almost fifty years were required for the Lincoln monument to be planned and built. During this period Lincoln's standing as one of the most vilified presidents in history changed radically.[8] Lincoln, whose election spurred Southern secession, was termed one of America's "immortals" when his memorial was dedicated in 1922. On the other hand, Garfield's status has been compromised by his short, four-month tenure as president. This is reflected in the marking of his assassination site. For twenty-five years the site was marked in the lobby of the Baltimore and Potomac Railroad station where the attack took place. When the station was demolished, the small star was removed and never replaced. When the National Gallery of Art was later erected on this site, no attempt was made to restore the marker.

A Sense of Community Loss

Sanctification can ensue when communities are struck by accidents and tragedies such as natural disasters, fires, explosions, crashes, and other accidents. In these cases sanctification is a natural response to the grief of community loss. The creation of memorials both honors the victims of the disaster and helps the community to mourn. Relatively few tragedies result in sanctification, however. Many factors are involved, but the most important is whether the tragedy touches a single, relatively homogeneous, self-identified community, one that comes to view the tragedy as a common, public loss. Members of such communities share a sense of identity based on civic pride, ethnic or religious affiliation, and occupation that encourages them to view the disaster as a loss to the group as a whole rather than as losses to isolated individuals and families.

Most disasters strike heterogeneous populations whose allegiances are divided among many separate groups. Losses may be great, but the victims are not identified with one group and, as a consequence, are mourned individually and memorialized at the grave site. In cases where accidents draw victims from a group or community with a sense of identity, however, a large public memorial is usually consecrated, either at the disaster site itself or at a site of civic prominence. The memorial to the unknown dead at Johnstown, Pennsylvania, is a good example (Figure 1-6). The flood of 1889 was one of the largest "natural" disasters in American history and claimed over two thousand lives. The flood became significant not just for its size but because it devastated a fast-growing industrial community with a strong sense of civic identity. The memorial represents an effort by the entire community to recognize its loss. Although I say more about disasters of this sort in Chapters 3 and 5, I want to note two points here. First, the magnitude of a disaster does have a bearing on whether it will be memorialized, but is only one consideration. A sense of community loss may arise from events that claim far fewer lives than the Johnstown Flood did if the victims belong to a group with a strong sense of self-identity. I present a wide range of events of both sorts in Chapter 3, including the Cherry, Illinois, coal mine fire of 1909, the New London, Texas, school explosion of 1937, the Our Lady of the Angels School fire of 1958 in Chicago, and the Collinwood, Ohio, school fire of 1908, as well as some natural disasters such as the Xenia, Ohio, tornado of 1974. Second, certain types of "accidents" I discuss in Chapter 5 leave few marks on the landscape even when they devastate a community. These accidents are, so to speak, "explained away" and result in rectification, even when they claim incredible numbers of lives.

DESIGNATION

Designation is closely related to sanctification in that a site is marked for its significance, but this response omits rituals of consecration. In essence, designated sites are marked but not sanctified. They arise from events that are viewed as important but somehow lacking the

Figure 1-6. The monument to the unknown dead of the Johnstown Flood of 1889 at Grandview Cemetery in Johnstown,
Pennsylvania. Here the community banded together to dedicate a memorial to the almost eight hundred victims who
could not be identified. The town closed on the day of the
dedication, 1 June 1892, and almost 10,000 citizens gathered at the cemetery for the ceremony.

heroic or sacrificial qualities associated with sanctified places. Creating a park, erecting a sign, or building a marker are ways of designating a site, but such a site gains little long-term attention and is rarely the focus of regular commemorative rituals. Usually there is agreement as to why the site is important, but these reasons are rarely the subject of an elaborate dedicatory address: designated places are unveiled rather than dedicated. Along the continuum running from sanctification to obliteration, designation lies squarely between active veneration and direct effacement. This is a pivotal position, and designation is sometimes best viewed as a transitional phase in the history of a tragedy site. The meaning and marking of a designated site may change through time, either toward sanctification or toward rectification or obliteration, for reasons I mention below.

The Minority Cause

Some sanctified sites begin as designated places, often marking minority causes. They may assume meaning immediately for the minority group, but time must pass before the minority cause symbolized by the site is accepted by a larger constituency. In the meantime the site may be venerated informally by the minority. Martin Luther King Jr. was assassinated at the Lorraine Motel in Memphis, Tennessee, in 1968. Not long afterward the site was marked by the motel's owner (Figure 1-7). Efforts to do more began almost immediately thereafter, attempts to create some sort of public monument to King as a martyr to the cause of civil rights. Beginning at the grass-roots level, these efforts paid off two decades later in the creation of a civil rights museum and educational center at the site of the Lorraine Motel funded by local, state, and national authorities. In the intervening years King became a national hero whose birthday is commemorated as a national holiday, and the goals of the civil rights movement came to be accepted by a broad spectrum of Americans. The transformation of the assassination site from designation to sanctification mirrored these changes. There are many places that, like the King assassination site, are associated with the cause of minority rights and history. The present political climate allows these long dormant sites at last to be commemorated. Similar sites can be found relating to Native Americans and a wide range of other ethnic and racial minorities, including Chinese Americans and Japanese Americans. In addition causes such as

Figure 1-7. The Lorraine Motel in Memphis, Tennessee, looking up toward the place where Martin Luther King Jr. was assassinated on 4 April 1968. The memorial tablet positioned on the wall next to the room Dr. King occupied was erected by the motel's owner.

the rise of American labor have produced designated sites that may be on their way toward sanctification. I draw on the stories of many of these rallying points in Chapter 9.

Places in Process

Some sites are set apart and marked because they are on their way toward sanctification but still "in process." There is little disagreement about the significance of these sites, and it is only a matter of time before public financial support is forthcoming. In a metaphorical sense, these places are undergoing a sort of "canonization," insofar as the reasons for their veneration are being assembled, confirmed, and cataloged. Many national shrines associated with the Revolutionary and Civil Wars followed this path to sanctification. They were recognized immediately as significant sites, but time was required to enlist the resources needed for proper consecration. The Bunker Hill Memorial is one such example, for commemoration on a fitting scale took seventy-five years (Figure 1-8). The site's designation was begun by veterans of the battle, and the major monument now located there was funded privately. Dedicated in 1843, the monument was ceded to the commonwealth of Massachusetts in 1919 and eventually to the National Park Service in 1976. Designation is not uncommon during periods in which such sites pass from private ownership to public stewardship.

The Unforgettable Event

Apart from marking transitional places, designation is the final outcome for what can only be termed "unforgettable" events. These are unique occurrences, "freak" accidents and tragedies that would lead to rectification or even obliteration if they were not so unusual. These events may claim many lives, but the loss is neither specific to a particular community nor heroic enough to warrant consecration. Designation ensues only by reason of the remarkable circumstances of the tragedy—a one-of-a-kind disaster unlikely to happen ever again such as the crash of the *Hindenburg* airship or the loss of the Donner party in the Sierra Nevada. Some of these, such as the *Eastland* disaster in the Chicago River, are marked—much later—as the worst events of their kind (Figure 1-9).

Figure 1-8. The Bunker Hill Memorial in Charlestown, Massachusetts, just across the Charles River from Boston. Veterans of the battle lobbied for a memorial for many years, and the monument was begun with private donations in 1827. Only much later did the site pass into public hands, first to the commonwealth of Massachusetts in 1919 and eventually to the National Park Service in 1976. The monument is atop Breed's Hill, just below Bunker Hill proper, but part of the original battlefield.

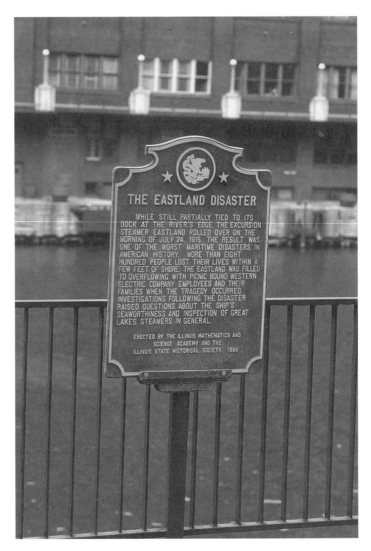

Figure 1-9. The site of the *Eastland* disaster in the Chicago River. The *Eastland* capsized here in 1915, claiming over eight hundred lives. The site remained unmarked for many decades. This is the only tribute to this tragedy, one of the greatest maritime disasters in American history.

RECTIFICATION

Rectification is the process through which a tragedy site is put right and used again. The site gains only temporary notoriety in the aftermath of the tragedy. Associations with the fatal event eventually weaken, and the site is reintegrated into the activities of everyday life. No sense of honor or dishonor remains attached to the site; it is, so to speak, exonerated of involvement in the tragedy. Of the four outcomes I outline, rectification frequently produces the least activity at the tragedy site—often only the cleaning up of visible evidence of an accident or tragedy. Sometimes neglect and abandonment ensue before the site is put to a new use, but changes are little noted and rarely discussed. Rectification is the rule for the vast majority of sites touched by tragedy and violence. These are the sites of events that fail to gain the sense of significance that inspires sanctification or designation and lack the shameful connotations that spur obliteration. Rectification, then, is the most common outcome when tragedies come to be viewed as accidents and when violence is interpreted as senseless.

The Accidental Tragedy

Of all tragedy sites, those associated with accidents are the ones most likely to disappear from the landscape and to prove difficult to find. These sites are exonerated of blame and assume a role analogous to that of the innocent bystander. The tragedy could have happened anywhere. That it afflicted a particular site is purely a matter of chance. These events are always followed by a search for a cause, usually in an official investigation and/or in heated litigation. The focus of the investigation is both to determine blame and to propose preventive measures. As soon as this is accomplished, any notoriety attached to the site usually dissipates. Thus, when an airplane or train crashes, the public focuses on the cause with an eye toward preventing similar accidents and loses interest in the site itself. Attention continues to focus on the site only in those situations, discussed above, where the tragedy claims many victims from a single group and induces a sense of community loss.

I noticed somewhat unexpectedly that, although these scars disappear from the immediate site, the accidents frequently lead to visible changes elsewhere. This is because once the cause of an accident is determined, remedial action may be taken all over the country or, indeed, all over the world. The great urban fires of the nineteenth century—the Chicago Fire of 1871 being just one of many—resulted in new building codes requiring brick and masonry construction where wood had previously been the norm. Requirements for fire escapes, emergency lighting, and fire doors can all be traced to specific disasters. New technologies have been a key to America's rise as an urban and industrial society, but at the cost of many lives. The safety measures in effect today are almost all after the fact. They endure long after evidence of the precipitating accidents has disappeared.

Senseless Violence

Rectification is also the rule in cases of "senseless" violence. These are events such as spontaneous riots at sports events or stray acts of terror that neither attain significance as ethical or heroic struggles nor induce a strong sense of community loss. These are acts of violence that come to be interpreted as "accidents." An example is the Wall Street bombing of 1920, when a powerful, shrapnel-covered bomb was detonated in the heart of New York's financial district, killing thirty, wounding two hundred, and causing tremendous property damage. The crime was never solved, nor was it claimed, even anonymously, as an act of revenge or terror. Without a sense of meaning, and since its victims were struck at random, the event faded from public attention. The site was "cleansed," rectified, and returned to use. All that remains are stray shrapnel scars in the stone of a few Wall Street buildings. Most acts of homicide eventually come to be viewed as senseless, or rather, as lacking the deeper meaning that would result in sanctification or even designation. Rectification is the outcome in these situations. Only in situations where the violence induces a great sense of shame is another outcome possible—obliteration.

OBLITERATION

Obliteration entails actively effacing all evidence of a tragedy to cover it up or remove it from view. Obliteration goes beyond rectification, for the site is not just cleansed but scoured. The site is not returned to use but more commonly removed from use. If the site is ever occupied again—usually after a long period of time—it will be put to a wholly different use. In many respects obliteration is the opposite of sanctification. Whereas sanctification leads to the permanent marking of a site and its consecration to a cause, martyr, or hero, effacement demands that all evidence of an event be removed and that consecration never take place. Whereas sanctification is spurred by the wish to remember an event, obliteration stems from a desire to forget. Sanctification leads to veneration of a place, whereas obliteration leaves only stigma. As is to be expected, events that lead to obliteration are nearly the opposite of those that inspire sanctification. Rather than being tied to heroes and martyrs, obliterated sites are associated with notorious and disreputable characters—mobsters, assassins, and mass murderers. Instead of illustrating human character at its best, obliterated sites draw attention to the dark side of human nature and its capacity for evil.

A curious feature of obliterated sites I noticed is that, once stigmatized, they stand out as much as sacred spaces. They are breaks in the texture of landscape that are noticeable by way of contrast with their surroundings—for instance, the vacant, trash-filled lot along an otherwise ordinary suburban street that was once the home of mass murderer John Wayne Gacy (Figure 1-10). Some societies and cultures have rituals that serve to lift stigma, guilt, or blame, ceremonies that symbolically cleanse people and places and allow them to return to full participation in day-to-day life. This is not true of American society; there is no easy way for stigmatized sites to be returned to use. Occasionally they will be reused, but only after lying fallow for years or decades. Most remain scarred indefinitely.

The equivocal status of stigmatized places can lead to some unusual outcomes, some of which I might even term pathological. Stigmatized sites attract graffiti and vandalism and, because there is no easy way to remove the stigma, remain targets of abuse for long periods of time. Here again lies an interesting contrast with sanctification. When a site is sanctified after a great community tragedy, the dedication of a memorial often marks the end of a period of grieving or acts as the focus of a cathartic release of grief. The shame attached to stigmatized sites circumvents this process; people are discouraged from caring for the site, even if the violence—say, of a mass murderer— claimed many innocent victims who may deserve memorialization. In such situations where public attention is out of bounds, stigmatized sites may attract furtive interest, since open discussion is taboo. They become the subject of stories and jokes and are pointed out to visitors

Figure 1-10. The site of the home of serial murderer John Wayne Gacy in suburban Chicago. Gacy buried many of his victims under his house and garage. Little remained of the house after the police completed their search for victims during 1978–1979. What remained was bulldozed shortly after the completion of the investigation. Gacy was executed in 1994.

surreptitiously. Prevented as they are from being marked publicly and openly, they slip into the realm of popular culture and oral tradition—dark stories and legends—that keep memory alive. This recourse to oral tradition for sustaining memories of shameful events is the topic with which I close Chapter 6.

Mass Murder

Mass murder is the most common event to result in obliteration. Other outcomes are possible but unusual. The shame of the mass murder stems not only from the crime itself but from the realization by a community that one of its own members was capable of committing such violence. The shame of the murderer radiates outward to the community at large. A community will often attempt to minimize its connection to a killer, to maintain, for example, that the murderer was only a drifter or an outsider. When this is impossible, a community may attempt instead to distance itself from the killer by other means, such as burning, demolishing, or vandalizing the murderer's home or the murder site to efface as much evidence as possible. This has occurred after mass murders in a wide variety of locations stretching back into the nineteenth century—for although the frequency of mass murder is growing in recent decades, it has long been part of the American scene.

Notorious Places

Apart from mass murder, there is no single type of event that leads regularly to obliteration. Events associated with organized crime—"hits" and massacres—sometimes fall in this category, as do some terrorist acts. I will examine a few sites associated with the mobsters of the 1920s and 1930s in Chapter 6. Notorious criminals such as John Wilkes Booth can even stigmatize places unassociated with their crimes. Finally, there are some "accidental" tragedies that reflect so badly on a group or community that their sites are obliterated. This is the case in situations such as Boston's Cocoanut Grove Nightclub fire of 1942, where investigations discovered that civic authorities had been lax in enforcing existing building, fire, and safety codes. Other events fall in this category when government authorities or private citizens ignore repeated warnings of impending disaster. These include some explosions, fires, and transportation accidents, as well as unusual events such as the Salem witchcraft executions.

THE INVENTION OF TRADITION AND THE LAND-SHAPE OF MEMORY

To know that the fate of a tragedy site will be resolved in favor of one of these four outcomes overlooks one important fact: a site's treatment and interpretation may change through time, sometimes radically. Sanctified sites may be deconsecrated, defaced, or effaced. Obliterated sites may be brought back to life as shrines. Most sites change very little, but when they do, the process of change is as interesting as the original outcome. As John Bodnar notes in his recent book on commemoration and patriotism in America in the twentieth century, this is because "the shaping of a past worthy of public commemoration in the present is contested and involves a struggle for supremacy between advocates of various political ideas and sentiments."[9] Times change, and as they do, people look back on the past and reinterpret events and ideas. They look for patterns, for order, and for coherence in past events to support changing political sentiments, as well as changing social, economic, and cultural values. Often this debate focuses on place—on the actual site of the event—and whether it deserves to be remembered or forgotten. This struggle over meaning and memory reveals how individuals and society come to terms with violence and tragedy. Reinterpretation is common in a number of situations.

The Representation of Local, Regional, and National Identity

Many sites of violence are shaped to commemorate significant moments in the national past or formative events in the histories of cities, states, and regions.[10] At the national level, all the major battlefields of the Revolutionary and Civil Wars have been commemorated. The state of Texas, as one example, has sanctified the Goliad, Alamo, and San Jacinto battlefields, all sites of massacres marking Texas's fight for independence as a republic in 1836. The flag of the city of Chicago displays four stars, two symbolizing significant civic tragedies: Fort Dearborn, whose garrison was massacred in 1812, and the Chicago Fire of 1871. Despite the grand monuments that now grace the sites of all these events, each was shaped gradually over many decades, in some cases being transformed from derelict sites into sacred shrines. All now serve as emblems of national, regional, and local identity. They are cared for with pride, are the objects of rituals of commemoration, and serve as pilgrimage sites for thousands of Americans every year.

The key to understanding these sites lies in the question of what counts as "significant," a question whose answer can be determined only retrospectively. Time must pass before the protagonists, participants, historians, and general public look back and assess the significance of events and struggle with their meaning. The Boston Massacre of 1770 is seen today as a watershed event—the first blood of the Revolutionary War period—even though it was no more than a minor street fight.[11] Over a hundred years passed before it was permanently marked, and even then, in the nineteenth century, people continued to argue that it was an unheroic, undignified point from which to date the start of the Revolutionary War.[12] Similarly it took many years for Texas to mark the Goliad, Alamo, and San Jacinto battle-fields; indeed the Alamo was almost lost to urban development before it was rehabilitated and enshrined (Figure 1-11).[13] The same delay oc-curred in the case of Chicago's civic tragedies. Over time these inaus-picious events came to be reinterpreted as emblematic of Chicago's phoenixlike ability to rise from the ashes of its tragedies through hard work and enterprise.

To assert that the Boston Massacre, for example, would have meant something quite different if Americans had lost the Revolution-ary War only begins to hint at the complex debates that can arise over the significance of "historical" events. The basic point seems to be that commemoration cannot occur until there is a past worthy of com-memorating. Not only did commemoration have to wait until after the final peace accord was signed in 1783, but time had to pass before a consensus developed that the United States had succeeded in be-coming a viable nation. Annual rituals came first, then designated sites, and then monuments—often with peaks of activity correspond-ing to significant anniversaries at ten-, twenty-five-, fifty-, and hundred-year intervals. The sites of the significant battles of the Texas Revolu-tion were derelict at the time of the fighting, and they returned to that condition soon thereafter. The first real monuments did not appear until the 1880s—fifty years after independence—with a tremendous burst of commemoration coming during the centennial year of 1936.

In recent years a tremendous amount of historical scholarship has detailed the ways in which conceptions of the national past, patrio-tism, and regional identity evolve through time. Close study reveals that what is accepted as historical truth is often a narrative shaped and reshaped through time to fit the demands of contemporary society. This is not to maintain that history is merely myth and legend—al-though these sometimes play a role; rather, it is to claim that facts and events are filtered, screened, and interpreted to fit certain contempo-rary demands. Eric Hobsbawm and Terence Ranger term this process the *invention of tradition,* insofar as nation building in the last two cen-turies has been accompanied by the creation of canons of interpreta-tion—traditions, myths, and legends—that serve to explain the past in terms of romantic or heroic struggles for identity and to justify the quest for nationhood.[14] Other writers have applied the term *making histories* to this process by which nations and social groups make the past coherent so as to develop a sense of identity and continuity.[15] The

Figure 1-11. The Alamo in San Antonio, Texas. This is the chapel of the abandoned mission compound, which was fortified by Texas troops and defended against the Mexican army during the siege lasting from 23 February to 6 March 1836. All Texan troops died in the defense of the compound. The chapel did not pass into public ownership until 1883, with more land added from 1905 onward. The site is now maintained as a shrine to Texas liberty and independence by the Daughters of the Republic of Texas.

interesting thing is not only that the shaping of landscape is consistent with these ideas but, further, that particular sites often spur the invention of such traditions of interpretation. John Bodnar's previously cited work provides excellent examples of the ways in which public memory and patriotism often focus on particular sites that demand commemoration. Gaines Foster, in his *Ghosts of the Confederacy*, provides additional examples of the interplay of ritual and commemoration in the creation of the South's regional identity.[16]

The invention of tradition has powerfully influenced the American landscape. Over time virtually every significant site has been marked, including not only watershed events but places associated with the lives and works of great Americans. Today people take many of these sites— battlefields, tombs, and shrines—for granted, when in reality their selection for commemoration was far from inevitable. In Chapters 7 and 8 I consider this process and the factors that guide the enshrinement of sites emblematic of national, regional, and local identity.

The Commemoration of a Historical Struggle

Earlier in this chapter I mentioned that some designated sites mark the progress of a minority cause such as the civil rights movement. Such sites may, over time, be sanctified to mark the course of such a struggle, but usually only after a movement has attained a portion of its goals. Again, as with the process of marking sites of national, regional, and local identity, the selection of sites that will be used to outline such historical struggles is retrospective. These movements must also invent traditions and make histories that are consistent with their goals. As these traditions develop, certain key events will be singled out for sanctification.

Until quite recently the civil rights movement lacked major monuments and memorials. This was to be expected when the movement was in its early stages. As certain goals have been reached, more of its sites have been marked, such as the Martin Luther King Jr. assassination site in Memphis and his tomb in Atlanta, as well as the Civil Rights Memorial in Montgomery, Alabama. But the civil rights movement is not the only struggle to be marked in the American landscape. The struggle to organize and fight for the rights of labor resulted in some of the most violent episodes in American history. These periodic confrontations and massacres did not result from a single plan or strategy and arose as much from local circumstance as they did from broader notions of human rights and dignity. Nevertheless, by the early twentieth century organized labor had achieved many of its major goals. Gradually retrospective appraisals began to focus on certain specific confrontations as watershed events in the overall struggle. The sites of these were shaped and sanctified.

In the United States struggles such as those for civil and labor rights are common. Native Americans, ethnic minorities, and religious sects have all sought to mark sites that demonstrate their battle for identity and self-determination. For instance, recent debate over the renaming of the Wounded Knee Massacre site and of what used to be called the Custer battlefield reflect friction over the way the histories of Native American tribes are interpreted. The Church of Jesus Christ of Latter-day Saints can be singled out as one religious sect that has been particularly sensitive to its historical traditions and aware of its struggle for religious freedom. In the twentieth century branches of the Mormon churches have self-consciously assumed stewardship of virtually all the sites associated with their early history, including all the sites marking their violent confrontations with "Gentiles" on their journey from New York State, through Ohio, into Missouri and Illinois, and on to the Great Basin of Utah, cases I include in Chapter 7.

The Creation of Rallying Points

One last type of site can be altered radically in the aftermath of violence and tragedy: the rallying point. In these cases a site associated with some past wrong or act of violence becomes the focus for further agitation in pursuit of a goal. The Wounded Knee Massacre site in South Dakota, symbolizing one of the last great acts of genocide in the suppression of Native Americans during the nineteenth century, became the rallying point for the Sioux uprising of 1973. The site of the Kent State killings of 1970 became a rallying point for the anti–Vietnam War movement. In some cases these sites are merely a step along the path toward the sanctification or the first stage in the process through which a group marks its history and traditions. In other cases these rallying points fade from view after a short period in the public eye. Regardless of the outcome, such rallying points are an important sidelight to my study. Their emergence often spurs extensive public debate over the meaning and significance of the original tragedy and, as a consequence, lends insight into the sentiments and social forces that shape landscape. I will focus on these rallying points in Chapter 9, where I take up the issue of the marking of these sorts of struggle.

LANDSCAPE AND MEMORY: WHAT IS FORGOTTEN?

The relationship between tragedy and the negotiation of meaning suggests an important connection between landscape, culture, and social or collective "memory." In one sense *culture* refers to collective beliefs and values, the social conventions and traditions that bind individuals to a group or community. These are values that shape everyday life but transcend the individual and surpass the individual's ability to change them. They are values that build gradually, change slowly, and sweep from generation to generation. Culture is, in this sense, a sort of collective or social memory.[17] This concept of memory provides an important bond between culture and landscape, because human modifications of the environment are often related to the way societies wish to sustain and efface memories. More to the point, the very durability of the landscape and of the memorials placed in the landscape makes these modifications effective for symbolizing and sustaining collective values over long periods of time. Landscape might be seen in this light as a sort of communicational resource, a system of signs and symbols, capable of extending the temporal and spatial range of communication. In effect the physical durability of landscape permits it to carry meaning into the future so as to help sustain memory and cultural traditions.[18] Societies and cultures have many other ways to sustain collective values and beliefs, including ritual and oral tradition, but landscape stands apart from these—like writing—as a durable, visual representation.

The sites of violence examined in this book are inscriptions in the landscape—a sort of "earth writing" in the sense of the etymological roots of the word *geography*—that help to explain how Americans have come to terms with violence and tragedy. For the most part, I am concerned in this book with those sites that are marked, but I cannot entirely overlook those that are not. They are just as informative in spelling out the values society does not wish to remember. The question of what has and has not been marked is important. I will return to it in Chapter 9 when I will turn to sites that now lie hidden and almost

Figure 1-12. Site of the Manzanar Relocation Center in California's Owens Valley. During World War II Japanese Americans were interned at Manzanar and nine other relocation centers under Executive Order 9066. The site has been abandoned for years, but the success of redress legislation contained in the Civil Liberties Act of 1988 may lead to the transformation of the site, which is now marked with a historical plaque.

forgotten in the landscape. Apart from particularly shameful sites that are quite consciously effaced, there is a wide range of sites that seem as if they should be marked but are not. Perhaps the answer is that, with respect to many events of violence and tragedy, American society itself has yet to reach consensus. There seems to be, for example, little consistency in the marking of sites representing either the conflicts between Native Americans and whites or racial violence. These sites remain difficult to assimilate with heroic notions of the national past, and the sites themselves demonstrate a sort of collective equivocation over public meaning and social memory. Perhaps still more time must pass before the tensions raised by such events can be resolved. In Salem almost three hundred years had to pass before a public memorial was erected, that is, before Salem as a community could look back and find a lesson to be learned from the witchcraft episode. What will be the fate of other places of equally equivocal meaning—the internment camp at Manzanar (Figure 1-12) or the sites of the Rock Springs or Ludlow Massacres? These are places that may long remain in limbo before American society comes to terms with their meaning and a past marred by violence and tragedy.

Chapter 2

The Veneration of
Heroes and Martyrs

The most common motive for sanctification is to honor a martyr, fallen hero, or great leader, irrespective of how they died. The tradition of venerating heroes has a long history in Western societies and almost always results in their commemoration in landscape. Veneration may extend to every place associated with a hero's life—birthplace, childhood home, residence, office, sites of great accomplishment, and burial site. Sites like these can be found in every village and town that has had one of its children succeed in politics, business, or industry. American tourist guides are chock-full of such sites, including Thomas Jefferson's Monticello, George Washington Carver's lab, Emma Goldman's grave, Charles Lindbergh's boyhood home, and the last residence of Harriet Tubman.

When one of these heroes dies violently or tragically, the death site may come to be venerated. Sometimes, however, the veneration of a death site may be a difficult task, because such sites carry a burden of shame. This is not a problem when a soldier dies heroically on a battlefield, but only a small portion of America's national heroes are cloaked in such glory. Assassinations may take place anywhere, as may other tragic deaths—in a theater, railroad station, motel, or office. These sites may be far more difficult to sanctify because the shame engendered by the violence may stand in the way of veneration. The assassinations I discuss in this chapter provide a measure of how unpredictable the results may be.

The success of veneration also hinges on the victim's fame and its durability after death. The likelihood of veneration rises with a victim's stature, but subsequent assessments are important, too. Some grow in stature, whereas others decline, and these changes are usually reflected at the death site—even if the changes are made years or decades later. Critical to the process of veneration is the question of whether the victim deserves to be commemorated as a martyr or hero. This cannot always be answered in the immediate aftermath of a violent death, particularly when the victim's fame is tied to a controversial or unpopular cause, as Abraham Lincoln's was to the Civil War or Martin Luther King's was to the civil rights movement. Veneration may then lead to fractious and prolonged public debate between the victim's supporters and detractors. Delay is inevitable. The time required to create a monument at an assassination site is often measured in decades, and the victim's reputation may change substantially during this interval, sometimes for the better and occasionally for the worse. The most interesting part of this process is that the question of *whether* a victim should be commemorated is often fought out over the issue of *how* commemoration is accomplished at the death site.

THE VENERATION OF GARFIELD AND MCKINLEY

Four American presidents have been assassinated: Lincoln (1865), Garfield (1881), McKinley (1901), and Kennedy (1963). Memorials were built to each of these presidents in the cities where they were shot, but in quite different ways. Rather than begin with Lincoln, whose assassination raised a number of complex problems for commemoration, I begin with the simpler cases of James Garfield and William McKinley. The responses to their assassinations outline the general issues that usually arise in debate over the commemoration of death sites.

Garfield was wounded in an attack on 2 July 1881 as he was on his way to board a train at Washington's Baltimore and Potomac station, then at the southwest corner of 6th and B Streets on a site now occupied by the main building of the National Gallery of Art.[1] His assassin, Charles Guiteau, was frustrated over not receiving a position under the spoils system then employed to dole out jobs in the federal government after presidential elections. Garfield's two wounds were not immediately fatal.[2] The president succumbed of complications eleven weeks later in New Jersey, having been moved from Washington to escape the city's summertime heat and humidity. Guiteau, judged by many to be insane, was tried and convicted in a brief trial and then hanged on 30 June 1882.

There was no immediate, popular ground swell of interest in memorializing Garfield, for two reasons. First, apart from William Harrison, who served only a month after catching pneumonia at his inauguration in 1841, no president held office as briefly as Garfield; he had scant opportunity to leave a mark on national policy. That his assassin had been infuriated by the political spoils system did spur the government toward implementing its present system of civil service through the Pendleton Act of 1883, but only after Garfield's death. At the time of his death, Garfield's reputation rested exclusively on his earlier accomplishments as a college teacher, Civil War general, and member of Congress. Second, he died in a relatively peaceful period of American history, and his career was never bound to a watershed event, as was Lincoln's to the Civil War, McKinley's to the Spanish-American War, or Kennedy's to the domestic and foreign upheavals of the 1960s. As novelist Thomas Wolfe commented many years later, Garfield was—with Presidents Arthur, Harrison, and Hayes—one of "The Four Lost Men":

> Their gravely vacant and bewhiskered faces mixed, melted, swam together in the sea-depths of a past intangible, immeasurable, and unknowable as the buried city of Persepolis.
> And they were lost.
> For who was Garfield, martyred man, and who had seen him in the streets of life? Who could believe his footfalls ever sounded on a lonely pavement? Who had heard the casual and familiar tones of Chester Arthur? And where was Harrison? Where was Hayes? Which had the whiskers, which the burnsides; which was which?[3]

Yet Garfield had led an impressive life, and his accomplishments seemed to demand commemoration. He completed a college degree at Williams in a period when few young people attained a higher education and then returned to Ohio to become the head of a small college. In the Civil War he rose to the rank of major general and served as chief of staff of the Army of the Cumberland. Later, during his seventeen years in Congress, Garfield took part in virtually every debate of national importance and as party leader was instrumental in reshaping the Republican Party in the post–Civil War era. As one of his biographers has written: "His career seemed to embody the national ideal of the self-made man, rising from log cabin to White House in unbroken ascent."[4] Given his accomplishments, tribute was forthcoming, including a massive and lavish mausoleum in Cleveland's Lakeview Cemetery.

In Washington the move for commemoration came during the term of Chester Arthur, Garfield's successor. In March 1884 Arthur asked Congress for funds to erect a pedestal for a statue of Garfield to be placed at the foot of the capitol grounds at 1st Street and Maryland Avenue. Arthur was acting at the suggestion of the secretary of war, who in turn was forwarding a request from Colonel Almon Rockwell, Garfield's army comrade and deathbed nurse. Indeed it was the Society of the Army of the Cumberland—the veterans of the army in which Garfield had served—that commissioned the statue destined for the pedestal. Congress approved the funds, and the statue and pedestal were dedicated on 12 May 1887. The nine-foot statue depicts Garfield holding his inaugural address in his left hand (Figures 2-1 and 2-2). The inscription reads, "Law, Justice, Prosperity." On the statue's pedestal are seated three five-foot statues representing Garfield's three careers as scholar, soldier, and statesman. This was a period when Civil War veterans were erecting great numbers of monuments to their comrades and leaders on the battlefields of the war (a point discussed in Chapter 4). Garfield's memorial seems to have derived from the same impulse. The statue remains on the same site today, although access is difficult because it is perched on a traffic island in a busy thoroughfare. A resolution was introduced in Congress in 1959 to move the statue and pave over the site to improve traffic flow around the capitol.[5] The resolution failed, but it is perhaps a measure of Garfield's weak fame that by the middle of the twentieth century, some people considered his memorial to be no more than a traffic obstacle.

Figure 2-1. The Garfield memorial at the foot of the capitol in Washington, D.C. The placement of the memorial stresses Garfield's accomplishments as a member of Congress rather than his short tenure as president. The memorial is offset to the south of the centerline of the Mall, a symbolic axis running from the capitol building to Arlington National Cemetery and connecting the far more visually prominent Washington Monument and Lincoln Memorial.

Figure 2-2. A view of the Garfield memorial looking toward the rotunda of the National Gallery, once the site of the Baltimore and Potomac Railroad station where Garfield was fatally wounded. A small plaque marked the site until the station was demolished after the opening of Washington's new Union Station in 1907. The plaque was never returned to the site, the only presidential assassination site not now marked.

The site of the attack also faded from attention. Not long after Garfield's death, the Baltimore and Potomac Railroad laid a star in the floor of the station where the president had fallen. Directly above the spot a marble plaque bore his name, title, and the date of the shooting. This simple tribute was maintained for over two decades until 1907, when Washington consolidated its rail depots in Union Station, just to the north of the capitol. The Baltimore and Potomac station, never a permanent structure, was razed shortly thereafter. The star and marble tablet were removed for safekeeping, pending decisions concerning the future use of this government property. The star and tablet were never returned. In the 1930s the National Gallery of Art was built on the site. The designers thought it inappropriate to reposition the star and tablet within the gallery. As a result, the tragedy site has remained unmarked. As I argue below, there always tends to be resistance to marking the site of an assassination because of the sense of shame that surrounds it. In Garfield's case, the site is now unnoted.

The commemoration of William McKinley after his death in Buffalo closely parallels that of Garfield's in Washington. McKinley was shot on 6 September 1901 while visiting the Pan-American Exposition.[6] Leon Czolgosz, the assassin, made the attack after waiting in a long reception line until he was within range of the president. Captured immediately, Czolgosz was tried and convicted in a brief trial and executed on 29 October 1901. Modern medical techniques might have saved McKinley, but he died of complications eight days after the attack in the private home where he and his wife had been staying during their visit to Buffalo. His body lay in state in Buffalo and Washington before entombment in Canton.

Calls for a monument arose almost immediately after the assassination. The first, in early November of 1901, came from the directors of the Pan-American Exposition.[7] They proposed developing a small park around the Temple of Music. The temple was not built to last, however; plans were already afoot to redevelop the grounds of the exposition when the fair closed. Retaining the temple would have upset these plans and required rebuilding it as a permanent structure. The proposal would also have had the unintended effect of glorifying the assassination. This was an important point, more so than it had been in Garfield's assassination. McKinley's supporters had good reason to worry about such perceptions. Czolgosz's attack had been politically motivated. The assassin felt that McKinley's platform of "peace, progress, patriotism, and prosperity" predicated on the "sanctity of contracts" and "national honor" was a sham. Versed in the literature of anarchy and socialism, Czolgosz believed that the McKinley administration was in the pocket of the nation's oppressors. He would have agreed with Almont Lindsey's assessment of this elite: "Their creed was the creed of the moneyed interests—that property was the highest good and the chief end of society. They believed that social justice and human rights should remain forever subordinate to considerations of property."[8] Some radicals actually claimed Czolgosz as a martyr, as Emma Goldman remarked: "The boy in Buffalo is a creature at bay. . . . He committed the act for no personal reasons or gain. He did it for what is his ideal: the good of the people. That is why my sympathies are with him."[9] Given that Czolgosz acted from these motives, McKinley's supporters were keen to distance the president from his assassin. There was even the sense that raising a mighty memorial to McKinley would serve as a slap in the face to radicals.

Within two months a second and eventually successful bipartisan proposal was put forward in the New York Assembly to build a monument in Buffalo's Niagara Square. The choice of Niagara Square was significant, as one politician noted:

> It is no idle spot in which it is proposed that this monument shall be erected. Niagara Square is in one of the largest arteries of traffic that the State holds. It is the pivotal point of a municipality that has in itself a population of nearly half a million and it borders a highway through which tens of thousands daily pass to and fro on their journeys between the city and its adjacent towns and villages.
>
> There is an impressive sentiment hanging in the atmosphere of this locality, too. Niagara Square lies not only on the line of a busy thoroughfare but it lies upon the line and towards the base of Delaware avenue, where died our President, and through which his funeral cortege passed on its way to the City Hall where his body lay in State. It is in full view of our City Hall also, and from the spot where the city of Buffalo has laid a golden slab marking the place where the body of the martyred President lay. You could, were it not for intervening walls, look out upon the tree-studded acres where it is proposed that this monument, in memory of William McKinley shall be built.[10]

Niagara Square also happened to lie at the center of Buffalo's original street plan as surveyed in 1804, a radiating pattern of streets embedded in a grid reminiscent of (and related to) the plan of the District of Columbia. Advocates also stated a forceful rationale for the monument itself:

> It is well that we should build a monument in honor of our dead. A monument is symbolic. It is symbolic of the greatness of the man whose memory is honored and even the hurrying, busy

thousands who pass must have their thoughts drawn to the qualities that made that greatness and inspire in them the spirit of emulation. A monument such as is proposed in this bill would become a living lesson. It would be a rebuke to those who sympathized with the foul crime by which our great President died and it would show to our children the love and veneration in which the people of this land hold their chosen rulers. It would inculcate in them the spirit of National pride. It would bare that honest pride to the people of foreign nations and would prove to them that a loyal people had sought so far as lay in their power to make amend for the crime of the disloyal assassin. . . .

It is meet, Mr. Chairman, that the State of New York should do something in honor of the memory of one who fell within her borders, by the hand of an assassin, while he was the chosen ruler of our Nation. And I will venture that you and your fellow members in this committee will agree with me that it is fit and proper that the tribute that our Commonwealth should pay shall be laid in the city that was the scene of his martyrdom.[11]

State support was sought in part because some money remained from New York's allocation for the Pan-American Exposition. Despite the support of every civic-minded organization in Buffalo, the city's government, and its churches, state legislators at first balked at reallocating these funds. Some maintained that Buffalo itself should fund the monument and that state appropriations would set a costly precedent for funding other monuments. This last matter was of no small importance, because during this period Civil War veterans were lobbying state legislatures for battlefield memorials, often quite successfully. Furthermore Ohio's McKinley Memorial Association had announced plans to construct a monument in Canton, leaving the feeling that Buffalo's would be redundant. The necessary legislation finally passed in March 1902, but not without misgivings and much election-time politicking.

Statewide elections were scheduled for fall, and few assemblymen and senators wished to alienate voters. The governor was worried at the prospect of losing in the state's second-largest city, and in Buffalo popular support for the monument appeared to be overwhelming.

Still,

> there was a distinct feeling of hostility against the McKinley
> monument measure in the governor's mind and, naturally, in the
> minds of the Republicans prominent in affairs of the legislature.
> They wouldn't say so, for publication, of course, but, speaking
> privately, they declared it was ridiculous for Buffalo to ask the
> state to build a monument to the martyred president. If Buffalo
> wanted to erect a monument to him, Buffalo should pay for it,
> but, really, they couldn't see why Buffalo should desire thus to
> perpetuate the shame she must—or, at least, should—feel in
> having permitted the president of the United States to be
> assassinated while her guest.[12]

As the governor saw it, Buffalo wanted to wallow in its shame at state
expense. Such perceptions can be an effective barrier to commemoration because tensions arise between the desire to honor the martyr and
the wish to hide a community's sense of shame. These tensions can
waylay commemoration for lengthy periods, as it was about to do in
New York. Even after the governor signed the bill, McKinley's supporters soon found that they had other hurdles to surmount.

The monument, by Daniel Burnham of Chicago, is of uncontro-
versial design, a sixty-nine-foot obelisk resting on a pedestal ninety-six
feet in diameter (Figure 2-3). As they rise to meet the obelisk, the steps
of the pedestal define the basin of a fountain whose water is divided
into four pools under the repose of four fifteen-ton marble lions. It
proved to be more difficult to gain clear title to all the land needed,
something not accomplished until June 1905. By then many people
had expressed second thoughts about the monument.[13] As is common
in such civic spats, the opponents avoided questioning the plan directly but nipped around its edges instead. They took issue with the
funds Buffalo would have to invest, the rearrangement of the familiar
Niagara Square, the rerouting of trolleys, noise, safety, and even the
felling of the square's canopy of shade trees. The McKinley Monument Commission responded to these criticisms as best it could, even
when one property owner took the city to court.

When the last legal obstacle was cleared in late 1904, supporters
moved forward as quickly as possible to circumvent other possible delays. The dedication was finally set for 5 September 1907, the sixth

Figure 2-3. The McKinley monument in Buffalo's Niagara Square. The square is considered to be Buffalo's birthplace and was selected for the monument to pay special honor to the fallen president. Despite inevitable delays, the monument was dedicated in 1907, just six years after the assassination.

anniversary of McKinley's keynote speech at the Pan-American Exposition the day before his shooting. New York's new governor spoke to the monument's message: "In memory of his martyrdom, in memory of an heroic death, in testimony to the futility of insensate envy and the lasting supremacy of law and order, in memory of a worthy life crowned by its sad sacrifice, this monument has been erected."[14] The timing of the ceremony was a boost to Buffalo's pride because the city dedicated its monument a full month before Canton finished its shrine to McKinley. These would be the largest McKinley memorials, but other cities dedicated smaller monuments. Buffalo had set an important precedent, however, by redeeming its shame over the assassination through the creation of a major memorial. As was true of the Garfield memorial, Buffalo's monument was positioned away from the place of assassination in a prominent civic location.

Even though the assassination site was not marked at the time, it was never entirely forgotten. The Temple of Music was razed, along with the other buildings of the Pan-American Exposition (save for the New York State pavilion, which became the home of the Buffalo Historical Society), and the grounds were reused for residential development. After a two-decade delay the Buffalo Historical Society marked the site in a small, quiet ceremony on 28 June 1921 with a simple granite boulder bearing a bronze tablet with the following inscription: "In the Pan-American Temple of Music which covered this spot President McKinley was fatally shot Sept. 6, 1901" (Figures 2-4 and 2-5). The society placed the marker not at the exact spot where McKinley was shot but only within the precinct of the former temple. The site was resurveyed and a small plot was appropriated in the median of a residential boulevard facing 30 Fordham Avenue. Marking the site had been of interest to the Buffalo Historical Society for many years, but resistance was sufficient to stall its plans. The society's secretary alluded to the difficulties in his report on the dedication but left the reasons unstated.[15] I assume that the objections continued to revolve around the sense of shame attached to the site and the inappropriateness of such a marker in a residential neighborhood.

Lincoln: Marking an American Immortal

Abraham Lincoln was honored by the city where he died, but oddly not until the 1920s, long after Garfield and McKinley. Lincoln was

Figure 2-4. The former site of the Pan-American Exposition's Temple of Music, where McKinley was shot on 6 September 1901. Save for one permanent building, all the exposition's pavilions were demolished to make way for residential development. The granite boulder marks the approximate point of the assassination.

the first American president to be assassinated, and there was no clear precedent for dealing with a tragedy of this sort. Furthermore the conspiracy cast a shadow over more than just the assassination site at Ford's Theatre, and the disposition of these collateral sites was difficult to resolve. Finally, Lincoln's fame and reputation were inextricably tied to the Civil War, the most divisive event in U.S. history. As much as did Robert E. Lee's surrender at Appomatox five days earlier or the subsequent capitulation of the rebel government and its remaining military forces, Lincoln's death came to signal the end of the war. It is particularly ironic that on the day of his death Lincoln ordered the Union flag raised again over the remains of Fort Sumter, the anniversary of the fort's capture by Southern forces in 1861 in the first engagement of the war. In commemorating Lincoln Americans also had to face the Civil War. This was a task that would take many decades and involve many compromises of memory.

Figure 2-5. The boulder marking the site of McKinley's assassination opposite 30 Fordham Avenue in Buffalo, New York. The plaque was placed here in 1921. The plaque was placed not at the precise location of the attack but rather within the site once occupied by the Temple of Music and the new residential street plan.

Lincoln was shot by John Wilkes Booth on the night of 14 April 1865 in Ford's Theatre.[16] The president died early the next morning in a back bedroom of the Petersen House, just across from the theater on 10th Street. Booth was pursued through Maryland and into Virginia, where he was trapped and killed by a cavalry detachment on 26 April. His coconspirators were arrested, tried, and hanged soon thereafter. Others implicated in the assassination plot—even tangentially—were dealt with harshly. Unlike the case with the Garfield and McKinley assassinations, memorialization of Lincoln was slow to arrive, and the sites associated with the assassination took on lives of their own.

The most striking difference is that Washington's Lincoln Memorial was not completed until 1922. Critical to this long delay was the difficult issue of how to memorialize Lincoln. Even at the time of Lincoln's death in the mid-nineteenth century, little consensus existed as to the proper way to commemorate America's national heroes. Cities and states sometimes funded elaborate tombs for their leaders, but these efforts did not stretch to building common memorials in the nation's capital. In must be remembered that the Washington Monument was not begun in the capital until 1833 (thirty-four years after the first president's death) and was still incomplete when Lincoln died.[17] It was not finished until 1885. A memorial to Thomas Jefferson in Washington was not dedicated until 1943, the bicentennial of his birth. It was only during the mid- to late-nineteenth century that Americans began to look back on their history with a view toward proper commemoration. Calls were heard for a memorial to Lincoln in the nation's capital almost immediately after his assassination, but the plans did not move far forward.

This did not prevent memorialization from occurring at a rapid pace elsewhere. Union states and major Northern cities all began to raise memorials to the fallen president. His home state of Illinois took the lead, particularly Springfield, where Lincoln's elaborate tomb was dedicated in 1874.[18] Lincoln was by no means totally ignored in Washington. The Freeman's Monument depicting Lincoln emancipating the slaves was unveiled in 1874. Nevertheless the heart of the problem of building a larger memorial was that Americans did not agree on how Lincoln should be remembered. The first memorials were clearly partisan and confined to the Northern states. Any results at the national level would require bipartisan support, and this would be difficult to achieve until Americans reached some consensus on how the Civil War was to be commemorated.

It is difficult now in the late twentieth century to understand the animus Lincoln engendered during his term as president. Today he is celebrated as one of the greatest of all American presidents, the defender of the Union, but this high regard is largely a product of retrospective assessments carried to the point of mythmaking during the late nineteenth and early twentieth centuries. Lincoln was in fact the surprise nominee of a radical minority party who was elected president because the Democrats split over the issue of slavery. The Southern states were so alarmed by his election that they began to secede from the Union the month after he was inaugurated. Then, rather than accede to the loss of the Southern states, Lincoln led the nation into the bloodiest war in U.S. history to force their return to the Union. During his term of office, Lincoln was one of the most vilified presidents in history. Certainly he had his supporters, but he remained a controversial figure long after his death, much to the detriment of attempts at commemoration.

It took a long time for Lincoln's fame to rise posthumously. Roy Basler's *Lincoln Legend*, Lloyd Lewis's *Myths after Lincoln*, and Merrill Peterson's *Lincoln in American Memory* are accounts of how Lincoln's reputation was slowly reversed after his death.[19] The process required almost two generations. Lincoln's fellow Republicans provided an important first push. Their eulogies and memoirs set the tone for later mythmaking and inspired the first efforts to depict the president in heroic terms in literature, history, biography, portraiture, and statuary. The cause was then taken up by a second generation of historians, writers, and poets—such as Carl Sandburg—who gradually immortalized Lincoln. Such efforts succeeded in rehabilitating Lincoln's reputation only because attitudes toward the Civil War were changing as well. This change began around the time of the fiftieth anniversary of the war's end.

Gradually, over several decades, the Civil War came to assume new meaning for Americans in both the North and the South. Whereas early assessments stressed only the issue of victory and defeat, by the late nineteenth century the war was being cast in heroic terms by both sides. That is, both North and South could maintain that they had fought the good fight for causes each side held dear, even though this involved, as Frederick Douglass feared, a certain forgetfulness about the institution of slavery. Only a step separated this view from seeing the war as a struggle that tested—and strengthened—the nation. I find it difficult to say exactly when these interpretations took hold, but the transformation was expressed on some battlefields. At Gettysburg in 1892, the High Water Mark of the Rebellion Monument was erected by Northern states but also paid tribute to the heroism of their opponents in Pickett's Charge, an unprecedented honor in an era of partisan monuments. The fiftieth anniversary encampment at Gettysburg in 1913 attracted thousands of Union and Confederate veterans who proposed building a monument to peace. Not actually dedicated until the seventy-fifth anniversary in 1938, the Eternal Peace Light Memorial is inscribed as follows: "Peace Eternal in a Nation United. An enduring light to guide us in unity and friendship." Washington's Lincoln Memorial was eventually dedicated about midway between these two anniversaries.

It was still a slow process, but efforts to commemorate Lincoln began again as his stature rose and the war was reinterpreted.[20] In late 1901 Senator Cullom of Illinois restarted the lobbying on Lincoln's behalf with a bill "to provide a commission to secure plans and designs for a monument or memorial to the memory of Abraham Lincoln, late President of the United States."[21] Unsuccessful in this first effort, Cullom tried again in 1902. Neither Cullom's lobbying nor four more attempts in 1908 and 1909 achieved their goals, however, even though 1909 was the hundredth anniversary of Lincoln's birth, a coincidence that might have been expected to help rally support. Finally, in December 1910 Cullom was able to muster the support he needed. His bill was passed and then signed by President Taft in February 1911.

The Lincoln Memorial Commission met for the first time on 4 March 1911, and President Taft was elected chair. First concerns were the selection of the location, design, artists, sculptors, and architects; these decisions took almost two years. The commissioners settled on a site in Potomac Park where an extension of 23d Street intersected the centerline of the Mall, placing the memorial in line with the Capitol and the now-completed Washington Monument. The design, by Henry Bacon, was in the form of a temple with thirty-six columns supporting its pediment, one column for each of the states in the Union when Lincoln died (Figure 2-6). Ground breaking for the foundation of the memorial took place on 12 February 1914, Lincoln's birthday, but without special ceremony. Over the next two years construction continued apace, with Daniel Chester French being selected to sculpt the statue of Lincoln that was to be the memorial's centerpiece. Dedication was scheduled for September 1920, but complications arose: the sculpture had to be enlarged, landscaping fell behind schedule, and the foundations under part of the memorial had to be reinforced because of subsidence. The dedication ceremony was finally held on Memorial Day 1922 before an audience that included President Harding; members of the cabinet; Senators and Representatives; the judiciary; high civil and military officials; officers of various patriotic and veteran societies; and distinguished citizens, including Robert T. Lincoln, the only surviving son of the late president.

The dedication of the Lincoln Memorial marked an upswing in Lincoln's reputation as one of the nation's greatest leaders. Now he and George Washington were both honored with major monuments along the central axis of the Mall: Washington as the father of the na-

Figure 2-6. The dedication of the Lincoln Memorial in Washington, D.C., in 1922. Only President Washington, America's "founding father," is honored with a more impressive monument, and his took a long time to complete, too. Reservations about honoring presidents in such regal styles slowed both projects. From Edward F. Concklin, *The Lincoln Memorial in Washington* (Washington, D.C: GPO, 1927), 88.

tion and Lincoln as its defender. To this point the Lincoln Memorial paralleled to some degree the Garfield and McKinley monuments insofar as all were placed away from the death site in prominent civic locations. Differences arose over the treatment of the death sites, however, for as Lincoln's stature increased, so did interest in the sites shadowed by the assassination: Ford's Theatre, the Petersen House, the boarding house run by Mary Surratt where the conspirators often met, the farm where Booth was killed, and other sites associated with the conspiracy and Booth's life and flight. On the one hand, it seemed inappropriate to reuse or destroy them, but on the other, it seemed equally inappropriate to turn them into memorials.

First and foremost, the assassination ended John Ford's hold on his theater, and the building was not used to stage another play for over a century (Figure 2-7).[22] At the time of Lincoln's death, the theater was less than two years old. John Ford, owner and proprietor, had opened his new theater in August 1863 to replace a building that had burned the year before, a remodeled church that Ford had opened as a theater in 1861. Immediately after the assassination, the theater was closed, guards were posted, and John Ford was arrested. Soon released, Ford was not allowed to reopen the theater until after the hanging of four conspirators on 7 July 1865. He tried to resume his schedule where he had left off, but he began to receive threats. One letter dated 9 July read: "You must not think of opening tomorrow night. I can assure you that it will not be tolerated. You must dispose of the property in some other way. Take even fifty thousand for it, and build another and you will be generously supported. But do not attempt to open it again. [Signed:] One of many determined to prevent it."[23] Anticipating trouble, the secretary of war closed the theater again, this time permanently. Ford stood at the door on the evening of 19 July and refunded tickets.

Now that the structure was unusable as a theater, some expected it to be demolished. Instead the War Department rented the building from Ford and began converting it into a three-story office during the summer of 1865; the War Department then purchased it outright in 1866. Effacement of the assassination site began when souvenir hunters descended to strip the theater of its furniture and fixtures before conversion. The shell of the theater survived into the twentieth century, but almost all the other relics of the tragedy were lost. The surgeon general and a War Department records office were the first occupants. By 1893 the entire building was used by the War Department's Office of Records and Pensions.

The Office of Records and Pensions continued to occupy the building until 1893, when a second tragedy ended its stay. Additional renovation work in June resulted in the collapse of all three floors, killing twenty-two workers and injuring another sixty-eight. The interior was rebuilt after the disaster, but instead of housing offices, the building was used as a warehouse and publications depot from 1893 to 1931. By then interest in the theater was growing, as was concern for the fate of the Petersen House, where Lincoln died (Figure 2-8). William and Anna Petersen continued to live in their boarding house until their deaths in 1871. The house was purchased from the Petersens' heirs in 1878 by Mr. and Mrs. Louis Schade as a home and office for Mr. Schade's newspaper, *The Washington Sentinel*. The Schades had many visitors who wished to view the bedroom where Lincoln died,

Figure 2-7. A view of Ford's Theatre in Washington, D.C., today. John Ford was never allowed to reopen his theater, but the building proved too valuable to destroy. It survived into the twentieth century as a government office building and warehouse. Preparations for the Civil War centennial led to its complete restoration. It was reopened as a museum and theater in 1968, administered by the National Park Service.

but the house itself remained unmarked. Official recognition arrived in 1883 when a small publicly funded marble tablet was affixed to the building's front façade. This was the first time any of the events surrounding the assassination were marked and appeared at the time when the Garfield tablet was added to the Baltimore and Potomac Railroad station.

Ten years later the Petersen House was taken over by Osborn Oldroyd, a fervent fan of Lincoln. Oldroyd had spent the years since the war collecting every bit of Lincoln memorabilia he could find. In 1883 he moved to Springfield, Illinois, rented Lincoln's former home, and opened his own museum, remaining there even after the house was deeded to the state of Illinois in 1887. When the Petersen House became available for rent in 1893, Oldroyd moved his collection to Washington and opened the house to the public. Oldroyd lobbied hard for preserving the house, and in 1896 he was able to persuade Congress to purchase it from the Schades. Oldroyd was allowed to continue running his museum, but now the U.S. government owned both sites associated with Lincoln's assassination. When Oldroyd died, the government again intervened in 1926 to purchase his collection.

In 1928 both the Petersen House and Ford's Theatre were placed under the jurisdiction of the Office of Public Buildings and Public Parks. When the Adjutant General's Office vacated Ford's Theatre in 1931, Oldroyd's collection was moved to the theater's first floor, and the second and third floors were converted into a library and offices. The museum opened on 2 February 1932. The Petersen House, now cleared of Oldroyd's collection, was refurnished through the efforts of a number of women's patriotic organizations and reopened to the public in 1932 as "The House Where Lincoln Died." Both properties were transferred to the care of the National Park Service in 1933, as were many other sites associated with the Civil War. Minor repairs and renovations were made after 1933 and during World War II, but the buildings remained during this period in much the same condition as when the park service had inherited them. The Petersen House was largely intact, but only the three outer walls of Ford's Theatre were original because of the remodeling of 1865 and the collapse of 1893.

Calls for more extensive restoration arose in Congress in 1946 and 1954, but without success. Only as interest in the Civil War centenary grew in the late 1950s did this situation change. In 1958 the

Figure 2-8. The Petersen House in Washington, D.C., where Lincoln died in a back bedroom on the morning of 15 April 1865. After passing through many hands, the house is now a National Park Service property. The ground floor has been restored to its approximate appearance on the night of the assassination. The Petersen House was the first of the sites associated with Lincoln's death to be publicly marked, a small marble tablet having been placed there in 1883.

National Park Service moved forward with a major structural rehabilitation and restoration of the Petersen House under the service's Mission 66 program. By the time the house was reopened on 4 July 1959, $30,000 had been spent on the work. Ford's Theatre was next but demanded far more work and funding. Over $2 million was approved on 7 July 1964. Work began in November, and the theater remained closed during the renovation. The building was rededicated in January 1968, and in February, for the first time in over a hundred years, a play was again staged in the theater. The thoroughly restored theater was reopened to the public and has remained both a museum and active theater ever since. A few years later the first-floor rooms of the Petersen House were restored to their appearance on the night of 14 April 1865.

Nothing like this was ever attempted at the Garfield and McKinley assassination sites. The association of the Lincoln sites with the history of the Civil War may have stalled veneration for many decades, but when the time came, it actually worked in their favor by pushing away any lingering sense of shame. Only by looking back on their history can the extent of the transformation be appreciated. In the course of a century, two rather unremarkable buildings, both of which would almost certainly have been demolished under other circumstances, have been converted into national historical shrines in which the federal government has invested millions of dollars. Even secondary sites associated with assassination conspiracy and Booth's escape route attract public attention, designation, and conservation. Maryland's Surratt Society, dedicated to defending the reputation of Mary Surratt, who, they and other historians claim, was unjustly executed as a conspirator, leads annual tours along Booth's escape route from Washington.[24] Many of the sites along the route are marked (Figure 2-9). The spot where Booth died now lies in the median of a divided highway that runs through Fort A. P. Hill. On most days cars can be seen stopped along the road for visits to his death site (Figure 2-10). These and almost every site associated with Lincoln's life and professional achievements are all marked.

KENNEDY IN DALLAS

The treatment of President Kennedy's assassination site in Dallas has parallels with McKinley's in Buffalo and Lincoln's in Washington.

Dallas's memorial was erected to the scale and with the speed of Buffalo's, whereas the treatment of the collateral sites was more in keeping with what eventually happened to Ford's Theatre and the Petersen House. The similarity of the Kennedy and McKinley episodes stems in part from the fact that both presidents were guests in the cities where they died, whereas Lincoln and Garfield were shot in Washington. McKinley was in Buffalo to deliver a keynote address at the Pan-American Exposition. Kennedy was on a swing through Texas to help salve wounds within the state's deeply divided Democratic Party.[25] Both killings left a deep sense of shame. As hosts, Buffalo and Dallas failed their guests and the nation. Perhaps the sense of shame was slightly stronger in Dallas because some conservative citizens had made clear before he arrived that Kennedy was an unwelcome guest. After the assassination, one resident wrote: "I think Dallas feels shame, not guilt. Many people here are ashamed to have been caught acting like fools—as they had been doing for many months—at the moment when the nation, and their President, needed the best they could give in thought, action and coherent criticism."[26]

A memorial was being discussed within a week of the 22 November 1963 assassination. It seemed clear to many that the wreaths collecting in Dealey Plaza spoke to the need for a more lasting memorial. The day after the assassination a county judge, Lew Sterrett, suggested that a memorial would be wise.[27] Exactly a week later a local attorney and Democrat named Mike McCool and local Republican leader Maurice Carlson announced that they would make the first appeal for a memorial before the Dallas City Council the following Monday. As McCool said: "I will suggest to the City Council that this monument doesn't have to be dedicated in any sense of shame or guilt. It should be a symbol of this city's real love and deep grief over the President's death. This monument could be the rededication of the deep conviction and sincere belief of the people of Dallas in the teachings of Almighty God, in human compassion and in tolerance toward our fellow man."[28] The idea was received by some with a measure of trepidation. As former Dallas Mayor R. L. Thornton stated: "For my part, I don't want anything to remind me that a President was killed on the streets of Dallas. I want to forget."[29] Still, it seemed clear that public sentiment favored a memorial. The cause was taken up in editorial in one of the city's papers: "Regardless of the eventual designation of a monument, the spot itself will be marked, where Pres-

Figure 2-9. A roadside marker along Highway 101 in rural Virginia just to the north of Fort A. P. Hill. Almost all the sites associated with Lincoln's assassination and Booth's flight from Washington are now marked and are the subject of an annual tour.

Figure 2-10. The place where John Wilkes Booth died after being cornered and shot by the U.S. Cavalry on 26 April 1865 on the Garrett farm in rural Virginia. The site is not formally marked but is easy to find within the wooded median of Highway 101, which runs through Fort A. P. Hill. A beaten path leads to the site, evidence of continuing interest in all aspects of the Lincoln murder conspiracy.

ident Kennedy was struck down. Of this we may be assured. History will demand it be marked, just as momentous events—even tragic ones—are noted for the future everywhere."[30] Perhaps J. M. Shea Jr. best stated the dilemma facing Dallas and the reason a memorial was needed:

> We are rich, proud Dallas, "Big D" to Texas, and we have never wanted a lesson in humility from any man. Not even from a murdered President of the United States. We have lived for three months with national tragedy, and I won't be popular for bringing this subject up now. But somebody must. To say nothing, more important, to do nothing, only says to the rest of the world that, as they have read, we shrugged the whole thing off.
>
> For weeks after President John F. Kennedy was killed, the city fathers almost refused to admit that such a thing could happen, not here. While cities all over the United States dedicated memorials, our leaders could not bring themselves to think about marking the site of the national tragedy. They would, some said, contribute heavily to a memorial on condition that it be built in Washington—not here. . . .
>
> But the organized forgetting didn't work. The tragedy would not go away. Day after day, I drove down to the slopes in front of the Texas School Book Depository, and always, no matter when I got there, or whether it rained or snowed, groups of people stood as at a shrine among the madonnas put up by children and the fresh flowers brought by nameless citizens. It still goes on. As I write this, not so much as a street, let alone a stone monument, has been dedicated to Kennedy, but the people have built their own memorial out of their patient presence.
>
> Now, some of our ablest citizens have begun to understand that we can't make sense out of the future until we confront the past. Kennedy's death is a fact. I hope that out of our many arguments will come a memorial that is more than a statue. If we are to learn the lesson that President Kennedy came to teach, we must build a living, searching memorial. . . .
>
> Big D's penance for its silly years should lead to a meaningful memorial to its dead teacher. Or his death will be, for Dallas, in vain.[31]

Even as Shea wrote, Dallas was taking steps in the direction of a memorial.

By 17 December a committee formed and elected officers. Its attention turned to deciding what type of memorial would befit the assassination, where it would be sited, and how it would be funded. The committee did not feel constrained to select an architectural monument and even considered the possibility of "living" memorials. Foremost among suggestions for the latter was the idea of purchasing the Texas School Book Depository and converting it into an institute of advanced study in an area related to Kennedy's interests, perhaps in the realms of political or sociological research. Over the winter of 1963–1964, the idea of a living memorial gave way to plans for a conventional architectural monument, for two reasons. First, the federal government planned to establish a presidential library for Kennedy, and this library was to assume the character of a living memorial by promoting public service among the young through active programs of scholarships, lectures, and public events. Second, discussions with the Kennedy family established that they intended the presidential library to be the primary focus of memorial efforts. They did not object to Dallas raising a monument, but they indicated that they wished it to be modest and dignified.

From the beginning the committee conceived of the memorial as one funded by private subscription, with the city contributing no more than a site. The most desirable location was assumed to be Dealey Plaza, along the short stretch of Elm Street extending from the Dallas County Records Building, past the Texas School Book Depository, and to the nearby railroad overpass. This site had the disadvantage of already commemorating George Dealey, a once prominent Dallas journalist, philanthropist, historian, and civic leader. Dealey Plaza was also encumbered with roads and a nearby rail yard. Despite these disadvantages, the site had the benefit of marking the birthplace of Dallas. It was here that the city's first log cabin was built by John Neeley Bryan when he began a ferryboat service across the Trinity River in the nineteenth century. All too ironically, the plaza had also seen many brutal lynchings,[32] but the Dealey memorial was built in 1949 to stress the site's positive associations. The Bryan Colonnade in the northwest corner of the plaza (now famous as "the grassy knoll" in accounts of Kennedy's assassination) marked the site of Dallas's first log cabin. The Cockrell Colonnade in the southwest corner of the plaza opposite Bryan's was a tribute to two other Dallas pioneers, Alexander and Sarah Horton Cockrell. That Kennedy was shot in a place of civic pride was a sad twist of fate. The coincidence made it all the more difficult for Dallas to distance the memorial from the death site.

The issue was resolved in April 1964 when the memorial committee and city announced plans to place the memorial in a new park that would be developed expressly for this purpose and situated adjacent to the city's courthouse and two blocks removed from Dealey Plaza.[33] The land was already owned by the county. Fundraising commenced at the end of May with a goal of $200,000. The memorial committee made clear its intention to contribute some of this money (eventually $75,000) to the planned Kennedy Library in Massachusetts for a Dallas memorial there. The remainder would be used to fund the Kennedy Memorial Plaza in downtown Dallas. It was hoped that the memorial could be dedicated in 1966. Contributions by fifty thousand people pushed the drive past its goal in September. Attention turned to securing the land for construction and choosing the design of the memorial. Both tasks took longer than expected. In the end the location of the memorial had to be moved one block south because the land could be cleared more rapidly than the original site. Bounded by Commerce, Market, Main, and Record Streets, just to the east of the old county courthouse and immediately north of a new courthouse, this site was only one block further from Dealey Plaza than was the original.

Philip Johnson agreed to donate his services to design a cenotaph for the plaza. The design was a fifty-foot-square boxlike structure bounded by thirty-foot concrete walls (Figure 2-11). The structure's two million pounds rest on eight small supports, giving the cenotaph an unusual feeling of both lightness and gravity, as if its great mass were suspended in space. The walls are open to the sky. At the center of the cenotaph is an eight-foot-square slab of polished gray-black granite engraved with Kennedy's name. As Johnson later explained:

> The cenotaph, which means empty tomb, is an empty room where anyone can walk in and be separated from life around. You can look up and see the sky, look down and see the plaque— and most important meditate in solitude.
>
> This cenotaph in honor of President Kennedy I conceive as

a place of quiet refuge, an enclosed place of thought and contemplation, separated from the city around, but near the sky and earth. To commemorate the man John Fitzgerald Kennedy there is, within, only a stone marker and the engraved name.[34]

On the sidewalk to the north of the cenotaph a touching tribute is inscribed on another granite slab (Figure 2-12):

The joy and excitement of
John Fitzgerald Kennedy's life belonged to all men.

So did the pain and sorrow of his death.

When he died on November 22, 1963, shock and
agony touched human conscience throughout the world.
In Dallas, Texas, there was a special sorrow.

The young President died in Dallas. The death
bullets were fired 200 yards west of this site.

This memorial, designed by Philip Johnson,
was erected by the people of Dallas. Thousands
of citizens contributed support, money and effort.

It is not a memorial to the pain and sorrow
of death, but stands as a permanent tribute to the joy
and excitement of one man's life.
John Fitzgerald Kennedy's life.

As the cenotaph was being designed, the Dallas Park Board was setting its own plans to mark the assassination site. The board wished its plan to be considered not as a memorial but rather as a guide to help visitors understand what happened in Dealey Plaza. The plan was to place an etched-bronze mural on the east edge of Dealey Plaza along Houston Street (Figure 2-13). The park board installed the mural in the spring of 1966, before the cenotaph was ready, because the city was running behind its original schedule.

As had been the case in Buffalo at the turn of the century, not everyone was pleased with the plans for a memorial. Critics focused on the "waste" of a valuable $1 million parcel of county land. County commissioners argued that they were being asked to contribute too

Figure 2-11. The Kennedy memorial in Dallas, Texas. An entire block of land was cleared to provide space for the memorial. The site is just a short distance from the assassination site in Dealey Plaza. The design by Philip Johnson stands atop an underground parking garage, one of the compromises that had to be made to complete the memorial in 1970.

much because, once the memorial was in place, the plaza would be off-limits to further development. This issue led to a three-year delay while a compromise was worked out. It was agreed that an underground parking garage would be built under the plaza, with ramps confined to the outer edges of the block. A good deal of reengineering had to be undertaken to crown the car park with the massive memorial, but the compromise allowed the entire project to continue on course.

The monument was dedicated in June 1970. The ceremony was short, only twenty minutes, and attracted only a small crowd. Neither Dallas's mayor nor members of the Kennedy family attended. Today the Kennedy Memorial Plaza is flanked by the Dallas County Historical Plaza, completed in 1971, on the block originally intended for the presidential memorial. To this square was moved a replica of the Bryan log cabin, and other memorials have since been added. It is perhaps ironic that Kennedy's assassination led the city of Dallas and

Figure 2-12. A view of the Kennedy cenotaph showing the inscribed granite tablet that greets visitors to the shrine. Referring to the cenotaph, the inscription closes with the following words: "It is not a memorial to the pain and sorrow of death, but stands as a permanent tribute to the joy and excitement of one man's life. John Fitzgerald Kennedy's life." The tension between pain and joy, between shame and honor, is often at the heart of debates over such memorials.

Figure 2-13. This etched-bronze mural commissioned by the Dallas Park Board in 1966 was the first public marker to be installed after Kennedy's assassination. It depicts the route of Kennedy's motorcade and was intended only as an aid to the thousands of visitors to the site. It was added to the existing memorial to George Dealey, a prominent Dallas journalist, philanthropist, historian, and civic leader. In the distance can be seen the now-infamous "grassy knoll," which is really the Bryan Colonnade, honoring Dallas's first white settler.

Dallas County to create this new two-block square to celebrate their origins and history.

Dealey Plaza continued to hold fascination for visitors, however, just like Ford's Theatre and the Petersen House. Crowds gathered daily to study the route of Kennedy's motorcade (Figure 2-14). To guide them, they had the mural constructed by the Dallas Park Board and a marker placed on the Texas School Book Depository in 1980 by the Texas Historical Commission. The fate of the Texas School Book Depository remained uncertain and became the subject of heated debate. After the assassination the book depository itself moved out, and

Figure 2-14. A view across the Kennedy assassination site looking toward the Bryan Colonnade (the "grassy knoll," on the extreme left) and the former Texas School Book Depository (first building from left). Kennedy's limousine was at the approximate position of the truck when the last, fatal bullet struck. Some of the many visitors can be seen in the distance. The book depository is now used as the administrative offices of the Dallas County government. A controversial exhibit, "The Sixth Floor," was opened in the building in 1989.

the building had a number of owners. The Dallas County Commissioners Court approved its purchase in 1977 for county offices and re-named it the Dallas County Administration Building. The sixth floor, Oswald's aerie, remained empty. To avoid having tourists disrupt staff to get to the sixth floor, the commissioners sought, without success, to develop a museum there, isolated from county offices. Many people were infuriated by the plan, seeing it as a glorification of Kennedy's assassin. The Dallas County Historical Foundation took up the cause and tried to gain funding for an exhibit in the building to be entitled "The Sixth Floor." [35] The plan nearly died. After a tremendous amount of discussion, the exhibit was opened to the public in 1989. The exhibit remained controversial but sought to silence critics by broadening its interpretation to include the entire assassination period, touching on some of these controversies. The exhibit remains popular, as much so as Ford's Theatre.

On the whole the shaping of all the presidential assassination sites has been guided by a desire to honor the victims and to downplay the violence of the killings as much as possible. All four martyred presidents were memorialized in the cities where they were shot, but the memorials were not placed at the sites of the assassinations. They were all positioned in some other place of civic prominence. Of the assassination sites themselves, three are marked, but only two attract much attention today, Lincoln's and Kennedy's. And these were both marked with great reluctance, Ford's Theatre after a delay of almost ninety years and the Texas School Book Depository after twenty-six. This reluctance to draw attention to attack sites extends also to attempted assassinations. Presidents have been attacked in Washington, Milwaukee, Miami, Sacramento, and San Francisco.[36] To my knowledge, not a single one of these sites has been marked.

THE VENERATION OF OTHER HEROES

Apart from presidents, battlefield heroes, and what might be termed "local heroes," individuals who meet violent deaths are memorialized only rarely. If sites of everyday murders and accidental deaths occasionally gain such attention, it is often short-lived (Figure 2-15). In some unusual situations an ordinary murder site may evolve into a rallying point for a cause, but this too is rare. For the most part, murders are different from assassinations, and the former usually go unmarked. Yet there is no easy way to know in advance whether a person's death site will be sanctified. President Kennedy's brother Robert was killed in the kitchen of the Ambassador Hotel in Los Angeles as he was leaving a campaign rally during his bid for the presidency in 1968.[37] Robert Kennedy had served in a number of high elected and appointed government positions, but his assassination had no effect on the death site. No marker or shrine exists at the Ambassador Hotel, and Los Angeles did not build a major memorial. Similarly no marker notes where presidential candidate George Wallace was paralyzed in

Figure 2-15. The remains of a small memorial in Palo Alto, California, marking the site of an accident that claimed the life of a school child at a railroad crossing. This photograph, which was taken in 1995, just three years after the accident, shows how such roadside memorials are gradually effaced as memories fade.

Figure 2-16. Huey Long's tomb and memorial before the
Louisiana Statehouse in Baton Rouge. Long had helped to
get the statehouse built during his tenure as governor, and
the front gardens were a natural choice for his tomb. The fatal attack occurred in a ground-floor corridor toward the rear
of the building. The location is marked with a small plaque.

Figure 2-17. The small garden in New York's Central Park dedicated to the memory of John Lennon. Lennon was killed in 1980 in front of his home just across the street from the site of the garden. Named "Strawberry Fields," the memorial is an example of the shrines that arise occasionally to honor popular figures other than political leaders.

an attempted assassination in the parking lot of a shopping center in Laurel, Maryland, in 1972.

But a person does not have to be a president or general to be commemorated. Every city and state has its local heroes who are memorialized regardless of whether they die violently. One example is Senator Huey Long of Louisiana. Long was shot in a back hallway of the Louisiana Statehouse in Baton Rouge in 1935.[38] He was one of the most popular political figures in Louisiana history. His supporters marked the assassination site with a small plaque and built a memorial. It was a coincidence that Long was shot in the statehouse, since it was one of the building projects he implemented during his two terms as governor. His tomb and memorial were placed in its front garden in a fashion befitting a president's memorial (Figure 2-16).

Figure 2-18. The Stevie Ray Vaughan memorial in Austin, Texas. Vaughan was a popular local musician gaining a large national audience when he died in a helicopter crash in 1990. The memorial in a public park is adjacent to a concert stage where Vaughan performed.

Death site shrines are not confined to political figures. Musician John Lennon was killed outside his New York City home, the Dakota Hotel, on 8 December 1980. Lennon's fans lobbied to create a small memorial garden—Strawberry Fields—just opposite the Dakota death site in Central Park (Figure 2-17). Popular figures do not require a following as large as Lennon's to be memorialized, however. Local heroes of all walks of life may have a following large enough to lead to commemoration closer to home (Figure 2-18).

Finally, not all martyrs gain widespread popular acclaim immediately after death. As in Lincoln's case, for some of these individuals many years must pass before they are honored at the death site. Their death sites may become rallying points for their supporters and their cause. The best example I can cite is Martin Luther King Jr.'s death site at Memphis's Lorraine Motel. Since King's assassination the Lorraine has been completely redeveloped as a national civil rights study center and museum, but the project took over two decades to complete. During this time King's following swelled and his reputation was burnished in the face of quite vocal opposition. King was transformed from the leader of a minority cause to a national hero, and the effects were felt at the assassination site in Memphis.

The changes began with private tributes to King. On the Memorial Day following the assassination of 4 April 1968, a marble tablet was set into the balcony window frame of the room in the Lorraine that King had occupied the night before his death.[39] The tablet was erected by the owner, Walter Bailey, who inherited the motel from his wife, Lorraine; she died of a stroke on learning of the assassination. Bailey turned room 306 into a small shrine to King. His additions included a glass enclosure extending from the room to where King fell on the edge of the balcony, a small display of King memorabilia, and some plastic wreaths (Figure 1-7). Bailey could do little more. The motel was heavily mortgaged and he was not wealthy. Contributions by visitors helped only to keep the motel open. To his credit, Bailey resisted profitable offers to turn the motel into a tourist attraction.

The Lorraine Motel continued on its precarious financial footing for the next fourteen years (Figure 2-19). By 1982 Bailey was unable to meet mortgage payments and chose to declare bankruptcy to forestall foreclosure and possible demolition of the Lorraine. Bailey hoped to gain time to mount a rescue effort. To this end the Martin Luther King, Jr. Memphis Memorial Foundation was incorporated, and its

Figure 2-19. The Lorraine Motel in Memphis, Tennessee, in 1986, when planning and fundraising were underway for the National Civil Rights Museum. Walter Bailey, the motel's owner, can be credited with spurring on the effort. The shrine he constructed on the upper balcony helped to elicit subsequent city, county, state, and national support for the memorial. Rather than compete with the King Memorial in Atlanta, the foundation that guided the transformation decided to use the Lorraine to pay tribute to the entire civil rights movement.

members, knowing of Bailey's predicament, struggled to raise money to buy the Lorraine. They were offered an extended deadline by the bankruptcy judge, but to no avail. The Lorraine was put up for foreclosure in December 1982. A last-minute donation saved the day, and the foundation submitted its successful bid of $141,000 at the foreclosure auction. The last $50,000 was a loan secured from the union that King had been representing in Memphis on the day he was shot, the American Federation of State, County and Municipal Employees, Local 1733.

The foundation took possession in January 1983 and changed the building's name to the Lorraine Civil Rights Museum Foundation to better identify its goal for the structure. The foundation envisioned developing it into more than a memorial to King and wanted to use the opportunity to commemorate the entire civil rights movement and all its heroes. King's tomb was already enshrined in Atlanta, so the devel-

Figure 2-20. The Lorraine Motel just after the opening of the National Civil Rights Museum in 1991. Although the museum's exhibits trace the entire history of the civil rights movement, Martin Luther King Jr.'s room has been restored to its appearance on the day of his death, 4 April 1968.

opment of the Lorraine seemed to be a good opportunity to state a broader message. Funding these plans remained the major hurdle, and nothing could be done at the site for many years. As fundraising continued, the motel was kept open. It was feared that closure would lead to vandalism, so Walter Bailey stayed on as its proprietor while paying token rent to the foundation.

The foundation sought seed money from Memphis business and government leaders in February 1985.[40] Although support was slow to materialize, the foundation pushed ahead with some of its plans in the hope of having something ready in time for the twentieth anniversary of the assassination. As plans became more definite, it was realized that $8–10 million would be required to bring the foundation's plan to completion.[41] The foundation expected to be able to count on no more than $2 million in private donations, so it made a major effort to appeal to government sponsors: the city of Memphis, Shelby County, the state of Tennessee, and federal authorities. The state of Tennessee took the first step by approving $4.4 million for the museum in April 1986. Other support followed, but not without objection.

There was some opposition to the plan, just as there was some resistance to making King's birthday a national holiday. As was the case in Buffalo with regard to the McKinley monument, the squabbling circled around a host of peripheral issues.[42] Some people felt that enough money had already been raised to honor King, particularly to fund the shrine in Atlanta. Others maintained that the Lorraine project would reopen the social wounds of the 1950s and 1960s by calling attention to events better left forgotten. If money was to be spent in King's honor, some people argued that it would be better invested in programs to aid Memphis's African American population. Finally, it was maintained that too much money was being siphoned from critical urban projects by the Lorraine plan and other downtown development projects.[43] Supporters of the museum responded that the project represented much more than just another social-welfare or urban development scheme. They appealed to Memphis's sense of pride, pointing to the elaborate tribute to King that Atlanta now boasted. The chair of the Memphis Convention and Visitors Bureau, Harry Miller, felt that squabbling over the Lorraine might reinforce negative perceptions of the city:

> It is a fact that tourists do seek out the Lorraine Motel. As a Southern city, people come here with all sorts of preconceived notions anyway, and I cringe at the negative image we give to these tourists. I don't know how to measure the negative impact the site has now.
>
> It's a historical fact that Dr. King was assassinated here. We can't change that. We can control the image we now give outsiders.[44]

As one editorial stated:

> The center would tell the nation that something good— perhaps something great—is happening in Memphis. It would be far more persuasive than any amount of rhetoric by public officials or private leaders.
>
> It would mean that the city is willing to put down hard cash on the proposition that Memphians will work together to build a bright and shining future.[45]

County and city funding for the project was forthcoming in June and July of 1986. The motel was closed and totally transformed. It was re-opened to the public as the National Civil Rights Museum in September 1991 (Figure 2-20).

At the Lorraine, in Washington at Ford's Theatre, in Dallas at the former Texas School Book Depository, and at many other sites discussed in this chapter, the fight over place had much to do with the fight over history—who will be remembered, how, and why. A quarter-century after King's death, the Lorraine Motel was being used to tell the story of the entire civil rights movement. A century after Lincoln's assassination, Ford's Theatre was reopened to retell the closing episode of the Civil War. In all cases the death site posed problems for commemoration. The sense of shame engendered by assassination is always difficult to dispel. Separating the site of commemoration from the site of death is a solution sometimes employed. Even then the death site cannot always be ignored. Tensions will remain until it is sanctified, designated, or obliterated. The same tensions are the focus of the next chapter, which deals with disasters that claimed far more lives. Their commemoration revolves around paying tribute to the sacrifices of everyday people rather than presidents, heroes, and martyrs, but the issue of how to come to terms with tragic and violent death remains the same.

Chapter 3

Community
and Catharsis

Sanctification can occur when a community is struck by disaster. Just as assassination induces a sense of community loss, so too does the loss of miners trapped in a coal pit, children lost in a school fire, or families swept away in a flood. The afflicted community commonly seeks to memorialize these victims and pay tribute to their sacrifice at the site of the disaster, at the plot where the victims are buried, or in a public place. The process of planning and erecting such memorials is also a way for communities to come to terms with a disaster. They serve as a focus for public outpouring of grief that can help a community to overcome its sense of loss.

The creation of memorials can play a healing role in times of community distress for many reasons. Planning and funding a memorial is a way for a shattered community to act again as one. In the aftermath of a disaster, creating a memorial is often one of the acts that bring all groups back together to work toward common, collective goals other than survival alone. The dedicatory ceremony—often held on one of the first anniversaries of the tragedy—can be a similarly important moment, an opportunity for all survivors to gather again as a community. Disasters often fragment communities, and a dedicatory service may be one of the first chances survivors have to renew acquaintances and share experiences. A dedicatory ceremony makes grief public, setting an example for survivors who may otherwise have difficulty facing their losses in private. Such public ceremonies also give official sanction to private grieving by acknowledging the magnitude of the community's loss. Finally, a group memorial sometimes helps to assure survivors that victims did not suffer alone, that their deaths meant something more to the community, and that the entire community grieves their sacrifice. In this sense the dedication of a memorial can offer a sense of closure, a sense that the worst is behind and the first stage of recovery is complete. The durability of a memorial means that it can serve as a focus for ritual commemoration long thereafter, even when all other evidence of a disaster has disappeared. These are all ways in which the creation of memorials can help a community come to terms with a great tragedy. In a variety of combinations, these factors have helped to inspire memorials to many different types of community disaster.

THE HEALING PROCESS

The general outlines of this process can be found in the history of Cherry, a small town in north-central Illinois, not far from the Illinois River and about a hundred miles west and slightly south of Chicago. Cherry was once a major coal-mining town. Even though it is far to the north of Illinois's largest mines and produced lower-quality fuel than they did, Cherry had the advantage of lying considerably closer to its single customer, the Chicago, Milwaukee, and St. Paul Railroad. The railroad created the company that opened the mine in 1905 to supply its locomotives. By 1909 the mine was producing 300,000 tons of coal annually from two veins, the deepest 485 feet below ground. The mine's work force of five hundred supported a boomtown population of about fifteen hundred.

Mules were kept underground to move coal and supplies. Their stables were at the bottom of the shaft; feed and supplies were lowered from the surface about once a day. On Saturday, 13 November 1909, at about 1:00 P.M., a load of hay on its way down to the stables was set ablaze by burning oil dripping from an open lamp. The hay was extinguished in the sump of the shaft, but only after it had ignited some of the wooden beams supporting the roof. The miners thought they could damp these flames but underestimated the danger. After an unsuccessful forty-five-minute fight, the 484 workers who had gone below before 7:00 A.M. were told to evacuate the mine. Many were able to escape, but the majority were trapped far back in the mine. When those on the surface tried to reenter the mine to pull more miners to safety, they were held at bay by the fire, which killed twelve of the rescue party. The shaft was sealed temporarily to slow the fire, but from that point forward only twenty-one more miners were saved, a group that spent eight days underground before their rescue on 20 November. Rescue attempts became more and more futile. Every time the temporary cap was lifted, the fire grew larger. On 25 November the rescuers admitted defeat. Both shafts of the mine were sealed with concrete to smother the fire. The caps were not removed until 1 February 1910, when the remaining bodies were removed from the mine.

The disaster claimed 259 miners in all, about half the male population of Cherry, and left the town with 170 widows and 469 fatherless children.[1] Relief from local, state, and national sources was fast and generous. The United Mine Workers Union, the *Chicago Tribune,* and the American Red Cross all sent relief workers to Cherry, and almost $450,000 was raised through public and private donations. Additionally the mine owners gave $400,000 to the victims' families, a settlement unprecedented in American mining history and far beyond the slim compensation offered workers in turn-of-the-century industrial disasters.[2] Wrongful death suits brought two years later in New York City against defendants in the Triangle Shirtwaist Factory Fire yielded only $75 per plaintiff.[3] The relief committee in Cherry was able to pay $3,261 to each family that lost a member in the disaster. The Chicago, Milwaukee, and St. Paul Railroad, through its coal company, was particularly generous because it wanted to continue mining at Cherry. Some consideration was given to closing the mine, liquidating company assets, and surrendering the proceeds to claimants—then a common means of evading liability claims—but the value of the mine's remaining coal deposits convinced the railroad to retain its holdings. The mine was reopened in late 1910, and the mine continued in production until 1927.

One aspect of the relief effort focused on the proper care of the dead. Cherry did not have a cemetery large enough for all the victims, and in many cases the purchase of a private plot would have taxed the resources of the families overmuch. Establishing a cemetery became a focus of community concern. It was an activity around which the whole town rallied as it began to regroup after the disaster. The own-

---

ers of the mine stepped in during the winter and donated five acres of land on the south edge of Cherry within view of the mine. Here were buried most of the bodies recovered in November and February, although some were interred in the nearby town of Ladd. Townspeople also rallied around plans to erect a memorial in the new cemetery to pay tribute to all the victims. On the second anniversary of the disaster, a monument was dedicated there "to the memory of the miners who lost their lives in the Cherry mine disaster of November 13, 1909" (Figure 3-1). That the monument was contributed by the local branch of the United Mine Workers of America, but placed on former "company" land, is a measure of the degree to which animosities were put aside in the interest of honoring the dead. The sculpture still stands as the largest marker in the Cherry Memorial Cemetery and has long been the anchor for annual memorial services, including large ceremonies on the fiftieth and seventy-fifth anniversaries of the disaster.[4]

Although the Cherry cemetery was sanctified, the mine itself has since been marked. After closure in 1927, the mine remained easy to find—its huge tip towering over the prairie—but unmarked. On Memorial Day 1986 this changed when an interpretive plaque was placed close to the site of the abandoned mine by the Illinois State Historical Society and Illinois Department of Transportation. It was positioned at the front of a small city park facing Cherry's main street and adjacent to the town's war memorial (Figure 3-2). The plaque recounts the disaster, the generosity of relief, and the consequences of the disaster. After seventy-seven years the Cherry mine disaster was being recognized—and marked—as a significant episode in Illinois history. And much good did come of the Cherry disaster. In its aftermath the state legislature enacted a number of laws designed to prevent mine fires, improve rescue operations, and increase the training of miners. The litigation leading to the monetary award to families spurred passage of a liability act that came to serve as the basis for the Illinois Workmen's Compensation Laws. These laws were the beginning of a new wave of legislation in Illinois and elsewhere that made it much more difficult for employers to avoid liability for accidents, which they previously had done. The plaque was a public acknowledgment of these gains, perhaps as significant at the state level as was the dedication of the original memorial by the people of Cherry in 1911.

Figure 3-1. The memorial to victims of the Cherry, Illinois, mine fire of 1909. The creation and dedication of such memorials can serve an important cathartic function in the aftermath of community disasters. In honoring the dead, community members can gather together to overcome their sense of loss.

Figure 3-2. The historical marker placed near the abandoned Cherry coal mine in 1986 by the Illinois State Historical Society and Illinois Department of Transportation.

New London, Texas, is another small American community that experienced a trauma as great as Cherry's, but this time the victims were children. On 18 March 1937 a natural gas explosion lifted the town's junior-senior high school off its foundation and destroyed the building.[5] Just under three hundred died—teachers, visitors, and students from the fifth through eleventh grades, the youngest students being in overflow classes from the nearby elementary school. New London was at that time a prosperous and quickly growing community thriving in the oil country of northeast Texas. Derricks and pumps dotted even the school grounds. The school also had a leaking natural gas supply that filled the building's poorly ventilated crawl space with an explosive mixture. Natural gas was then often piped to customers in its raw form, without the odorizing agent now added so that leaks can be sniffed out. A spark from a switch ignited the gas while classes were in session, killing the greater portion of New London's youth.

New London is in some ways still grappling with the explosion. The decision was made almost immediately to rebuild on the site; a new *memorial* school opened in time for the start of the 1938 school year. Classes resumed in temporary quarters within weeks of the disaster. Plans for a community memorial also emerged at the same time. A memorial association formed, fund raising began, and a contract was in hand by the fall of 1938. Donald Nelson designed a memorial of Texas pink granite similar to the one he had just finished for the Texas centennial at the Goliad, Texas, massacre site of 1836 (discussed in Chap. 7). The memorial was erected in the center of the main highway running through New London in a grassy, landscaped median directly before the new school (Figure 3-3). Atop the shaft is a bas-relief depicting teachers and students in study. Below on the pedestal are inscribed the names of 270 victims, not quite all the dead, since some families did not wish to have their children listed.

Even with the monument in place, the explosion remained an uneasy topic in New London. No high school reunion was held in 1937 or in subsequent years. A memorial service was held on the first anniversary, but as the superintendent had remarked not long before, "We have mapped our school program expressly to keep the minds of our students in normal channels and away from the depressing thoughts of a year ago."[6] As one survivor noted, "When anybody brought it up, I would leave the room. It was something I could not face."[7] The well-tended memorial remained, however, and gradually attitudes changed. In 1977 some of the survivors scheduled a lightly attended reunion in the face of local criticism. Subsequent reunions held every two years have attracted more and more survivors, and in 1987 a second, smaller, fiftieth anniversary marker was added at the base of the main memorial (Figure 3-4). Now many survivors look forward to these gatherings in New London around the memorial: "It's real, real touching to all of us to reunite again. Because we have something in common that most people don't have. We're survivors."[8]

Other school disasters have been equally devastating, some long before New London's.[9] One of the memorials I find most poignant lies in the 400 block of East 152d Street in Cleveland, Ohio (Figure 3-5). This is the address of the former Lakeview School in the suburb of Collinwood, which burned on 4 March 1908, claiming the lives of about 170 students and teachers. When a new school was built just

Figure 3-3. The monument to the victims of the New London, Texas, school explosion of 1937. Behind the monument is the new school that was built on the site of the old.

Figure 3-4. A small fiftieth-anniversary marker placed at the base of the original New London monument. Such indications of continuing care demonstrate the power of such memorials to draw communities together in the wake of major disasters.

Figure 3-5. The memorial garden outlining the foundation of the Collinwood, Ohio, elementary school that burned in 1908. The new school that was built adjacent to the garden has since closed, but the garden itself is still maintained.

next door to the original, a small memorial garden was planted over the ruins. The garden outlines the foundation of the building that burned. More impressive than the garden itself is the fact that it remained well tended and cared for, certainly into the mid-1980s, when I last visited—this despite the fact that the school that replaced the original had long since closed and fallen into disrepair. Eighty years after the fire, the disaster remained a focus of community care and attention, as it perhaps still does.

On the whole, however, responses such as these are the exception rather than the rule. Community memorials such as those in Cherry, New London, and Collinwood are rare. As I argue in Chapter 5, most sites of disaster are rectified and reused. Sanctification occurs in only those few situations where disaster inspires a sense of communal, collective loss. There seem to be distinct limits on the types of communities where disaster induces such feelings. All the examples in this chapter come from small communities, ones where the disaster claimed a large portion of the population. Memorials arise far less frequently in communities where loss is distributed over a larger population. The communities I have brought into discussion were also relatively homogeneous, socially and economically. The greater social and cultural diversity of larger cities means that disasters there rarely impinge on one group more than others. Tragedies can, of course, be selective and devastate a single neighborhood or parish of a larger community; these consequently have a greater chance for memorialization. There is a chance within larger cities for disasters to fall on self-identified communities, but again, this is relatively rare. Finally, when community memorials arise in larger cities, their creation sometimes hinges on other factors. As I argue in Chapters 7 and 8, some cities (e.g., Chicago) and states (e.g., Texas) have gone back, long after the fact, to mark the sites of tragedies such as the Fort Dearborn Massacre of 1812, the Chicago Fire of 1871, and the fall of the Alamo in 1836. These memorials have more to do with a community creating—and marking—its origins than with the cathartic release of emotion engendered by memorial building.

SUBTLETIES OF PLACEMENT AND MEANING

Not all community memorials end up in such prominent or meaningful places as those discussed above. Sometimes memorials are erected in out-of-the-way places or do not appear at all. Subtle shades of meaning can sometimes be seen in these variations in placement. One such case is the memorial garden marking the Texas City explosion of 1947, one of America's largest industrial accidents.[10] The disaster began on the morning of 16 April when a French freighter loaded with ammonium nitrate caught fire and exploded in the middle of the harbor at the center of Texas City's maze of refineries and chemical plants. Used as fertilizer, but with half the explosive power of an equal weight of TNT, the 2,200-odd tons of ammonium nitrate itself was enough to devastate the port, but the explosion set off a still-deadlier chain reaction. As debris and flame rained down, two oil refineries, a chemical plant, and numerous petroleum storage tanks were set afire. A second freighter full of ammonium nitrate exploded the next day. By the time the last fires were put out days later, the death toll was just

Figure 3-6. The memorial to the Texas City, Texas, explosion of 1947. The garden is on the edge of town, far away from the areas that were devastated by the explosion and fires. The fire fighters who lost their lives are honored at a small memorial at the central fire station, as well as on the grounds of the state capitol in Austin, where their names have been inscribed on the fire fighters' memorial.

shy of six hundred, including twenty-seven fire fighters. The harbor and industrial complex were a wasteland.

After some initial uncertainty, companies including Monsanto Chemical, Humble Oil, and Republic Oil decided to rebuild. Texas City, so dependent on these industries, began to clear the ruins and start over. The last of the unidentified dead were not buried until late June. The small cemetery on the edge of town at the corner of 29th Street and 25th Avenue was made into a memorial garden (Figure 3-6). A small memorial plaque to the fallen fire fighters was placed at the main fire station later; no memorial was positioned in the center of town or close to the epicenter of the disaster. The garden is still used for memorial services, but it stands isolated now by busy roads and has the forlorn air of an abandoned roadside cemetery. Its position on the edge of town almost suggests that the explosion should be viewed as an event outside the bounds of day-to-day life, an unfortunate act of God. It is an event for which Texas City may still grieve, but not one around which the city's life revolves.

THE JOHNSTOWN FLOOD(S)

The placement of the Texas City memorial mirrors that of the great monument raised to the Johnstown Flood of 31 May 1889. One of the largest disasters of the nineteenth century, the flood claimed over 2,200 lives in Johnstown and nearby communities. Before the flood Johnstown was a flourishing iron- and steel-making city of about 30,000, one of the most prosperous industrial centers in a booming region. The story of Johnstown's one-night fall from grace and its struggle to rebuild caught the attention of the nation and emerged as one of the great legends of American history.[11]

The disaster was only partly natural. It was caused by the failure of an earthen dam on the South Fork of the Little Conemaugh River after a day of record rainfall. At the same time, the dam was an accident waiting to happen. Completed in 1838 to balance water levels along a Philadelphia to Pittsburgh canal, by 1889 the dam was poorly maintained. Abandoned by the canal company, purchased by the Pennsylvania Railroad, and then passed on to private owners, the dam had been not only neglected but also improperly modified. When the property was purchased by wealthy Pittsburgh business executives for a summer retreat in 1879, the dam was spruced up. Its height was lowered a few feet to widen the crest for a road, and its spillway was screened. The grating of iron rods was intended to prevent the escape of a fresh stock of game fish, but it tended to clog and block the flow of water. The dam's incorrectly repaired sagging and a water level that was allowed to rise right to the brim of the dam were more serious hazards. The people of Johnstown were not unaware of the threat posed by the reconstructed dam before its collapse, but its deficiencies went unremedied. No one had the sense to notice that continuing deforestation and farming behind the reservoir were increasing runoff and allowing the water to attain faster, higher crests. Moreover, urban and industrial development was pushing further up the tributaries of the Conemaugh. Channels were narrowed to make room for buildings, roads, and railways, leaving them more prone to flooding.

With the heavy rains washing in, the South Fork Dam failed at about 3:10 P.M. on 31 May. The reservoir—three miles long, up to a mile wide, and sixty feet deep at the dam—emptied into the South Fork in about forty minutes. The crest of this wave hit Johnstown just under an hour later after washing away the villages of South Fork, Mineral Point, East Conemaugh, and Woodvale. Telegraphed messages of danger from the little town of South Fork had been discounted throughout the afternoon; no one was prepared for the onslaught. In Johnstown the Little Conemaugh meets Stony Creek almost at a right angle below steep bluffs to form the main branch of the Conemaugh. The floodwaters rushed across this confluence, crashed into the bluff, and divided, flooding Stony Creek upstream and the Conemaugh downstream. With its energy dissipating, the crest of the flood was unable to dislodge a stone railroad bridge just north of town. It instead deposited a thirty-acre mass of debris thirty feet deep. At about 6:00 P.M. this huge pile caught fire and burned for the next three days.

Johnstown's population spent a terrifying night trapped by flood waters that were being fed by runoff and thus slow to recede. As survivors waited for dawn, word of the disaster reached the outside world and relief was on its way. Major shipments of supplies had to await the rebuilding of railroads, but money and goods were being collected across the nation and world. As aid poured in through the summer months, no one questioned the decision to rebuild. One of the town's major employers, the Cambria Iron Company, was not badly damaged by the flood, and its reopening during the summer provided additional encouragement. With employment available and relief arriving daily, Johnstown's reconstruction was marred only by an outbreak of typhoid that claimed several dozen lives during the summer. Essential services were restored by the fall of 1889, and Johnstown was completely rebuilt within a few years.

After the flood many people noted survivors exhibiting symptoms of stress that are recognized today as common responses to disaster.[12] Reconstruction was seen as therapeutic, but many townspeople, having lost so much, moved away permanently. Those who stayed made changes. Until the flood Johnstown was organized into separate boroughs that guarded their political independence. After the flood borough rivalries dissolved and political consolidation was achieved under a new city charter adopted in November. This sort of convergence behavior is commonly seen following a disaster. Social rivalries dissipate as groups work together to meet the tasks of rescue and reconstruction. Private and public ceremonies honoring victims are often a focus of convergence behavior. In the case of Johnstown, plans for memorialization were closely interwoven with the task of reconstruction.

Plans for a memorial arose first from the practical need for burying and marking the graves of the hundreds of unidentified flood victims. The relief commission conceded that it could never hope to identify all the victims and that many bodies would be discovered only much later, if at all. To solve part of the problem, the relief commission purchased a 20,000-square-foot plot for the unknown dead in Grandview Cemetery, a relatively new burial ground atop one of the valley's highest hills. For the next three years unidentified bodies were moved from temporary graves to Grandview for reinterment in what became known as the Plot of the Unknowns; 755 bodies were buried there. Marble markers were placed on the graves, and in an effort to make the plot symmetric, a few extra stones were added to bring the number to 777 (Figure 3-7). A twenty-one-foot granite monument was placed at the head of this field of graves, the statuary group depicting Faith, Hope, and Charity. Significantly the monument was positioned in a cemetery high above the valley of the Conemaugh, a place where the victims would never again be touched by flood.

On 31 May 1892, the third anniversary of the flood, virtually the entire population of Johnstown turned out for the unveiling and dedication of this marker, called the Monument to the Unknown Dead. The governor of Pennsylvania was on hand to assess the lesson learned from the flood: "We who have to do with the concentrated forces of nature, the powers of air, electricity, water, steam, by careful forethought must leave nothing undone for the preservation and protection of the lives of brother men." [13] The dedication of the marker symbolically closed the reconstruction period. As the editor of the local newspaper remarked, the unveiling of the monument was "the last public act of the tragedy of the Conemaugh." [14]

The Monument to the Unknown Dead was the only public memorial raised to the flood of 1889. The general feeling seemed to be that going further would be unwise. Many residents felt that it was now

Figure 3-7. The Monument to the Unknown Dead in the Grandview Cemetery in Johnstown, Pennsylvania. Buried here are almost eight hundred victims of the 1889 flood. The memorial is high above the town, safe forever from the floodwaters of the Conemaugh.

time for Johnstown to put the flood behind it and move forward with reconstruction, that further memorialization would only prolong painful memories. As editor George Swank wrote in the *Johnstown Tribune:* "We cannot help things by repining. We cannot bring back the lost loved ones by giving way to our feelings which will now and again swell in spite of our endeavor to keep them down. But in the activities of business and industry we can find a solace and it is there we find it today. All eyes forward then. Look the other way." [15] This desire to downplay the memory of the flood is related to the monument's location. Rather than being placed in a central location, it was erected at Grandview Cemetery. The cemetery was high above the city and not visible from it, and the city could just barely be seen from the edge of the cemetery. Johnstown does have a public square containing monuments to the city's founder and the town's Civil War dead. The flood memorial was placed elsewhere, however, in the distant Grandview

Cemetery. The placement of the monument symbolically expressed Johnstown's final view of the flood: it was important to honor the victims but without letting the tragedy overshadow the future.

This interpretation is congruent with the final judgment of the cause of the flood—an act of God. Following the disaster, people were quick to blame the South Fork Fishing and Hunting Club, but this view was never sustained in court. No one was ever fined or punished for the collapse of the South Fork Dam. There were in any case two immediate barriers to compensation. The engineer who supervised the dam's reconstruction was dead, and the South Fork club was almost bankrupt. The few cases that went to court got nowhere. The defense argued that the flood was a "visitation of providence" and that the dam, even if adequately maintained, would have failed because of the record rainfall. These findings confirmed the view of many that the tragedy could not have been prevented. If there was a lesson to be drawn from the tragedy, it was, as John Wesley Powell put it, that "modern industries are handling the forces of nature on a stupendous scale. . . . Woe to the people who trust these powers to the hands of fools!" [16]

The curious thing is that Johnstown's Central Park does now contain a flood memorial, but one dedicated to the inundation of 20 July 1977 (Figure 3-8). The monument is a simple obelisk of modest height inscribed with the names of the flood victims, a verse from the Old Testament (Isaiah 9:2), and its sponsors. The obelisk was funded by gifts from local schoolchildren in 1979, the International Year of the Child, under the sponsorship of the Southern Allegheny Flood Recovery Association and the Greater Johnstown Clergy Association. I do not believe that the 1977 memorial could have been erected without a significant change of attitude toward Johnstown's floods between 1889 and 1977. The monument stands as a decidedly public acknowledgment of the power that floods continue to hold over the city. It conveys a message that is at once both fatalistic, because it admits that floods are likely to occur no matter what the city does to prevent them, and realistic, because it finally admits that floods are a part of Johnstown's past, present, and future.

To understand this change of attitude, it is necessary to consider Johnstown's response to the St. Patrick's Day Flood of 1936. Long after the failure of the South Fork Dam, Johnstown continued to have problems with flooding, because it was exposed to the runoff from a

Figure 3-8. A memorial to the victims of Johnstown's 1977 flood in the town's central plaza. This was the first flood memorial erected in central Johnstown. No memorial was erected at all after the 1936 flood, but a flood museum was established in the early 1970s a few blocks from this plaza.

large catchment area. The 1936 flood killed 25 people, left 16,000 homeless, and caused $44 million in damage, including 77 buildings destroyed and 4,500 damaged. The damage amounted to one-third the assessed value of property in the city. The flood again attracted national attention, and President Franklin D. Roosevelt visited the city that summer to survey the damage and discuss federal relief.

The judgment was that, once again, Johnstown had experienced a "visitation of providence," but the city responded far differently than it had in 1889. This time around the city decided it could beat nature by floodproofing the city. This was 1936, the heyday of public works and flood-control projects intended to subjugate nature. A month after President Roosevelt's visit, Congress approved $7.6 million for flood control in the Conemaugh Valley. Work began in 1938 and continued for five years, the cost eventually totaling $8.3 million. The Army Corps of Engineers made the final inspection of its work on 27 November 1943 and declared Johnstown "floodproof."

The inspection marked the start of a six-month celebration of Johnstown's "victory" over the threat of flood. At the close of the festivities all high-water markers were to be removed from local buildings. These small rulerlike reminders running up the sides of buildings were commonplace in the Conemaugh Valley. Now that Johnstown was floodproof, the markers were removed as a symbol of the city's new-found freedom. The celebration also saw the organization of the Flood Free Johnstown Committee, which began a nationwide campaign to bring in new businesses. Lost in the hoopla was any thought of raising a memorial to the 1936 flood. Johnstown chose to see the 1936 flood as a challenge to be conquered, not as an event to be mourned. Rather than build a memorial, community leaders placed flood control at the head of their public works agenda.

For several decades Johnstown's hubris was vindicated in a modest record of flood damage. All that changed in the summer of 1977. In one eight-hour period twelve inches of rain fell in southwestern Pennsylvania, breaking seven dams in the Conemaugh watershed and spilling down on Johnstown with a flow 44 percent greater than the flood of 1889. Although the flood-control works of the 1940s were claimed to have reduced the flood peak eleven feet, the storm still caused seventy-seven deaths and left eight missing. Suddenly Johnstown was faced with the reality that no amount of floodproofing could ever stop the Conemaugh; nature simply could not be subjugated by either the city or the Army Corps of Engineers. With this realization came a more open acknowledgment of the floods' destructive power, and a monument was raised not in a distant cemetery but in the town square. Now, for the first time, a flood gained the same sort of tribute hitherto reserved for the town's founder and its Civil War dead. The memorial was an admission that Johnstown's floods are a part of the town's history, not an exception. Implicit in the monument's placement was recognition that a lesson was to be learned from the flood, one of humility, of pride humbled by the forces of nature.

Before leaving Johnstown, one last visit should be made to the South Fork Dam. Federal legislation in 1964 authorized funds to acquire the ruins as the Johnstown Flood National Memorial, to be administered by the National Park Service. The legislation was amended in both 1972 and 1978 to enlarge the park further. The ruins had lain little disturbed since the nineteenth century, save for construction of a rail line through the gap ripped in the dam by the flood (Figure 3-9). The South Fork Fishing and Hunting Club had abandoned the property, and it eventually found its way back into private hands through public auction. The area around the club's still intact cottages and clubhouse was developed as the small town of St. Michael. The dam was left alone.

The changes at the South Fork Dam paralleled developments in Johnstown proper. The Johnstown Flood Museum Association was formed in 1970 with the goal of founding a museum. The association was motivated in no small measure by the fact that Johnstown was on the verge of losing the last of its steel industry. Tourism was seen as a way to turn a past catastrophe into a present-day asset. When the public library moved to new quarters in 1971, the old building was acquired, and the museum was dedicated on 31 May 1973. The association's membership has grown since, as have the scope and quality of the museum's displays. Although the flood of 1889 is still highlighted, the museum portrays other dimensions of Johnstown life and history. In 1982, for example, an exhibit on coal mining was added to stress mining's importance to Johnstown's prosperity, and after the flood of 1977 displays were updated to reflect that flood's effects on the city.

I think there was a certain symbolic dimension to the decisions to create a memorial at South Fork Dam and to build a flood museum in

Figure 3-9. Looking across the South Fork Dam from the Johnstown Flood National Memorial, which is administered by the National Park Service. A breach of this earthen dam during heavy rain caused the 1889 flood. The property was abandoned in the aftermath, and a rail line was eventually laid across the floor of the reservoir.

Johnstown. All these decades later the Johnstown Flood was being canonized as a key moment in American history. No longer an event of largely local significance, the flood was positioned as one of the critical events of the nineteenth century, one that demonstrated how Johnstown and all America faced adversity together as a nation. Far deeper sentiments are expressed in this new park than might be supposed. Now the subject of a national memorial and a local museum, the Johnstown Flood was being fitted into a highly selective and carefully shaped vision of the national past. It is a vision that resonates with the virtues of heroism, sacrifice, and fortitude, which are now read into Johnstown's history. I consider the invention of such interpretive traditions in more detail in Chapters 7 and 8, and look at local, regional, and national traditions that have been inscribed on landscape. It is enough here to say that the creation of the National Flood Memorial and the Johnstown Flood Museum expresses a significant change of attitudes about the 1889 flood. No longer a source of grief and suffering to be forgotten, the flood became an event to be celebrated as a symbol of Johnstown's—and America's—heroic past.

RETROSPECTIVE MEANING

Other sites of community disasters have been marked long after the event, sometimes on the order of a century later. Sometimes the delay is necessary for an event to be viewed in a favorable light. At other times memorialization does not take place until a community begins to celebrate its origins and history, perhaps during its centennial. In Peshtigo, Wisconsin, a memorial and museum commemorate the largest forest fire in American history (Figure 3-10).[17] This vast fire in the lumbering region of northern Wisconsin on 8 October 1871 has never attracted as much attention as the great Chicago Fire, even though the two were burning at the same time, the Chicago Fire beginning just a bit earlier the night before. Property loss was greater in Chicago, but the Peshtigo Fire claimed far more lives, perhaps as many as 1,100, and destroyed a far larger area, in the range of 2,400 square miles. Peshtigo gave its name to the fire only because it was the largest settlement burned and experienced the greatest loss of life. By all contemporary accounts, the fire's speed and ferocity were terrifying.[18] In Chicago the fire moved slowly enough from block to block for people to flee, and—more important—they had somewhere to flee to. Peshtigo was consumed by a firestorm that was already at full force as it swept out of the surrounding forests and into the town. The only refuge was the Peshtigo River, where those who survived lay submerged for almost six hours.

Peshtigo rebuilt after the fire and soon reclaimed its position as a thriving entrepôt and manufacturing center for the wood products and lumber industry. The dead were buried, but no common memorial was erected, as would be done in Johnstown two decades later. It was not until 1951 that the Peshtigo Fire was commemorated with a modest marker in the cemetery where many of the victims were buried. Remarkably a hundred survivors of the fire were in attendance at the dedication on 3 June. A decade later a museum was established adjacent to the memorial in a former church. Dedicated on the anniversary of the fire in 1963, the museum is not as ambitious as Johnstown's,

Figure 3-10. The Peshtigo Fire Museum, commemorating the great forest fire of 1871. The memorial is in a cemetery just to the left of the museum and was not erected until 1951, long after the largest forest fire in American history.

even though it seems inspired by the same motives. Again, many decades had to pass before the disaster was commemorated.

In Memphis, Tennessee, a memorial in Martyr's Park pays tribute to the yellow fever epidemics of the 1870s (Figure 3-11).[19] Few people today realize the battles Americans fought against massive epidemics in the eighteenth, nineteenth, and early twentieth centuries. The South in general, and the Mississippi Valley in particular, was faced with yellow fever, malaria, cholera, smallpox, dysentery, and dengue fever. Disease was such a problem that some scholars have argued that it had much to do with shaping the regional culture of the South.[20] Many of the epidemics spread along rivers, railroads, and roads. Memphis, as an important hub of commerce, was particularly hard hit. The city experienced a rash of epidemics from 1827 onward through the nineteenth century. The city's growth after the Civil War meant a larger population and greater fatalities every time disease struck, with the 1870s being particularly brutal. Yellow fever, cholera, and smallpox struck in 1873, claiming over two thousand lives. Yellow fever returned in 1878 and 1879, infecting almost twenty thousand people and killing almost six thousand.[21] Although the cause of yellow fever was then unknown, southerners did recognize the expediency of abandoning settlements infected by the disease. Only after the arrival of the twentieth century would scientists learn that yellow fever is carried by a species of mosquito that lives only in habitats created by humans in towns and villages. Running away *was* effective, and the population of Memphis did just that, by the thousands. Starting in 1878 and continuing into the next year, the city was abandoned. The state of Tennessee took the unusual step of repealing the city's charter until prosperity returned in the 1880s.

The victims of the epidemics of the 1870s were often buried close together in Memphis cemeteries for practical reasons, but no common memorial was erected at the time. The first commemoration did not occur until 1955, when the Catholic Church dedicated a marker at Calvary Cemetery to honor men and women of religious orders who died fighting the epidemics. A group of nuns from St. Louis who volunteered to serve in Memphis in 1878 was singled out for special recognition. Attitudes to commemorating the epidemics changed still further in the 1960s. Gradually, as Memphis looked back on its past, the epidemics came to be viewed in a more heroic light, as events that

Figure 3-11. The sculpture in Martyr's Park in Memphis, Tennessee, paying tribute to victims of the yellow fever epidemics of the 1870s. So severe were the outbreaks that Memphis was essentially abandoned during 1878–1879. Small memorials can also be found in Memphis cemeteries honoring both the victims and the doctors and nurses who fought the epidemic.

shaped the city's social, economic, and political life in distinctive, positive ways. A decision was made in the mid-1960s to create a small memorial park along the riverfront just south of the central city. A sculpture honoring the victims, heroes, and heroines of the epidemics was commissioned for this new "Martyr's Park." At the ground-breaking ceremony for the park in 1969, dignitaries reflected on the meaning of the epidemics and the sacrifices made on behalf of the community by those who stayed to fight them. As the secretary of the memorial association remarked, "In the tragedy they all became one. . . . While others fled, they laid down their lives for their friends that the city and the people they loved might not wholly perish from the Earth. . . . The erection of this monument at this time takes on special meaning. . . . If people could once come together in tragedy, why can we not solve our differences today without tragedy?" [22] The park's sculpture was dedicated in 1971, a full century after the epidemics. Again, as in Johnstown and Peshtigo, time had to pass before the significance of the tragedy could be appreciated and commemorated.

Such a long delay is by no means necessary, nor are grand monuments required to give voice to community loss. Even humble monuments can speak eloquently of a town's suffering, as in Xenia, Ohio. With one small difference, the block around its city hall is reminiscent of hundreds of other midwestern town squares. The current city hall, built in 1938, is just across East Market Street from its predecessor, built in 1901. Around and between the two are memorial benches, a tablet noting the town's contribution to the 1918 savings stamp campaign, a copy of the Ten Commandments donated by the Eagles Club, and a flagpole contributed by the American Legion. The town's Civil War casualties are honored with their own memorial. The difference is found tucked against the corner of the new city hall—a small tablet placed there in memory of those who lost their lives in the Xenia tornado of 3 April 1974 (Figure 3-12). Inscribed on the tablet are the names of the thirty-two people who lost their lives in the tornado and two national guardsmen who died in the aftermath. Tornadoes claim many lives every year. Some particularly widespread weather systems, such as the Palm Sunday storm of 11 April 1965, can spawn dozens of tornadoes and kill hundreds of people in a single day in five different states. Relatively few storms brutalize a town as thor-

Figure 3-12. The memorial to the Xenia, Ohio, tornado of 3 April 1974. In the background is the city hall.

oughly as did Xenia's, however.[23] When this tornado touched down on the afternoon of 3 April, it moved straight across Xenia from southwest to northeast, from the suburban developments of Windsor Park and Arrowhead right across the downtown and into the Pinecrest neighborhood. Few parts of Xenia escaped damage, and given the devastation, it is remarkable that the death toll did not climb higher. Xenia was lucky afterward, for aid was available right around the corner in other large Ohio cities. Cleanup and reconstruction began almost immediately, and now, two decades later, little evidence of the tornado remains. The memorial tablet is the only official marker, but it holds a place of honor in the town square as a forthright reminder of the community's loss.

Hidden Grief

The response to community loss is not always as straightforward as those outlined above. The Our Lady of the Angels School fire of 1958

Figure 3-13. The Our Lady of the Angels parish on Chicago's West Side. The parish church is to the right. The school on the left was built on the site of the one that burned in 1958. There is no outward sign of the disaster in the parish.

in Chicago offers, as a final example, a more complex and perhaps incomplete response to the tensions arising from community disaster. This fire swept through a parochial school on the afternoon of 1 December. Although the cause of the fire was never determined, it left ninety-two students and three teachers dead and seventy-six students injured, a devastating blow to a modest Catholic parish. The school, located at 3814 West Iowa, on Chicago's West Side, and immediately adjacent to the parish church, was completely gutted by the fire. No sooner had a requiem mass been held than the decision was made to rebuild on the same site as quickly as possible. Unlike New London and Collinwood, no memorial was envisioned for the grounds of the new school. The new building was to honor the nuns and students who died, according to the parish pastor, but no note of this was made on the plaque placed next to the front door of the new school when it opened two years later, in 1960 (Figure 3-13).[24] Instead a small memorial was erected in the Queen of Heaven Catholic cemetery in Hillside, Illinois, where many of the victims were buried, quite distant from the parish itself.

This is, to me, an unexpected outcome, as if the parish sought to come to terms with the disaster by pretending that it had not happened. The stress was not on memorializing the victims at the site, and the only marker was placed at a distant cemetery, as if to keep the tragedy both out of sight and out of mind. Instead the stress was on beginning the new school and getting the surviving students back to classes—as quickly as possible—in rented and borrowed classrooms on the West Side. Perhaps the lack of a memorial at the site has something to say about how the parish chose to deal with its grief. The desire to put the tragedy out of mind may have been so great as to subvert the normal grieving process. Perhaps the element of shame was greater here than in New London or Collinwood because the fire burned a church school—with obvious religious overtones—and because the fire department had not been able to save more students once on the scene. I would not go so far as to call the response a cover-up, but I think the element of shame may have subverted efforts to come to terms with the disaster as effectively as other communities have.

My only evidence is anecdotal, an account of the fire by one of the survivors. Michele McBride was thirteen at the time of the fire; trapped in her classroom, she survived extensive burns. Twenty years later she wrote a book about the fire with a passionate introduction:

> I wish I could say that it was bravery, superhuman courage, some inner, heaven-sent strength that sustained me through the agony, but I cannot. It was anger, raging anger that made me survive. I was angry at the lack of authority in my classroom when the fire broke out. I was angry because the firemen's ladders fell short of the classroom windows, because I lost the skin of my birthright, because I had to endure ravages of pain that I had thought were reserved for those condemned to the torments of Hell. I was angry for having lived, and I was angry at those who did die and left me behind. I was angry at being treated like a child after I had witnessed millions of years of burning all condensed into a single moment. . . . All the horrors of the world were presented to me in one brief second and made me realize I am mortal, I shall die.

In writing this book I have had to come to terms with many unspoken fears and ideas. It has been difficult, because I was taught very early to think that fire was the mystical act of a lonely God, and that it should not be talked about or questioned. . . .

Through the fire and its aftermath, I learned that disaster does not breed those strong, jolly, humble heroes that we read about in newspapers and books. Real survivors experience anger, panic, jealousy, guilt, self-doubt—all those feelings people never like to talk about, but which are as important and as powerful as bravery, kindness, and love. . . .

I was often embarrassed by all my feelings because I did not understand it was necessary to let all emotions surface. When people told me how brave I was, I always resented it. Bravery is a matter of choice, and I never volunteered for my position in the disaster. I simply acquired it, for the most part, because I misjudged the danger of fire. I did not know how fast fire travels or that hot smoke can kill. I thought that walls were safeguards that neither fire nor smoke could penetrate. I thought that I could safely wait for the firemen to come. I did realize that time was precious, and I was shocked when the teacher told us to say the Rosary, the longest prayer in the Catholic Church. It was such an inappropriate command, and yet what else could she have said? We were trapped, and some of my classmates already knew it.[25]

McBride goes on to recount her experiences in the aftermath of the fire. Even as she lay bandaged in her hospital room after having watched her classmates engulfed in flames, adults would not answer her questions about the fate of her friends, as if she were too tender to be told what she had witnessed with her own eyes. This sense of denial, and of shame, was strong long after the fire. When McBride began researching her book in the mid-1970s, neither the archdiocese of Chicago nor the Chicago Fire Department would permit her access to their records.

A sense of shame hangs over the Our Lady of the Angels fire that did not appear in the other community tragedies considered in this chapter. Although I argue in Chapter 6 that shame is a frequent motive for obliteration, it is not fair to say that the Our Lady of the Angels disaster followed this path. Rather, the response was confused and uncertain because, as McBride notes, "In my community it was always felt that bringing up memories of the fire would just add new grief to the old." [26] This tension is what I believe shaped the landscape of this disaster. The scene was veiled by a new building, and the small memorial was placed out of sight, far from the parish.

But McBride also writes, "I could not recover from the fire until I had learned how to mourn, not only for my dead friends but for my skin as well. I think that discussing a disaster and remembering the dead can help to heal wounds and resolve anguish in any stricken community." [27] This sentiment touches on the real power of memorials. Not only do they express in tangible form a community's loss, but the very process through which they are created "can help to heal wounds and resolve anguish in any stricken community."

Chapter 4

Heroic Lessons

Heroic causes can spur commemoration as readily as martyrdom and community loss can. The sites created in this way are shaped to express heroic lessons about the triumph of freedom over tyranny or of justice over injustice. Martyrdom and community loss may also help to transform these sites into shrines, but special care is devoted to justifying these sacrifices in terms of moral and ethical values, such as freedom, justice, and equality. These motives may be intertwined at some sites to produce a rather complex layering of memorials, particularly on battlefields. Some of the memorials are dedicated to the heroes who led the fight or died there (Figure 4-1). Others note the sacrifices ordinary soldiers made for their comrades and communities (Figure 4-2). A special few are dedicated to the principles for which the battle was fought, and these are the ones about which I am most concerned in this chapter. This monument building can take place in several ways. As James Mayo has pointed out in his richly detailed *War Memorials as Political Landscape,* the motives for America's domestic and foreign wars have varied greatly, as have the ways in which they have been commemorated on the battlefields and elsewhere.[1] Edward Linenthal and Emory Thomas have both pointed out the range of attachments that Americans have developed for these sites.[2]

In this chapter I am most interested in attachments that arise from the meaning of the

Figure 4-1. Monuments to leaders and heroes, like this statue honoring General George Meade at Gettysburg, are a commonplace feature of Civil War battlefields. Like the presidential memorials considered in Chapter 2, these monuments arise from the desire to pay tribute to the accomplishments and sacrifices of great leaders. From Lewis E. Beitler, ed., *Fiftieth Anniversary of the Battle of Gettysburg: Report of the Pennsylvania Commission* (Harrisburg, Pa.: Wm. Stanley Ray, State Printer, 1913), 166.

struggle itself. These are the lessons that are said to lie behind a battle rather than the meanings invested in memorials to ordinary troops, distinguished commanders, or valorous soldiers. Sometimes it is difficult to abstract the lessons of a battle from these other acts of valor and sacrifice. My point is only that, whereas almost all struggles produce heroes and induce a sense of community loss, not all come to be viewed as illustrating lessons worth remembering. Within any struggle there may be as many indecisive engagements as there are decisive victories and momentous turning points. Contrast the indecisive, plodding character of the Fredricksburg and Peninsular campaigns of 1862 with the fall of Vicksburg and the retreat of Lee's army after Gettysburg in 1863. Vicksburg and Gettysburg glow a bit brighter in the landscape because they helped to turn the tide of the Civil War. There are also

Figure 4-2. A regimental monument at Gettysburg. These pay tribute to the sacrifices of the ordinary soldier. Many of the regimental markers like this one were erected by the veterans of the units themselves. From Lewis E. Beitler, ed., *Fiftieth Anniversary of the Battle of Gettysburg: Report of the Pennsylvania Commission* (Harrisburg, Pa.: Wm. Stanley Ray, State Printer, 1913), 178.

many memorials to the "Indian Wars," but most commemorate individual heroes or the sacrifices of a local community rather than a lesson to be learned from the destruction of Native American cultures.

Although my concern is with sites where lessons become inscribed on landscape, even in these cases the first impulse toward commemoration derives not from marking a *lesson* but rather from the desire to honor the site of a hero's death or a community's sacrifice. Lessons are always learned after the fact, in retrospect. Vicksburg and Gettysburg could not be interpreted as turning points of the Civil War until after the fighting was over. Time must pass before an event's meaning and heroic connotations can be assessed and then embossed on landscape. While this process of interpretation is underway, veterans, families, and communities move in and begin the process of sanctification. Their efforts set the stage for later memorials that articulate the lessons to be learned from the sacrifice.

Virtually all the battlegrounds of the Revolutionary War are memorialized, as are events such as the Boston Massacre, which led up to the principal period of conflict between 1775 and 1781. Interest has tended to focus a bit more on the opening and closing events than those in between—that is, on the first skirmishes in Lexington and Concord in 1775 and the surrender of Cornwallis's troops at Yorktown in 1781.[3] The Continental Congress resolved to build a monument at Yorktown as soon as news of the surrender reached Philadelphia, but a century passed before one was built (Figure 4-3). Other battle sites were enshrined in the meantime, including Lexington and Concord, which had memorials before the war was over.[4] The Yorktown monument remains the grandest of the lot, but it is rivaled by the obelisk erected in Charlestown, Massachusetts, on the Bunker Hill battlefield (Figure 4-4). This is fitting, insofar as the two battles are perceived today as the war's bookends, the starting and ending points of the struggle for independence. Concord and Lexington came first, but Bunker Hill was the first real fight in which a well-organized corps of American troops made a good showing in a pitched fight with the British. The value of the battle was not so clear at the time; "indecisive" would be perhaps the best way to describe it. Unsurprisingly, a long time passed after the battle of 17 June 1775 until the monument was erected. The ground breaking was in 1825, and the completed monument was dedicated in 1843. By this time the battle did hold a secure place in the heroic saga of the Revolutionary War and represented a lesson in patriotism and sacrifice. As this lesson was inscribed on the battlefield, all other earlier tributes to fallen soldiers were effaced.

The Battle of Bunker Hill was a rather improvised affair on both sides. In the spring of 1775 the British sailed into Boston Harbor, intending to capture the city by taking control of strategic positions on the high ground to the south and north: Dorchester Heights and Charlestown, respectively. Word of the British plans reached the Americans, who decided to fortify Charlestown in anticipation of the British strike. Troops were sent the short distance from Cambridge on the night of 16 June to build a defensive position in Charlestown. Commanded to build a redoubt on Bunker Hill, the highest of several hills in the village, the troops began their work closer to the harbor on the

Figure 4-3. The memorial commemorating American-French victory over British forces at Yorktown, Virginia, in 1781. The monument was approved by the Continental Congress just after news of Cornwallis's surrender reached Philadelphia, but it was not completed until 1884. Many Revolutionary War sites gained additional attention at the time of the 1876 centennial or, like Yorktown, the centennial in 1883 of the signing of the peace accord with Britain.

Figure 4-4. The Bunker Hill Monument in Charlestown, Massachusetts, one of the grandest memorials to the Revolutionary War. Begun in 1825, fifty years after the battle, the memorial was inspired by the desire to cast the war in a heroic light as a formative event in the birth of the United States.

somewhat lower Breed's Hill, where the greater part of the battle was fought.

By dawn the British could see the preparations from the harbor. Eschewing a landing below Dorchester Heights, originally their first goal, the British began to plan an attack against the hastily fortified American position on Breed's Hill. A naval bombardment throughout the morning was intended to slow the American's work, weaken their fortifications, and most important, prevent additional troops from marching across the Charlestown neck from Cambridge to reinforce the somewhat beleaguered soldiers now concentrated on Bunker and Breed's Hills. Disembarking over 2,000 troops below the fortifications with the intent of breaking the American defenses at their weakest point between Breed's and Bunker Hills, the British attacked in the afternoon. The advance on the American stronghold was not well executed, and it took three assaults to break the defense. Most of the Americans were able to retreat toward Bunker Hill and then across the Charlestown neck to Cambridge. The British lost more troops than the Americans did, but by the evening of 17 June they had established control over the entire Charlestown peninsula and laid waste to what they found. The battle was by no means a victory for the Americans, but neither was it an astounding success for the British. The British remained in control of Boston until the following March but were prevented from expanding their perimeter by an American siege. The entire eight-month episode, from the Battle of Bunker Hill to the end of the siege of Boston, was largely inconclusive. The course of the war was decided elsewhere.

Given the ambiguous results, it is perhaps surprising that Bunker Hill was ever memorialized. Indeed the first efforts arose from a desire not to commemorate the battle itself but to honor one of its heroes. Major General Joseph Warren was one of the last defenders of the American redoubt on Breed's Hill. He remained to help cover the retreat to Bunker Hill and died as he made his escape. Warren, a local physician, had been an active and popular figure in the events leading toward revolution. He had helped to rally the minutemen at Lexington and was one of the American commanders at Breed's Hill. The Warren death site was marked in 1794 by the Masonic lodge of which Warren had been a member (Figure 4-5). The memorial was first proposed in 1776, just after Boston was retaken by American forces. It was a simple, eighteen-foot column surmounted by an urn, built of

Figure 4-5. The monument to Joseph Warren originally sited on Breed's Hill until the Bunker Hill Monument was begun. The monument was erected by Warren's fellow Masons and is typical of the memorials erected to heroes of particular battles. Its removal from Breed's Hill signaled a new conception of the meaning of the battle, one that stressed the importance of the engagement to the birth of the nation. From Richard Frothingham, *History of the Siege of Boston and of the Battles of Lexington, Concord, and Bunker Hill. Also, An Account of the Bunker Hill Monument,* 6th ed. (Boston: Little, Brown, 1903), 359.

wood on a brick pedestal with an inscription testifying to Warren's heroism and the valor of his "associates." This was a typical battlefield marker of the sort one would expect to honor leaders and fallen soldiers.

Apart from sporadic celebrations in Charlestown, none earlier than 1782, the monument to Warren and his colleagues was the only act of memorialization in the first generation after the war. The situation did not change until the 1820s, when work began at the local level to build a grander monument. These efforts seem to have been initiated by veterans of the battle and by those whose families fought in the Revolution. The motives involved paying tribute both to the battle itself and more generally to the entire Revolution. With the fiftieth anniversary of Bunker Hill approaching, Americans were beginning to look back with pride on what they had accomplished during the Revolution and since. The nation was now on a firm constitutional footing and growing economically. The urge to commemorate Bunker Hill was as much a desire to celebrate these achievements and announce them to the world as it was to remember the battle itself. Several Boston residents banded together to purchase the site of the battle in 1822, and the Bunker Hill Monument Association was formed the next year with the goal of raising a substantial memorial.

The plans took shape over the next two years. The monument was to be a grand 220-foot granite column towering over a fifteen-acre plot encompassing almost the entire area of the battle. To put this in context, the monument was planned as the most massive memorial to the Revolutionary War, even surpassing the 160-foot monument to Washington then planned for Baltimore (the one in Washington, D.C., came considerably later). By volume of stone, the monument would equal the Boston Custom House, one of the city's largest public buildings. Suffice it to say that the monument association's plans outstripped its purse. The final cost of the monument was just over $156,000, a tremendous sum that was far beyond the association's resources when the ground breaking occurred on the anniversary of 1825. Financing this grand plan was the major impediment to its completion, and the obelisk rose in fits and starts over the next eighteen years. The original plan had been to fund the monument by subscription, but this source was played out by about 1830 with only about half the final costs covered. Generous contributions by private donors, a smaller sum added by the state of Massachusetts, and the largess of women's patriotic groups that organized a fair to benefit the monument made up most of the difference. Thought had been given to calling the monument complete at 159 feet in the desperate financial hours of 1834, but the final fund-raising effort was sufficient to push the monument to its originally intended height. Nonetheless regrets were expressed that the association had been forced to sell some of its real estate—part of the battlefield—to raise money for the monument. The completion of the monument was celebrated in 1843, with the association taking possession from the contractor on 31 December 1844.

In retrospect there was positive benefit to the association's overly ambitious plans. The creation of the monument rallied citizens around the idea of a shared heroic past. This was important to building a sense of community and nationhood. The building of the Bunker Hill Monument was the largest voluntary communal act of its time. Donations came primarily from Boston and its immediate vicinity, but other states made contributions as well. Their citizens, too, had fought at Bunker Hill. The timing was important also. Veterans and their descendants were in the vanguard of the work to create the Warren memorial and the early efforts of the monument association. Only a handful of veterans remained alive by the time of the monument's final dedication, however. In the interval the story of the Revolutionary War had been passed on to a new generation, and this story had been transformed into a sort of fable, a David-versus-Goliath tale. By the time the monument was dedicated, it celebrated this story more than it did the individual heroes of the battle, like Warren, or the community's losses in the fighting. Tellingly the Warren memorial was removed from the battlefield during the construction of the new monument and never replaced.

This transformation was expressed in the words used to sanctify the Bunker Hill Monument. The change was already underway in 1825, when the cornerstone was inscribed "to testify the gratitude of the present generation to their Fathers, who, on the 17th June, 1775, here fought in the cause of their country, and of free institutions, the memorable battle of Bunker Hill, and with their blood vindicated for their posterity the privileges and happiness this land has since enjoyed." [5] The soldiers are mentioned, but it is their sacrifice to the *cause* that is highlighted. This changing emphasis is apparent in the addresses delivered at the ground breaking in 1825 and the dedication in 1843. Both were delivered by Daniel Webster, an early supporter and president of the monument association and, having been born in 1782, an articulate representative of a second generation of Americans interested in celebrating the fruits of nationhood.

The orations delivered at the laying of the cornerstone and the dedication of the completed monument paid tribute both to the heroes of the battle and to the immediate loss to the community. As

Webster intoned in his first oration: "We are among the sepulchres of our fathers. We are on the ground distinguished by their valor, their constancy, and the shedding of their blood."[6] One full section of the eight-part oration was a paean to the veterans of the Revolutionary War and to those who died. In Webster's view the Bunker Hill Monument was far more than a memorial to those who fought and died in 1775. Even in his first oration, he began to draw out the meaning of the monument as a symbol of the values of the new republic:

> No vigor of youth, no maturity of manhood, will lead the nation to forget the spots where its infancy was cradled and defended. But the great event in the history of the continent, which we are now met here to commemorate, that prodigy of modern times, at once the wonder and the blessing of the world, is the American Revolution. In a day of extraordinary prosperity and happiness, of high national honor, distinction, and power, we are brought together, in this place, by our love of country, by our admiration of exalted characters, by our gratitude for signal services and patriotic devotion.[7]

Webster developed this point further, to argue that American independence was a signal event for all of humanity:

> But our object is, by this edifice, to show our own deep sense of the value and importance of the achievements of our ancestors; and, by presenting this work of gratitude to the eye, to keep alive similar sentiments, and to foster a constant regard for the principles of the Revolution. . . . We consecrate our work to the spirit of national independence, and we wish that the light of peace may rest upon it forever. We rear a memorial of our conviction of that unmeasured benefit which has been conferred on our own land, and of the happy influences which have been produced, by the same events, on the general interests of mankind.[8]

In the first oration Webster dwelt at length on the currents of world history leading to the Revolution and to the bounty independence brought to Americans and the world. This was a theme to which he returned in even more depth in his dedicatory address eighteen years later, as if the monument had become a pivot of world history. In the dedicatory much less was said about the heroes of the battlefield, or even about the veterans. Instead Webster ranged still further across the history of civilization, the colonization of the New World, and the trouble then brewing between the United States and Spanish America, all to draw out the meaning of the monument. In weaving these themes together, Webster allowed that the monument

> brings to our contemplation the 17th of June, 1775, and the consequences which have resulted to us, to our country, and to the world. From the events of that day, and which we know must continue to rain influence on the destinies of mankind to the end of time. . . . Today it speaks to us. Its future auditories will be the successive generations of men as they rise up before it and gather around it. Its speech will be of patriotism and courage; of civil and religious liberty; of free government; of the moral improvement and elevation of mankind; and of the immortal memory of those who, with heroic devotion, have sacrificed their lives for their country.[9]

All these lofty words reinforce my point that Bunker Hill was commemorated less to honor the 140 soldiers who died there than to teach about the Revolution and its consequences. By 1843 the Bunker Hill Monument outweighed the reality of the battle. On a pound-per-casualty basis, the monument is one of the weightiest war memorials ever erected by Americans—to an indecisive battle. Although Americans lost this battle, however, they won the war. This is the point that Webster sought to drive home and the one that is inscribed on the landscape of Charlestown.

Gettysburg: High Tide of the Rebellion

Gettysburg is another battlefield where the lessons of a war have been embossed on landscape. All America's major and minor Civil War battlefields have been shaped extensively to commemorate those who fought and died there. Gettysburg has received more attention than most, being one of the most decorated battlefields to be found anywhere in the world. For the most part the memorials pay tribute to fallen heroes, leaders and martyrs, the travail of the ordinary soldier, and a sense of community loss. At Gettysburg and a few other major Civil War battlefields, virtually every corps, army, division, brigade, regiment, company, and battery that fought there has erected a memorial, often several. Visitors can sense the tides of the battles by walking the lines of the memorials. Heavily fortified positions are now anchored by massive obelisks and mighty bronze statues, and bloody skirmishes bring Union and Confederate monuments together shoulder to shoulder in otherwise vacant fields. These are fitting tributes to those who died in America's most destructive war. At a few battlefields such as Gettysburg, however, an additional layer of meaning overlays the landscape, one that reflects the lessons that Americans have sought to draw from the war. Here one finds memorials that allude to the war's immediate causes as well as its ultimate meaning.

Gettysburg is exceptional in this regard. Unlike some of the largely equivocal battles of the Civil War, Gettysburg was recognized as significant by both sides soon after it was fought. Once the war ended, retrospective assessments reinforced the judgment of Gettysburg as a turning point—even the midpoint—of the war. This judgment in turn allowed veterans on both sides of the conflict to use the Gettysburg battlefield as a point of reconciliation. These assessments resulted in memorials being erected on the battlefield: the national cemetery dedicated in 1863, the High Water Mark of the Rebellion Monument dedicated in 1892, and the Eternal Peace Light Memorial of 1938. These are the focus of my discussion, rather than the hundreds of other memorials that have been erected at Gettysburg and are amply documented elsewhere.[10]

The dedication of the national cemetery at Gettysburg was the first step in the battlefield's sanctification (Figure 4-6). Out of practical necessity, cemeteries were established during the Civil War on all the major battlefields. The bodies of soldiers were sent home whenever possible, but many had to be interred on site. These new burial grounds were usually dedicated within a few weeks or months of the fighting. Of the dedications held during the war, none is more famous than the one at Gettysburg. It was unusual for the president to attend one of these dedicatory ceremonies, and the short benedictory oration Abraham Lincoln delivered has since achieved enormous fame for its elo-

Figure 4-6. Gettysburg National Cemetery was dedicated in 1863 in a ceremony that Lincoln closed with the Gettysburg Address. The first impulse for sanctification of the battlefield arose from the practical need to bury and honor the dead. Lincoln used the opportunity to frame the battle as a test of the nation's resolve to defend its ideals.

quence. Lincoln was not invited to deliver the keynote oration, an honor awarded to Edward Everett of Massachusetts, but his presence at the ceremony signaled that Gettysburg was already viewed as a watershed event, although the battle was by no means an unequivocal victory for the North.

In three days of fighting early in July 1863, the great armies of the Union and Confederacy fought to a virtual standstill on the fields and hills around the small Pennsylvania town. After the collapse of a full-scale infantry charge on fortified Union positions—Pickett's Charge—on 3 July, the armies fell back into defensive positions, where they remained for a full day before General Lee's troops began a slow retreat south. This was the end of Lee's 1863 invasion of the North, but the Union's General Meade was given little credit for ending the offensive. Instead he was heavily criticized for failing to pursue and crush Lee's retreating army. To many it seemed that Union forces had again shied away from truly aggressive engagement with the Southerners, continuing a two-year streak of consistently plucking stalemate from the jaws of victory.

It did not take long, however, for these first assessments to be revised. The important point was that General Meade's forces had held together for a full three days. They took command of the high ground along the east of the battlefield on 1 July and sustained their positions against seasoned Southern troops for the duration. This was a dramatic turnaround from some earlier battles where Union troops had been caught in poor positions and forced to retreat in disarray. Furthermore, and despite his brilliant tactics earlier in the war, Lee was not at his best at Gettysburg. His infantry engaged before it had been massed and without adequate cavalry support. Lee failed to capture the high ground, and rather than flank or bypass the Union's fortified positions on the second and third days, he chose an infantry charge across open ground against a fortified army. Whereas Lee had seemed invincible before, after Gettysburg the North had hope, and despite tremendous casualties on both sides, the South paid a much higher price at Gettysburg than the North did. Its armies were already wearing thin after two full years of war, while the Union's were growing ever larger. Gettysburg cost the South troops and commanders it simply could not afford to lose in such numbers. Coupled with the fall of Vicksburg in the same week, Gettysburg signaled improving Union fortunes. Vicksburg constituted a major success in the Union's strategy to divide and conquer the South region by region, moving from the West. Gettysburg signaled success in the eastern theater.

This was the situation into which Abraham Lincoln stepped when he delivered his address at the dedication of the national cemetery on 19 November 1863. Here was an opportunity to reflect on the point of the war. In his two-hour oration Edward Everett had ample time to pay tribute to the dead and wounded. Lincoln was able to focus on the lesson alone. Although I quote the address in full in chapter 1, it is worth repeating the salient passages here:

> Four score and seven years ago, our fathers brought forth upon this continent a new nation, conceived in liberty and dedicated to the proposition that all men are created equal.
>
> Now we are engaged in a great civil war, testing whether that nation—or any nation, so conceived and so dedicated— can long endure.
>
> We are met on a great battle-field of that war. We are met to dedicate a portion of it as the final resting-place of those who have given their lives that that nation might live. . . .
>
> It is for us, the living, rather, to be dedicated, here, to the unfinished work that they have thus far so nobly carried on. It is rather for us to be here dedicated to the great task remaining before us; that from these honored dead we take increased devotion to that cause for which they here gave the last full measure of devotion; that we here highly resolve that these dead shall not have died in vain; that the nation shall, under God, have a new birth of freedom, and that government of people, by the people, for the people, shall not perish from the earth.[11]

Writers and scholars such as Garry Wills, Philip Kunhardt, and Frank Klement have argued that the speech represented a powerful shift in reasoning about the war and its purpose.[12] Lincoln articulated reasons for the North to fight—to defend the principle of a republican system of government and the ideal of equality voiced in the Declaration of Independence. The Civil War was a test of this vision of government and whether minorities had a "right" to break up government anytime they chose to squabble with the majority, as was happening in France and the new republics of Latin America. In earlier speeches

Figure 4-7. General view of Gettysburg battlefield with monuments, looking south along Cemetery Ridge. Civil War memorials were erected in great number through the end of the nineteenth century and into the twentieth. Most were constructed by Union veterans and states. Southern states began to erect major memorials only after the battle was assessed more impartially in ways that stressed the sacrifices of both Union and Confederate troops.

Lincoln had rather studiously employed the term *union* rather than *nation* in describing the United States. By Gettysburg he employed only the term *nation* and posed the war as test of its very conception. His words helped to transform the stigma of the battle into a lesson, a symbol of principle, purpose, and pride. These powerful sentiments gave special meaning to the Gettysburg battlefield itself.

Shrines began appearing on the major battlefields soon after the cessation of hostilities. Gettysburg was no different. Veterans returned for reunions and commissioned memorials to their comrades in arms, cities and communities paid tribute to their heroes, and states funded still larger monuments (Figure 4-7). In the first thirty years the work was almost entirely one-sided, with Union veterans commemorating the battle as an important turning point of the war. Pennsylvania veterans were the most active, because the battlefield was a good site for their encampments, and Southern veterans avoided the site almost entirely in favor of memorial building at battlefields in the South. This situation began to change gradually in the late 1880s and 1890s as new meanings were found in the battle. In the years immediately after the Civil War, veterans were active in purchasing land on many battlefields. At Gettysburg the Gettysburg Battlefield Memorial Association, founded in 1864, was the first to act to acquire land. Over time national veterans groups such as the Grand Army of the Republic (GAR) exerted control of these local organizations. They in turn lobbied strenuously for the federal government to assume stewardship of the site. This was possible only after the veterans groups began to adopt a more impartial, nonpartisan approach to marking the battlefields. The meaning of Gettysburg had to be reinterpreted in a way that would allow Southern veterans to take pride in the battle and participate in the commemoration of the battlefield. This was accomplished by stressing the pivotal role of the battle for both sides and playing down the idea that the battle was a unilateral Union victory.

As it turned out, some of the earliest assessments of the battle were borne out by subsequent events. After Gettysburg the Confederacy was never again able to mount a major invasion of the North. By the close of 1863 its resources were so depleted that even Lee's army had to settle into defensive positions around Petersburg and Richmond, only to emerge for the last desperate race westward toward Appomatox in the spring of 1865. Gettysburg was confirmed as the midpoint of the war. It might seem unlikely that such an assessment would have interested Southern veterans in marking the battlefield, but curiously the opposite was true. If Gettysburg was to be viewed as the midpoint of the war, then it must also have marked the high point of Confederate resistance. At no time during the war did such a powerful Southern army move as far north as Lee's did at Gettysburg. Even though they were turned back, the Southern veterans could take pride in their own heroism in pushing their cause to its limit deep in enemy territory.

As Oscar Handlin has written, the war was gradually assuming symbolic meanings not entirely aligned with reality but springing instead from "the will to believe that the war had been worthy of the communities that survived it."[13] Handlin continues:

The war became, in retrospect, an experience Americans had shared rather than one that had divided them. Interregional migrations, the growth of national consciousness, and the softening of sectional issues . . . tended to induce men everywhere to think back upon the war as the mortar that had cemented the fractured union and made it whole again.

Almost at once, the symbolic function of the war distorted men's understanding of what the conflict had been in actuality. The war was transmuted from the bitter conflict it had been into an episode of high adventure. Every base element vanished; only nobility remained.[14]

By seizing on this nostalgic vision of the war, however, Americans "grotesquely distorted the actuality of the war as it had been. And the continued preservation of that symbol also obscures the surviving problems left by the war."[15] Those, of course, were the problems of slavery, race, and the type of society the United States wished to become.

The monument that speaks to this conception of the battle as a peak of heroism on both sides was dedicated in 1892: the High Water Mark of the Rebellion Monument (Figure 4-8). This is a remarkable monument in the form of a tablet inscribed with the names of all the units, both North and South, that participated in Pickett's Charge and its repulse on the afternoon of 3 July 1863. The focus of the charge had been a small copse of trees just inside the Union lines on Cemetery Ridge. It was here that the last scattered survivors of the charge breached the bulwark of Union defenses in hand-to-hand combat. Here the charge was broken, and so too was Lee's army. The monument was one of the last major monuments erected on the battlefield before the land was assumed by the War Department in 1895. It is remarkable insofar as it was commissioned exclusively by Northern states but paid tribute to units of both sides. It was a critical step in reinterpreting the battlefield as a place in which all Americans could take pride.

The High Water Mark Monument and federal stewardship signaled a changing conception of Gettysburg, but they did not solve all the conflicts of interpretation. One of the reasons Southern veterans were reluctant to place regimental markers at Gettysburg was a rule that gave Union veterans an unusual advantage. Rules maintained

Figure 4-8. The High Water Mark of the Rebellion Monument at Gettysburg, which was completed in 1892, just before the battlefield park was turned over to the War Department. The monument was funded by Northern states but pays tribute to the Confederate forces who fought in Pickett's Charge. The monument signaled a changing, less partisan interpretation of the battle that stressed the heroism of soldiers on both sides of the fighting. The bipartisan spirit is captured here in a view of both Union and Confederate veterans gathered before the monument on the fiftieth anniversary. From Lewis E. Beitler, ed., *Fiftieth Anniversary of the Battle of Gettysburg: Report of the Pennsylvania Commission* (Harrisburg, Pa.: Wm. Stanley Ray, State Printer, 1913), 167.

that regimental markers were to be placed at the battle lines occupied by the units, not necessarily where the units fought. By the nature of the battle, with the Northern troops on the defensive for most of the three days, almost all the Union troops fought at their battle lines. The Southern troops had, on the other hand, been on the offensive. The acts of heroism the Confederate veterans wished to commemorate were often far removed from the point where the soldiers had formed their battle lines, almost a mile in the case of some of the units of Pickett's division. This did not seem fair to the Southerners and is one reason self-erected regimental markers for Confederate troops are rare at Gettysburg.

The new federal battlefield commission was sensitive to such slights. One of its early members, William Robbins, a Confederate veteran, worked to redress this disparity during his term on the commission. He acted to survey and mark almost all the Confederate positions with plaques and interpretive captions. Although these were not actually commissioned by the regiments engaged, his work helped to attain a balance between Northern and Southern commemorative efforts. By the time he finished, Confederate positions were more effectively marked than their Union counterparts, albeit far less grandly. This same spirit of reconciliation suffused the encampment held at Gettysburg on the fiftieth anniversary of the battle. The event was one of the grandest of Civil War battlefield reunions, attracting over fifty thousand veterans, both Union and Confederate, for the week-long ceremony. This was the era of the New South, and Americans on both sides of the Mason-Dixon Line were intent on stressing their commonalities rather than their differences. Indeed the warm feelings engendered by the fiftieth anniversary encampment eventually led to a third significant monument: the Eternal Peace Light Memorial (Figure 4-9).

This memorial extends the meaning of Gettysburg still further and draws out a third lesson: the fruits of unity and peace. The idea for the monument arose during the 1913 encampment but was slow to come into being; the plan lay dormant until preparations for the seventy-fifth reunion began in the mid-1930s.[16] Early efforts to solicit funds from all states whose soldiers fought at Gettysburg were not entirely successful, but states on both sides eventually contributed, Pennsylvania and Virginia being two of the first. The monument was placed in the northwest section of the battlefield, close to where the fighting began on 1 July 1863, and was dedicated on 3 July 1938 by President Franklin Roosevelt. Designed by the noted architect Paul Cret, the monument is faced with a bas-relief sculpted by Lee Lawrie depicting two figures holding a wreath and embracing, with an eagle positioned in the foreground. The symbolism is made clear by the inscription: "Peace Eternal in a Nation United. An enduring light to guide us in unity and friendship." A tall shaft atop the monument is surmounted by an eternal flame. Emphasized in this final monument was the successful reunification of the nation and its accomplishments since the Civil War. It is no coincidence that during this same period, between 1913 and 1938, Southern states began to erect monuments at Gettys-

Figure 4-9. The Eternal Peace Light Memorial at Gettysburg. Dedicated in 1938 and built with funds contributed by states on both sides of the conflict, the memorial carries the inscription "Peace Eternal in a Nation United. An enduring light to guide us in unity and friendship."

burg for the first time. Virginia was first in 1917, and North Carolina followed in 1929 with a statuary group by Gutzon Borglum, the sculptor of the Mount Rushmore memorial. In 1933 stewardship of the battlefield lands passed to the National Park Service. During the New Deal the National Park Service ceased to be confined to safeguarding the nation's natural wonders, its responsibilities having been expanded to encompass America's historical monuments. Care for Gettysburg, along with most other major Civil War battlefield parks, was transferred from the soldiers of the War Department and army to the historians of the National Park Service.

The monuments considered here are only three of the hundreds that grace the Gettysburg battlefield. They neither dwarf the others nor dominate the landscape. Yet I sense that they differ from the others in the motives behind them. Far more than do the dozens of markers that pay tribute to acts of heroism by individuals and individual fighting units, these three seek to draw out the meaning of Gettysburg. Each gives voice to a different message: Gettysburg as a rallying point for a war-weary North (1863); Gettysburg as heroic turning point for a nation at war (1892); and Gettysburg as a symbol of peace, unity, and friendship (1938). These differences were mirrored in the way each monument was executed. The 1863 monument at the National Cemetery was a unilateral act by the federal government. The 1892 monument was commissioned by Northern states but paid tribute to the heroism of Southern troops. The 1938 monument was funded by states on both sides of the conflict. Taken together these three monuments help to show how moral lessons come to be embossed on landscape through the process of sanctification.

The Lessons of Haymarket

The lessons of war are often marked in the landscape, but other struggles have as much potential to shape landscape as do battles such as Bunker Hill and Gettysburg. America has experienced many other struggles fought over far different issues, including civil and human rights and social and economic justice. The labor and civil rights movements have been particularly rich in ethical lessons. Not all have changed landscape, but the Haymarket bombing of 1886 is an example of one that has. Recognized today as a major setback for the cause of labor, a key event in the political history of Chicago, and a low point in American jurisprudence, the Haymarket affair is interesting also because two different and contradictory lessons were abstracted from the violence. Each is marked in a different place. The police and Chicago's business community enforced control of the riot site and erected a monument to the police, the "defenders" of Chicago. The labor organizers who were executed unjustly for the bombing were honored in a martyrium just outside the Chicago city limits. Each side sought to assert its view of the events of May 1886 and the aftermath.

The history of labor in the nineteenth century was a long series of successes and setbacks. Each time the cause rallied for a major advance, a crushing blow was delivered by industrialists through the police or military. The Haymarket affair was one of the first renewed rallies by labor since the Great Railroad Strike was crushed in 1877. After Haymarket, and the Pullman and Homestead strikes soon thereafter, the labor movement was not able to regain its influence until several decades into the twentieth century.

Haymarket was rooted in a national campaign for an eight-hour work day for industrial workers. Workers at the McCormick factory, one of Chicago's major industrial plants, went on strike in support of the campaign. During the first two days of May, workers demonstrated at the McCormick plant and elsewhere around Chicago without disturbance. On 3 May the strike turned violent. The McCormick plant had called in strikebreakers, and a riot ensued at the end of a shift when these workers tried to leave the factory into the midst of a demonstration. Police intervened, costing the lives of at least two strikers and perhaps more. The strikers and their supporters were outraged, and calls for revenge were immediate. A rally was called for 4 May at one of Chicago's public market squares—Haymarket Square, west on Randolph Street across the Chicago River.

Throughout the day the rally remained peaceful. As many as 3,000 people gathered to hear speakers decry the killings of the previous day and express support for the strike. Even Chicago's mayor, Carter Harrison, briefly joined the audience during the speeches. By evening the demonstration began to fizzle as the weather turned cold and rainy. After 10:00 P.M., with the last speaker appearing before the remaining group, events took a violent turn. Police had gathered at a nearby station, waiting to see what would happen during the demonstration. When police observers reported "inflammatory" language being used, the squad had the reason it needed to intervene. As many as two hundred police officers marched into the crowd and ordered it to disperse, just as the demonstration was ending. While police and demonstrators milled about, a bomb was thrown into the police formation. To this day the identity of the bomber remains a mystery, but the bomb was well aimed. The explosion wounded many officers and left the remainder in panic, firing into the crowd and chasing the demonstrators. The toll of the mêlée will never be known exactly, since many of the civilian casualties were spirited away for fear of police retaliation, but at least four demonstrators were killed and perhaps a hundred injured. The police lost seven dead and sixty injured, not all from the explosion. Evidence suggested that, in the chaos, many police were caught in their own crossfire. Regardless of the cause, the damage was done. The small bomb was enough to set back the cause of labor for decades.

Eight men were arrested for the killings, not because there was any evidence that they were responsible for the bomb, but because they were leaders of the strike and demonstration. In proceedings now recognized as one of the great travesties of American justice, all eight defendants were convicted; seven were sentenced to death and the eighth, to prison. From start to finish the trial was stacked against the defendants. Even the bailiff played a role in weeding out jurors sympathetic to the defendants, remarking: "I am managing this case, and know what I am about. These fellows are going to be hanged as certain as death. I am calling such men . . . [as jurors] as the prosecution wants." [17] Justice was not the point of the exercise, as the state attorney noted in his summation for the prosecution: "Law is on trial. Anarchy is on trial. These men have been selected, picked out by the grand jury and indicted because they are the leaders. They are no more guilty than the thousands who follow them. Gentlemen of the Jury, convict these men, make examples of them, hang them and you save our institutions, our society." [18]

Of the seven sentenced to death, four were hanged on 11 November 1887, a day that became known as "Black Friday." The governor of Illinois commuted the sentences of two of the men to life imprisonment the day before the executions under the pressure of local, national, and international opinion. A third committed suicide on the morning of the hangings, but under suspicious circumstances. The three men who escaped death were pardoned six years later, in 1893.

In the aftermath of the executions not one but two shrines were born. Supporters of the martyrs rallied around their fallen heroes. In one of the largest funerals ever held in Chicago, the five martyrs—the four who were hanged and the suicide—were buried on 13 November 1887. Civic authorities had banned their burial inside the city limits, so the bodies were interred together in Waldheim Cemetery, which lies to the west of Chicago in Forest Park. One of their attorneys, William Black, delivered the first of the eulogies, making clear the cause for which the men died: "The world knows how bravely, how unflinchingly, with what self-sacrifice these men went to their end. . . . Without a tremor of fear or doubt, without a shudder of regret, they offered up their lives. We do not stand here by the bodies of felons. There is nothing disgraceful about their death. They died for liberty, for the sacred right of untrammeled speech and for humanity. We are proud to have been their friends."[19] Another of the attorneys, Albert Currlin, closed the ceremonies even more forcefully: "Oh, workmen of Chicago, be one, be strong. Be one from this day. Vow it in the presence of these dead. Shake off the yoke which Mammon lays upon your shoulders. Be free!"[20] These sentiments were echoed by others throughout the nation and abroad, as one commentator remarked: "The time will come when mankind will look back upon the execution of the anarchists as we of this day look back upon the burning of the witches of New England."[21] The bodies, laid to rest in a temporary vault on 13 November, were transferred to their permanent resting place the next month.

A memorial was erected on the grave site in 1893 (Figure 4-10), funded by the Pioneer Aid and Support Association, a relief group for the families of the Haymarket Eight founded by one of the widows. The sculpture depicts justice in the figure of a woman placing a laurel wreath on the head of a fallen worker with her left hand while her right is poised to draw her sword as she gazes forward into the future. Thousands gathered for a dedicatory parade on 25 June in Chicago and for the ceremony at Waldheim. Chicago was at the time in the midst of its famous Columbian Exposition, which ensured that the dedication would receive worldwide attention. Once again the lessons to be learned from the Haymarket affair were the subject of orations:

Figure 4-10. The Haymarket Martyrs Monument at Waldheim German Cemetery in Forest Park, Illinois. This monument was dedicated in 1893 and depicts justice in the figure
of a woman placing a laurel wreath on the head of a fallen
worker with her left hand while her right is poised to draw
her sword as she gazes forward into the future.

"When the hatred and passions of our time resound no more, for you
too, who are resting here, the hour of a juster verdict will have come.
Until then, may this monument prove to the unbelievers, to the yet
doubting and hesitating ones, that those who fell in the struggle for a
better social order have left an honorable memory with all friends of
justice and liberty."[22] Inscribed on the monument's pedestal are the
last words spoken by one of the martyrs, August Spies: "The day will
come when our silence will be more powerful than the voices you are
throttling today." The monument remains to this day a pilgrimage site
and the subject of regular commemoration.

One reason such a grand memorial was erected in 1893 was because another, far different sort of monument had been raised in the

interim: one to the police. They too had their own martyrs, of course, the officers killed during the 4 May riot. Subsequent investigations into their behavior tarnished their heroic claims considerably, as did inquiries into corruption within the department beginning in 1889, but they still had their supporters. The probusiness *Chicago Tribune* announced a drive to create a monument to these martyrs in January 1888, the logical site being Haymarket Square. Fund-raising was not a wholesale success. Popular support was so low that the project was saved only by the intervention of antiunion businesses, many from outside Chicago. Their sizable contributions near the end of the year pushed the project forward to completion. The design selected featured a policeman with his arm raised atop a pedestal emblazoned with the city and state seals and flanked by lanterns (Figures 4-11 and 1-4). The statue was dedicated on Memorial Day the following year. Mayor Cregier intoned at the dedication: "May it stand here unblemished so long as the metropolis shall endure to say to the millions who come upon it: This is a free and lawful country with plenty of room for the people of all the earth who choose to come here to breathe the free air and to obey these laws, but not an inch of room or an hour to dwell here for those who come for any other purpose."[23] At the rear of the pedestal is the simple inscription: "Dedicated by Chicago to her Defenders in the Riot of May 4, 1886." For many years the statue was the focus for annual Memorial Day ceremonies honoring Chicago's police.

Many resented the police monument, particularly its location at the Haymarket site and the fact that it depicted the police as "defenders" of Chicago. For those involved in the events of 1886 and the Pullman strike of 1893, the police seemed to be little more than the hired hands of industrialists. The monument was the subject of repeated vandalism for the next ninety years. William Adelman has traced this strange history all the way back to 1890, when an attempt appears to have been made to blow up the statue.[24] The seals on the pedestal were first stolen in 1903, but competition over the site took a dramatic turn in 1927 when, on the anniversary of the demonstration, a streetcar driver deliberately crashed his trolley into the statue. The statue was repaired and transferred to Union Park, further west on Randolph Street, where it stayed until 1956. By this time Haymarket had changed considerably and was cut by a new freeway. An overpass now spanned Randolph Street at the Haymarket above the expressway, and a special platform was constructed to one side for the statue,

Randolph St. West of Des Plaines 1890

Figure 4-11. The Police Monument at Haymarket in 1890.
The monument was funded largely by antilabor businesses
and proved unpopular. The statue is no longer on view in
public. Photograph ICHi-16155 courtesy of the Chicago
Historical Society.

where it was repositioned. Little remains today; the statue had to be
moved again for its own protection.

This last episode began in 1968 as demonstrations against the
Vietnam War were mounted in Chicago and throughout the nation.
The statue was an easy target and on 4 May was defaced with paint,
but the vandalism escalated after that summer's riots at the Democratic convention in Chicago. Again, as in the Haymarket Riot, excessive
police force ended with protesters being indicted for inciting the violence. In response the statue was blown up on 6 October 1969. Blame
was placed on the Weatherman faction of the Students for a Democratic Society, and the mayor responded to this obvious affront by vow-
ing to restore the statue. Rededicated on 4 May 1970, the statue was
again bombed on 6 October. Mayor Richard Daley ordered another

restoration and around-the-clock police protection. The statue was never harmed again, but the cost of protection was too high to sustain. The statue was moved indoors in 1972 to the lobby of the police central headquarters and then in 1976 to a courtyard of the city's new police academy on Jackson Boulevard a few blocks south of Union Park. Only the badly defaced pedestal remains in public view, perched somewhat precariously above the Kennedy Expressway (Figure 4-12).

The Haymarket affair is somewhat of a rarity insofar as both sides of the conflict chose to draw—and inscribe on the landscape—very different lessons. It is the victor who usually gains the final say, but the lesson of "law and order" drawn by the police was in this case too much at odds with the facts. Contention over the site marked by vandalism and removal of the statue resulted. The cause of labor was validated by subsequent events, but even its lesson has been inscribed no further than Waldheim Cemetery. Some discussion was given to redesigning the Haymarket site entirely to mark the centennial of the bombing. A park and memorial were envisioned, ones that not only would give voice to labor's struggle for the eight-hour day and trade unions but also, and more generally, would honor the freedoms of speech and assembly. Nothing ever came of these plans, and the site remains derelict. The problem with inscribing these broader messages on Chicago's cityscape stretch beyond the issues of commemorating the Haymarket affair itself. In Chapter 9 I make the case that the American labor movement as a whole has equivocated over commemorating its past and has had a difficult time inscribing the story of its achievements on landscape. Quite apart from these difficulties, the Haymarket monuments derived from the same motives as those at Bunker Hill and Gettysburg. Attempts to memorialize these sites involved commemorating the sacrifices of the martyrs and heroes that they had generated. At the heart of these efforts was a desire to draw a lesson from each battle and tragedy, a lesson that transcended the immediate sacrifices and reflected on values of liberty, justice, and community. These are the lessons that have helped to guide the shaping of each site.

FURTHER LESSONS

A striking aspect of all three cases in this chapter is the length of time over which landscape shaping took place at them. The lessons that are

Figure 4-12. The remains of the pedestal of the Police Monument on the north side of Randolph Street at the Kennedy Expressway. After being severely damaged several times, the statue was moved indoors to the police academy. Only the scarred pedestal remains.

marked took time to develop—as long as seventy-five years at Gettys-burg—and such lessons can remain in contention even longer, as did the police monument at Haymarket. This slow emergence of meaning and inscription is an issue to which I return in the final chapters of this book. There the focus is on the invention of historical traditions, the development of stories, myths, and legends that help to cement bonds of community at the local, regional, and national levels. I mention this because, although I considered Bunker Hill and Gettysburg as sepa-rate cases in this chapter, their transformations are difficult to abstract from changing conceptions of national identity that have also been embossed on landscape, a particular concern of Chapter 8.

I do not wish to leave the impression that the moral lessons I have been discussing were an anomaly of the nineteenth century. Monu-ment building certainly received a boost in the nineteenth century as Americans began to look back on their past with an eye toward estab-lishing their place in history, but it did not end there. The twentieth century is just as rich in examples. I ended my case studies with the Haymarket affair because it leads discussion away from battlefields and toward contested sites that are more typical of the twentieth cen-tury. Lessons of this century include those of labor rights, civil rights, human rights, and the rights of Americans to protest an unpopular war. In a whole range of contemporary sites—most still evolving—the lessons drawn from particular events outweigh the sacrifices of the individual victims. And sometimes, even in the twentieth century, Americans are still grappling with events long in the past, such as the Salem witchcraft trials. As I mention in the first chapter, much of the debate over Salem's proposed tercentennial memorial revolved around the lesson that was to be drawn from the witchcraft episode.

To see this process at work, I am inclined to jump ahead to some sites that I consider in more detail in Chapter 9. At Kent State Uni-versity small markers erected first by B'nai B'rith Hillel and then by faculty to honor four students killed by national guardsmen on 4 May 1970 evolved into a much larger, institutionally sanctioned monu-ment that sought to reflect on the turmoil of the entire Vietnam War period. The monument, dedicated on the twentieth anniversary of the shootings, carries the inscription "Inquire. Learn. Reflect." In Califor-nia at Tule Lake and in the Owens Valley, in Utah at Topaz Moun-tain, and at the sites of seven other Japanese American relocation cen-ters used in World War II, efforts have been made to draw attention

Figure 4-13. The site of the Tule Lake Japanese American Relocation Center. Here the lesson inscribed on the tablet reads, in part: "The majority were American citizens, behind barbed wire and guard towers without charge, trial or establishment of guilt. These camps are reminders of how racism, economic and political exploitation, and expediency can undermine the constitutional guarantees of United States citizens and alike. May the injustices and humiliation suffered here never recur."

to the unjust incarceration of American citizens in an episode of wartime hysteria. The message that will be inscribed on these relocation centers is still in debate, but it will revolve around the lesson that is already marked at sites such as Tule Lake (Figure 4-13). Of the internees, the marker tells us, "The majority were American citizens, behind barbed wire and guard towers without charge, trial or establishment of guilt. These camps are reminders of how racism, economic and political exploitation, and expediency can undermine the constitutional guarantees of United States citizens and alike. May the injustices and humiliation suffered here never recur." Even events such as the consecration of the Memphis's Lorraine Motel as a civil rights educational center two decades after Martin Luther King Jr. was assassinated on its balcony (Chapter 2) speaks to a desire to draw broader meaning from his death. The Lorraine is intended as more than a tribute to a fallen hero; it seeks to honor the accomplishments of the entire civil rights movement, which King did much to inspire and lead. I have saved the discussion of these and similar sites of evolving and contested meaning for Chapter 9.

Chapter 5

Innocent Places

Most episodes of tragedy and violence never lead to sanctification. Their sites are instead rectified; that is, they are rehabilitated and returned to use. I often think of these rectified sites as *innocent* insofar as they happened to be in the wrong place at the wrong time. In the aftermath of these events, attention focuses less on questions of honor and shame than on finding the cause of a disaster and its remedy. The site is typically immaterial to the debate and fades quickly from view. One consequence is that sites of some of the largest accidents and disasters in American history, including fires, explosions, shipwrecks, and airplane and train crashes, are difficult to find in the landscape today. Pinpointing their locations can involve a good deal of detective work. When found, there may be no sign of the disaster whatsoever.

Rectification may involve prompt reuse of a site, although delays of a few years are not uncommon. The timing is less important than the process through which these places are relieved of blame—how attention shifts away from place and toward remedy. I can illustrate this blame shifting by turning to two of America's worst accidents.

The Iroquois Theater Fire

The Iroquois Theater fire occurred in turn-of-the-century America when drama and vaudeville attracted the same crowds downtown that nowadays

Figure 5-1. The Iroquois Theater on 30 December 1903. The auditorium where most of the fatalities occurred was in the interior of this block, perpendicular to the foyer seen here. Photograph ICHi-02590 courtesy of the Chicago Historical Society.

flock to suburban multiplexes. On 23 November 1903 the Iroquois opened as one of Chicago's largest and most ornate palace theaters. Its site in the middle of the north side of Randolph Street between State and Dearborn placed it at the heart of Chicago's theater district. To make the best use of the *L*–shaped property, a foyer led from the theater's entrance on Randolph Street to an auditorium stretching along the interior of the block (Figure 5-1). The north wall of the auditorium and its exits faced a midblock alley, running east to west perpendicular to the entrance. The theater's seating rose in three levels from the stage—orchestra, balcony, and gallery. The Iroquois proved to be an immediate success and drew large audiences during its first month of operation, including a crowd of between 1,800 and 2,000 for a matinee on 30 December 1903. Before the afternoon was over, between 582 and 602 people—about a third of the audience—were dead in a blaze that lasted little more than fifteen minutes.[1] The Iroquois disaster remains the worst theater fire in U.S. history.

Subsequent inquiries pinpointed the cause of the fire as a spark thrown from a spotlight to a curtain high above the set. Stagehands could not reach the blaze with their underpowered fire extinguishers, but they did release the theater's asbestos fire curtain as the flames swirled up into the flyway. If it had worked, the curtain would have confined the fire to the stage, and vents on the roof of the flyway would have opened automatically to draw the fire up and out of the auditorium. The curtain jammed midway down the proscenium arch, however, and the flyway vents never opened. Instead the fire was pushed under the curtain and into the auditorium by a blast of fresh air coming from a stage door opened by actors fleeing the heat and smoke. Once in the auditorium, the fire and smoke shot upward toward the theater's main ventilator above the gallery. The smoke and heat coursed along the ceiling into the audience seated in the gallery and in the balcony just below. Despite one actor's efforts to calm the audience, the crowd panicked and stampeded. This made matters worse, because the theater's aisles were narrow and the exits poorly marked, with some even hidden behind curtains. Many exit doors opened inward, and some were locked. The hallways to the foyer were so poorly planned that crowds collided and died in narrow doorways and in areas where passages from different parts of the auditorium intersected at sharp angles and pushed torrents of people headlong into others. The fire escapes into the alley along the north wall were equally treacherous. Many exit doors led onto each external gantry, meaning that each new wave of victims blocked the ones behind. Worse still, the gantries led past fire vents that began to burst open and spill flames into the struggling crowd.

The theater lacked its own alarm system, but a fire station was located just around the corner. Fire fighters received the first alarm at 3:32 P.M., about ten minutes after the start of the blaze. By the time they arrived, the fire was almost out. Fed by the sets on the stage and the upholstered seats of the balcony and gallery alone, the fire did not last long or cause great physical damage to the theater. On the lower orchestra level only the first few rows of seats were burned. The rest of the theater was left untouched and structurally sound, including the ornate foyer and exterior facade. Fully 70 percent of the casualties had been seated in the gallery, and most of the remainder had been in the balcony. The actors, stagehands, and orchestra-level audience escaped with few injuries. By the time fire fighters entered the theater, extinguishing the fire was less of a problem than removing the bodies that blocked almost all the exits.

Chicago and the nation were stunned by the disaster, not least because it had occurred in a supposedly "fireproof" theater. In a public proclamation of grief, Mayor Carter Harrison called for a subdued New Year's celebration, canceled all public events, and dedicated 2 January 1904 as a citywide day of mourning. In the long run, however, and despite the tremendous loss of life, no memorial was raised at the site, and the building was used again as a theater. Unlike disasters that strike small or self-identified communities, the Iroquois fire claimed victims from every stratum of Chicago society. Even though the fire claimed almost twice as many victims as the Chicago Fire of 1871, no single neighborhood or group bore a disproportionate share of the suffering. The victims were claimed by relatives and buried privately.

Of more interest were the investigations into the cause of the disaster. Inspectors discovered that the theater failed to meet many provisions of Chicago's existing fire code. The theater had been allowed to open before it had been completed, and building and fire inspectors had overlooked the lack of these finishing touches. The stage had no sprinkler system, no fire alarm, and no automatic controls to vent smoke and flame through the flyway roof. Without a proper smoke-damping system in place, the flames had naturally burst across the audience to the closest vent—the outlet above the gallery. The theater did have some of the required safety features, such as an asbestos fire curtain and onstage fire extinguishers, but these proved to be inoperative or ineffective. Once the curtain jammed, its wooden fittings caught fire and allowed it to rupture. The fire extinguishers did not have the power to reach high above the stage to the flames. Apart from these deficiencies in the theater, the fire code of 1903 was itself highly inadequate. It contained no prohibitions against some of the

---

traps that claimed the most victims. Like other theaters of its day, the Iroquois lacked an emergency lighting system, its exits were unmarked, some critical exit doors opened inward, some were locked or concealed by curtains, and some passageways from the auditorium led to dead ends.

Legal action was initiated almost immediately against the theater's owners, as well as against many city officials. Damages were sought from the Iroquois Theater Company in 272 lawsuits.[2] The courts yielded little satisfaction; none of the defendants was convicted of a crime, and the insolvency of the theater company prevented payment of damages. The legal battle left undecided the fate of the theater itself. It might have been easier for Chicago if the theater had been consumed by the fire, but the structure remained intact as a valuable asset. Tension arose between the company's creditors, who wanted to reuse the building, and members of the public who felt that reuse was almost sacrilegious. As the president of the newly formed Iroquois Memorial Association stated, "I for one will fight this theater all the rest of my life. It is a disgrace of the city. No other community would allow it to open."[3] Yet the insolvency of the Iroquois Theater Company placed the building in the hands of creditors who had an obvious financial stake in defending the reopening of the theater.

The conflict was resolved in favor of the new owners. Unlike Ford's Theatre, which was not allowed to reopen for business (or at least not as a theater until the 1960s), the Iroquois returned to business within a year. I think that the Iroquois would have closed as a theater, or even been demolished, except for two relatively minor factors: the postfire investigation demonstrated that the disaster could not have been prevented even if the theater had met the then-current fire codes, and the theater was under new management when it reopened. These are subtle points, but they meant that the disaster could be blamed in part on insufficient safety regulations and on the actions of the original owners and of fire and police officials. The disaster resulted from negligence rather than irremediable defects in the building itself. Remedies were available for all the theater's deficiencies and, once applied, provided assurance that similar accidents could be avoided in the future.

Renamed Hyde and Behman's Music Hall, the building reopened on 19 September 1904. Potential for trouble was anticipated by the new management. Police officers were posted around the theater, and ushers were instructed to prevent patrons from wandering away from

Figure 5-2. The former site of the Iroquois Theater in the 1980s. The theater was reopened after the fire under a different name. The entire building was replaced by a larger theater—the Oriental—in 1926. The Oriental closed as a theater in the late 1970s, and the foyer was converted into retail space.

their seats for sight-seeing inspections of the auditorium. Despite a full house on opening night, however, Hyde and Behman's Music Hall did not do well and closed in late 1905. Reopened soon after as the Colonial Theater, the building remained in service until 1924, when it was demolished to build a larger theater, the Oriental. The Oriental continued as a movie theater until 1981, when it was closed and its foyer remodeled as a clothing store (Figure 5-2).

By the time of the Oriental Theater's demise, only faint memories remained of the Iroquois disaster. Save for an occasional notice in local newspapers on the anniversary of the disaster, no reminder of the fire was left anywhere in Chicago. This was not always the case. The Iroquois Memorial Association raised considerable funds for a tribute, which were used to rent and renovate a small building on what is now Wacker Drive as an emergency hospital, just a few blocks from the disaster site. The hospital was completed in 1910 and donated to the city.[4] A commemorative plaque was dedicated there in a ceremony in 1911.[5] The memorial association hoped at the time to establish a second hospital but never did. This tribute to the Iroquois victims did not long endure. The city closed the hospital as an economy measure in early 1935.

The memorial association also convened annual commemorative services for many years, but not at the theater site. The services were held at the Chicago Public Library, a few blocks east on Randolph Street, where they continued to attract survivors and the families of victims for many decades. As part of the annual rite, a fire alarm was sounded at 3:32 P.M. from the same box that brought the first company of fire fighters to the Iroquois on the day of the disaster. For fifty-five years it was rung by the same fireman, Michael J. Corrigan, who sounded the alarm in 1903.

In the late 1950s the services were discontinued, as was the rite of sounding the alarm. Few survivors remained, and still fewer were willing or able to attend. Sometimes tragedies remain unmarked until the last survivors are near the ends of their lives. The last survivors are sometimes the most influential in agitating for monuments that will prevent the memory of their experiences from dying with them. This was not true of the Iroquois disaster. By the time of the last services, the Iroquois Memorial Hospital was long gone and the opportunity to memorialize the disaster in other ways was being lost. Nowadays, if the Iroquois is mentioned at all, it is by way of comparison to other, more recent fires. A small panel in a display case at the city's fire academy explains the disaster's effects on fire fighting and fire safety in Chicago.

THE *EASTLAND* DISASTER

Only a short walk separates the former location of the Iroquois Theater from the site of a second great accidental tragedy. On the morning of 24 July 1915, on the south bank of the Chicago River between Clark and LaSalle Streets, the excursion boat *Eastland* capsized, claiming 812 victims.[6] The *Eastland*'s capsizing remains one of the worst peacetime inland boating disasters in history. In the United States this record is perhaps exceeded only by the loss of the *Sultana* on the Mississippi just after the close of the Civil War, as that ship carried liberated prisoners of war north from Southern camps, and by the *General Slocum* disaster in New York City in 1904. The *Eastland* disaster actually rivals the great maritime tragedies of its period. The *Titanic* sank in the Atlantic in 1912, claiming approximately 1,500 lives; the *Empress of Ireland* went down in 1913 at the mouth of the St. Lawrence River, taking almost 1,000 lives; and the *Lusitania* was torpedoed in 1915 off the Irish coast, claiming over 1,000 passengers. Indeed almost as many passengers were claimed on the *Eastland* as on the *Titanic*, although far fewer crew. In addition to resulting in a tremendous loss of life, the *Eastland* disaster was all the more tragic because it occurred at dock in broad daylight in the middle of a busy city, yet no one was able to prevent the huge number of deaths. My concern is with the site of these deaths on the Chicago River, but to understand the fate of this place, I must turn briefly to the ship that caused the disaster.

The *Eastland* was a tall, narrow ship, 256 feet long, that had been built in 1903 as a passenger and excursion boat for the then-popular Great Lakes routes. At the time of its capsizing it was rated to carry 2,500 passengers on excursions on Lake Michigan, often from Chicago to the attractive beaches and dunes of Michigan and Indiana. Its capacity was set not by the ship's intrinsic seaworthiness but rather by the number of life jackets that were stowed on board. The *Eastland* was in reality not a completely seaworthy craft and had stability problems that had been noticed on some of its earliest cruises. Most ships rely on solid ballast for stability; the *Eastland* depended on water tanks that were filled and emptied as needed to adjust trim. Water ballast acts no differently than does solid ballast if the holding tanks are completely filled and sealed. When they are partially filled or left open, however, they can cause peculiar stability problems. Water can surge in the tanks almost like a pendulum and make a boat pitch erratically and without warning. Those on the *Eastland* were not easy to adjust and were often mishandled. Crews were especially inclined to mismanage the tanks when boarding heavy loads. They would leave the tanks almost empty and then begin filling them as the load increased—precisely when the ship was least stable.

The ballast system was only one of the *Eastland*'s subtle design flaws, faults that were sometimes made worse by the crew. The ship's gangway ports were close to the waterline and thus prone to swamping when the boat tipped. This would not have been a critical problem if the ports were always sealed when the ship was underway, but the crew often left them open, and the doors leaked even when closed. Furthermore, during its years of service the *Eastland* was modified in ways that exacerbated its stability problems—for example, some wood decking was replaced with concrete, and more lifeboats and safety equipment were added on its upper deck after the sinking of the *Titanic*. The consequences of this additional safety equipment are a major focus of George Hilton's recent history of the *Eastland*, which he tellingly subtitled "Legacy of the Titanic." His point is that the causes of the *Titanic* disaster were largely misunderstood and that this misunderstanding helped to precipitate the *Eastland* disaster. The *Titanic* had a far too small and ineffective rudder for a ship of its size, and actions on the night of the sinking—including stopping the central propeller, which lay directly ahead of the rudder—made the ship almost unmaneuverable.[7] Whereas other ships could have avoided an iceberg even at high speed in the dark, the *Titanic* could not. Official inquiries and the public focused not on this design defect but largely on the *Titanic*'s "inadequate" stock of lifesaving gear. Ships all around the world began to be retrofitted on their upper decks with additional lifeboats, rafts, and flotation equipment—even if they had not been designed to carry the extra load. Experts warned that these new regulations would cause a sinking. Hilton's position is that the *Eastland* was the boat fated to confirm these predictions. Already an unstable craft, the *Eastland* was refitted just before the disaster (although just slightly in advance of new U.S. regulations stemming from the sinking of the *Titanic*). Other design factors contributed, but the new equipment may literally have pushed the *Eastland* to disaster.

On 24 July the *Eastland* was improperly ballasted when it began to board passengers, a group of almost 2,500 Western Electric workers and their families, most from the suburb of Cicero. With less than half the passengers aboard, the ship gave warning of the tragedy ahead—it listed toward the dock. This was the beginning of its slow pendulum-like swing into the river. The crew compensated by pumping water into ballast tanks on the opposite (starboard) side, making the ship even less stable but correcting the immediate list. Boarding continued, and the *Eastland* prepared for departure even though it was becoming less and less stable by the minute. Then, just as the gangplanks were drawn up and lines thrown to a tug, the *Eastland* listed away from dock and

Figure 5-3. The *Eastland* capsized in the Chicago River on 24 July 1915. The disaster claimed over eight hundred lives. Photograph ICHi-02033 by Jun Fujita courtesy of the Chicago Historical Society.

rolled onto its side, about fifty minutes after the ship's first lurch. Passengers on the upper decks were thrown into the river; people below deck were trapped in the water and debris (Figure 5-3).

Crew and passengers on nearby boats and tugs, as well as bystanders on shore, did their best to rescue passengers, but the actual capsizing happened too quickly, less than ten minutes after the start of the ship's final roll. Passengers had no time to release lifeboats or even to find life vests, much less don them. A large portion could not swim. Along the banks of the Chicago River even strong swimmers hesitated to jump to the rescue for fear of being overwhelmed by panicking survivors. The river current pulled survivors away from the hull and the shore until locks could be closed to halt the flow. By then, most of the victims had drowned.

Days passed before all the bodies could be removed from the river and from the *Eastland's* inner decks. In the meantime Chicago mobilized relief for the families and began investigating the disaster. Pinpointing the cause of the disaster as improperly trimmed ballast tanks was the easy part. The more difficult question was who would be held responsible for this oversight, the ship's poor design, the modifications, and the fact that the ship's capacity had been rated far above what the vessel actually could bear. The issue revolved around more than the crew's competence and stretched all the way to Washington, D.C. The inspection service of the U.S. Department of Commerce had jurisdiction over inland shipping at the time of the disaster, but it had never set adequate safety regulations and lacked impartial and skilled inspectors. The service was required neither to test a ship's stability and seaworthiness nor to tie this rating to cargo and passenger capacity. One result was that lawyers for the victims were never able to prove that the *Eastland* had been overloaded. Inspectors had rated the ship for the number of passengers on board the day of the disaster, even though that rating bore little relation to its true capacity. Not long before the disaster, the *Eastland's* owners had actually increased its rating by simply notifying inspectors that they had added life vests to the boat's inventory.

There were other reasons to spread blame widely. The disaster occurred during a period of friction between seamen's unions and shipowners. In an amazingly prophetic message sent to Washington the year before, the Chicago Federation of Labor predicted a capsizing just like the *Eastland's* because so many passenger ships were being overloaded on a regular basis. The unions had a stake in expanding the scope of the inquiries beyond the negligence of the *Eastland's* crew and owners. They sought a reorganization of the Commerce Department's inspection service and sweeping improvements of safety standards. This agitation for change at the federal level came at an unfortunate time. The *Lusitania* had been torpedoed only two months before, and the nation was moving slowly toward war. Preoccupied with international diplomacy and other more pressing issues, President Wilson sent Secretary of Commerce William Redfield to Chicago to begin an investigation that amounted to little more than a whitewash. Redfield was so antagonistic to an impartial and comprehensive investigation that his stay in Chicago generated tremendous ill will. He was almost recalled but eventually filed an interim report before departing. He suggested minimal reforms: in the future, inspectors should visit ships before altering load limits and should be permitted to order tests of a ship's stability if it came into question.

Public indignation in Chicago was scarcely mollified by these recommendations. Criminal indictments were returned by state and federal grand juries against the top officers of the St. Joseph–Chicago Steamship Company, owner of the *Eastland;* the *Eastland's* captain and chief engineer; the president of the chartering agency that had booked the Western Electric excursion; and federal ship inspectors stationed in Michigan. The federal trials began in Michigan, where the St. Joseph–Chicago Steamship Company was headquartered. Setbacks for the prosecution began in early 1916 when a federal judge denied a petition to have the trial moved to Illinois. He ruled in the process that federal courts had no jurisdiction over the accident because it occurred outside federal waters in the Chicago River. The judge further maintained that the only actions that could be viewed as contributing to the accident were those of 24 July; federal inspectors could not be held responsible unless the accident happened as an immediate consequence of an inspection. The final blow fell when the judge dismissed the charge of conspiracy pertaining to the negligence of the owners. The judge's rulings cleared all defendants of federal charges and indirectly destroyed the criminal cases pending in Illinois courts. Of the more than seven hundred lawsuits filed in state and federal courts, none produced a resounding victory for victims and survivors. Just like the Iroquois Theater Company, the St. Joseph–Chicago Steamship Company went bankrupt as a result of the disaster and left few assets to settle claims.

Despite the legal frustrations, the *Eastland* disaster instigated remedial action, though nowhere near as sweeping in scope as the reforms stemming from the Iroquois fire. The U.S. Congress passed laws in 1918 and 1919 that required inspectors to submit to their supervisors any change in a ship's passenger load limit and permitted the appeal of inspection decisions by interested parties. The new regulations made inspectors more accountable for their decisions, thus correcting a weakness of previous laws. The Department of Commerce continued to view the cause of the disaster in the narrowest possible terms—as a problem of the *Eastland's* design and of poor seamanship on the part of its crew. Secretary Redfield was unwilling to generalize from the disaster and resisted a shake-up of the inspection service that might have yielded additional improvements in safety.

The site of the disaster was a bystander to this debate. No matter how one viewed the causes of the *Eastland* disaster, the capsizing could have occurred anywhere, and the particular site was a matter of chance. That it happened where it did on the Chicago River between Clark and LaSalle Streets produced no lasting sense of stigma. Since the reasons for the disaster were clear and remediable, just as they had been after the Iroquois fire, the focus of attention remained on them instead of moving to the memorialization of the innocent site. The loss of so many victims from one company and suburb could have inspired a memorial, but it did not. The citizens of Cicero and the workers of Western Electric chose to mourn privately.

To close this episode, it is worth noting that the *Eastland* was raised from the Chicago River and reused. Following the bankruptcy of the St. Joseph–Chicago Steamship Company, the U.S. government purchased the *Eastland* to have it cut down and entirely rebuilt and armed as a naval training vessel, the USS *Wilmette*. During World Wars I and II the *Wilmette* was used to train gunners stationed at the Great Lakes Naval Training Center. Between the wars it was sailed by the naval reserve and ROTC cadets. By 1946, however, the *Wilmette* had reached the end of its useful life. It was sold for scrap and cut apart along the south branch of the Chicago River. The immediate site of the disaster has been redeveloped substantially since 1915 under various civic improvement plans, but it remains easy to find (Figure 5-4). Perhaps the most interesting difference is that in 1988 a small historical marker was erected on the south bank of the Chicago River where the *Eastland* was docked on the day of the disaster (Figure 5-5). Erected by the Illinois Mathematics and Science Academy and the Illinois State Historical Society, the plaque is a good example of the designation of what comes to be viewed retrospectively as an important event.

SHIFTING THE BLAME FROM PLACE

The two examples previously discussed in this chapter outline the general process of rectification. Hundreds of other instances could be cited with little difference in outcome. Over many years I have sought out the sites of some of the worst accidents on record—explosions, fires, and crashes—and have found no sign of them in landscape. One

Figure 5-4. The site of the *Eastland* disaster in the 1980s looking east along the Chicago River from the LaSalle Street
bridge. The building on the left appears in the background
of Figure 5-3. This section of the riverbank was redeveloped
in the 1920s, eliminating many docks and wharves.

does not even have to leave Chicago to find more recent cases. Nothing is marked at the site of a crash between a street car and a gasoline
truck at 63d and State Streets on 25 May 1950 that claimed 33 lives
and injured many more; where two Illinois Central trains collided at
the 27th Street station on 30 October 1972, killing 45 and injuring
322; at the Lake Street–Wabash Avenue curve of the Loop, where
two elevated trains struck and derailed on 4 February 1977, killing 11
and injuring 200; or where a DC-10 crashed at O'Hare International
Airport on 25 May 1979, claiming the lives of 258 passengers, 13 crew
members, and 2 people on the ground. These were all transportation
accidents that occurred at random places, but examples of other sorts
of accidents stemming from less mobile sources can be found throughout the United States. Most are rectified, although some evidence may
remain in a few unusual cases, if only because a site is so inaccessible
or the remains are so massive that the debris cannot be removed or
reused. In 1963 a reservoir failed in Los Angeles, flooding five square

Figure 5-5. A historical plaque marking the site of the *Eastland* disaster on the south bank of the Chicago River between LaSalle and Clark Streets. This is the only remembrance of the *Eastland* disaster in Chicago, and it came late. It was not commissioned by survivors or the families of victims.

Figure 5-6. This water reservoir in the Baldwin Hills section of Los Angeles burst in December 1963. Water flooded five square miles of the city and killed three people. No effort was made to reuse or efface the massive structure.

miles of the city and claiming three lives (Figure 5-6). The concrete basin was neither reused nor removed.

Questions of cause and blame are strongly related to what happens to the sites of accidents such as these. For a site to be rectified, blame must be shifted away from the site to a cause unrelated to the place of the disaster, as is often the case in transportation-related accidents like the *Eastland*'s.[8] This principle is also why the fate of a site may be closely linked to the outcome of formal inquiries into cause of the disaster, as well as the public response to such investigations. For rectification to occur, it is important for the formal investigations to point away from the site and toward mechanical faults, human errors, or lapses of safety procedures that are not specific to the place where the disaster occurred. When investigators pin the cause on external factors like boat design or poor seamanship, the site is relieved of blame because the location of the disaster becomes little more than a matter of chance, happenstance, simple bad luck. Thus, as is the case in many crashes and sinkings, the site is really coincidental to the cause.

The fate of a disaster site can also be shaped by issues that lie entirely outside the scope of formal investigations. One practical concern is whether the ruins are sufficient to rectify, that is, whether there is anything left to reuse. The Iroquois Theater was still structurally sound after the fire, a common outcome at disaster sites. Even buildings that are totally destroyed may rest on valuable land, and the inclination is to reuse the land or the buildings if at all possible. The greater the value of the remaining assets, the greater is the tendency to reuse the site. The Iroquois was not only almost wholly intact but also one of the largest theaters in the Loop and brand new. A tremendous financial sacrifice would have been involved in pulling it down. In 1981 overhead walkways collapsed in the atrium of the Hyatt Regency in Kansas City, killing 114 people in the lobby below and injuring over 200 more. The hotel was a tremendous asset to the owners, and no thought was given to closing it. The site was rectified by removing the walkways and converting the entrances into small balconies overlooking the lobby. When I looked at material concerning a B-25 bomber that crashed into the Empire State Building in July 1945 or a blimp that crashed into the Illinois Trust and Savings Bank in the heart of Chicago in July 1919, I could find no indication that debate focused on anything other than repair and reuse of the buildings where the deaths occurred. A fire caused by nitrate-based X-ray film used at the Cleveland Clinic killed a hundred people in 1929, but the building was reused and is now part of a large hospital complex in Ohio (Figure 5-7). Nonetheless, although I think that the value of a building will always sway outcomes toward rectification, in the next chapter I discuss situations where a strong sense of shame does force the obliteration of reusable buildings and properties.

If a site is eventually reused, it is important that the original owners do not benefit from the disaster and, if they are at fault in any way, are made "to pay," either by compensating victims or by enduring punishment in court. The Iroquois and *Eastland* disasters put their owners out of business. The Hyatt Regency collapse cost almost $140 million in compensation. Even owners who are blameless will have a difficult time restoring their buildings if it appears that they stand to reap a windfall, in insurance or through litigation, at the expense of the victims.

In a few unusual situations a cause is never found. The explosions in 1993 at the World Trade Center in New York and in 1995 at the Murrah Federal Building in Oklahoma City are by no means the first terrorist bombings in American history. In these cases, however, just

Figure 5-7. In 1929 a fire in this building claimed a hundred lives. Home then of the Cleveland Clinic, the building is still in use and is now part of a far larger hospital complex in Cleveland, Ohio. The fire was caused by nitrate-based X-ray film. This was one of several fires that forced widespread use of "safety" film, but it left no scars at the site of the disaster.

like the Army Math Research Center bombing at the University of Wisconsin in 1970, the bombings were in support of a "cause" and the bombers were discovered. This was not the case when a huge bomb exploded on Wall Street in 1920. On 16 September a horse-drawn wagon of explosives and metal weights was wheeled into the heart of the financial district and detonated in the noontime crowd, killing thirty-two, wounding approximately two hundred, and causing tremendous property damage. No person or group ever claimed responsibility for the bombing, and the police came up empty-handed in their investigation. With no one to blame and no reason to commemorate this senseless act of violence, the site was quickly rectified. All that remains are the small shrapnel scars on the face of some of the buildings near the epicenter of the explosion (Figure 5-8).

The events at the World Trade Center and in Oklahoma City are different and have already provoked other responses, although it is not

Figure 5-8. Shrapnel scars on a building on Wall Street in New York City caused by the terrorist bombing of 16 September 1920. No one ever confessed to the bombing or was charged with it, and the area damaged by the blast was rectified, as if the explosion had been an accident.

entirely clear what will happen in the long term. The Trade Center tower has been rectified, although memorial services have been held there since to honor the victims. In Oklahoma City there is talk of creating a small memorial park at the site of the explosion as reconstruction proceeds. It is much too soon to know whether the park will materialize, yet the suggestion helps to make the point that, in some cases, subtle differences among seemingly similar events can sway responses away from rectification and toward sanctification or obliteration.

OTHER OUTCOMES

A fine line separates rectified sites from those that are either sanctified or obliterated. In the *General Slocum* disaster, the one most closely parallel to the sinking of the *Eastland,* a small memorial was erected. The

Figure 5-9. The former site of the Knickerbocker Theater on Columbia Road in Washington, D.C. The roof of the theater collapsed in 1922, claiming just under a hundred victims. The theater was rectified and reopened under a new name in 1923; it was razed for new development in 1969.

General Slocum caught fire while on a cruise in the East River on 15 June 1904, but the captain did not immediately turn to shore. His delay in running the ship aground, which he finally did on North Brother Island, cost hundreds of lives. Additional parallels exist between the rectified sites considered in this chapter and those that have inspired memorials, as discussed in Chapter 3. The New London School explosion in Texas in 1937 and the Collinwood School fire in Ohio in 1908 can be compared to the Iroquois disaster, and in both towns memorials were erected. In contrast, the collapse of the Knickerbocker Theater in Washington, D.C., in January 1922 left no mark in landscape (Figure 5-9). The Knickerbocker's roof had been improperly anchored and fell under the weight of accumulated snow, claiming just under a hundred victims. The theater, on Columbia Road, was rebuilt and reopened under a new name in 1923 until finally being razed for new development in 1969.

Figure 5-10. The Potomac River at the 14th Street Bridge, where a Boeing 737 crashed during takeoff from Washington National Airport on 13 January 1982. No sign of the crash remains where the airplane struck the bridge and killed passing motorists. Although a few airline disasters have been memorialized, most of the sites have been rectified, as was this one.

There is no easy explanation for why such similar events produce such dissimilar results. All things being equal, situations that induce a sense of community loss are likelier to proceed toward sanctification. But this assertion only begs the question of why some accidents are perceived as a community sacrifice whereas others are seen as no more than a group of strangers brought together by the same tragic fate, like the characters in Thornton Wilder's *Bridge of San Luis Rey*. Many of the memorials examined in Chapter 3 were the work of communities of fewer than ten thousand people. Some were experienced so acutely because they claimed so many victims from one segment of the population of these cities and towns—for example, the children of New London and Collinwood and the coal miners of Cherry, Illinois. The larger the city where the disaster occurs and the greater the mix of victims, the likelier rectification becomes. Airplane crashes often claim large groups of strangers, and very few such crash sites are marked (Figure 5-10).

Memorialization seems to be a slightly more common response now than it once was. Northwest Airlines flight 255 crashed in August 1987 during its takeoff from Detroit Wayne County Metropolitan Airport, claiming 156 of the 157 passengers on board. In less than a year a small memorial was placed at the center of the crash—a concrete slab bearing the flight number. The slab has attracted other remembrances—flowers and a wooden cross—and has been the focus for memorial services and visits by the victims' families. A memorial was also erected in a cemetery in Sewickley, Pennsylvania, to the victims of the crash of USAir flight 427 in Pittsburgh in 1994. Such memorials used to be exceedingly rare but now appear at least occasionally. Such memorials sometimes appear even after particularly shameful events, such as the mass murders discussed in the next chapter. Small memorials have been erected in San Ysidro, California, and Killeen, Texas, sites of two of the largest mass murders in American history. I do not know whether these markers reflect a passing trend or a more permanent change in attitudes toward such events. In any event, over the past decade or two Americans have become a bit more open and certainly more adept at handling such disasters and tragedies.

Trauma, loss, and bereavement are now recognized as psychologically stressful. Psychologists, psychiatrists, and other counselors are now called routinely to assist survivors and families of victims. With this openness has come recognition of the value of acknowledging loss in periodic services and gatherings, sometimes convened quite specifically at the site of the disaster. The creation of memorials and monuments is a natural outgrowth of these communal activities and a focus for many mourners. Also, over time precedents have been set for building such shrines and marking the landscape. Perhaps in this context proposals for a memorial to the 1995 terrorist bombing in Oklahoma City are less remarkable than they once were. Not so long ago, a memorial of this sort would have been considered improper, almost an affront to a community's self-image. Now such a memorial is viewed as reflecting respect for the victims and their families and paying tribute to the community's ability to constructively respond to adversity.

Along with this openness has come a greater willingness to look back and mark sites of long-ago tragedies. I mentioned that the site of the *Eastland* disaster was finally marked in 1988, seventy-three years after the event. Although I classify the marker an act of designation rather than sanctification, other examples come to mind. On 6 July 1994 members of the Hartford, Connecticut, Fire Department gathered on the site of a fire that claimed 169 lives fifty years earlier during a performance of the Ringling Brothers and Barnum & Bailey Circus. An elementary school now occupies the site, but the firemen contributed a small wooden plaque to be placed inside "in loving memory of those who perished on this location," extending "condolences to their survivors."[9] I mention in Chapter 3 that not until the twentieth century did the people of Peshtigo, Wisconsin, erect a memorial there to the largest forest fire in American history. This disastrous fire in the lumbering region of northern Wisconsin on 8 October 1871 has long been eclipsed by the great Chicago Fire, which started the day before but was still burning as Peshtigo was consumed. Up to eight hundred people died in the Peshtigo fire as it swept across almost 2,400 square miles of forests and farms. In Memphis a memorial begun in the late 1960s was dedicated in 1971 to the great yellow fever epidemics of the 1870s. So numerous were the losses that the city was virtually abandoned and its charter repealed until prosperity returned in the 1880s. Although the many victims were buried close together in the "no-man's-land" of the public cemetery, where a small memorial was erected in 1955, the new memorial pays tribute to this loss far more publicly along the banks of the Mississippi in Martyr's Park.

Although it is likely that other disasters will be marked retrospectively, accidental disasters shade toward obliteration in some situations, especially those where something clearly could have been done to avert a disaster or where someone gained at the victims' expense. Such disasters are the subject of the next chapter, but it is worth noting that events quite similar to the Iroquois disaster have resulted in obliteration. These incidents include the Cocoanut Grove Nightclub fire in Boston in 1942 and the Beverly Hills Supper Club disaster in Southport, Kentucky, in 1977, although in the latter case there was little left to efface. In both the Cocoanut Grove and Beverly Hills incidents there was a strong sense that the owners' almost reckless disregard for existing building and safety codes contributed substantially to the death toll. The perception that such accidents are less an "act of God" and more an act of manslaughter pushes them closer in meaning to homicide and mass murder—and toward obliteration.

Remedial Landscapes:
A Different Sort of Remembrance

Accidental tragedies usually leave few marks where they claim their victims, but they may have repercussions for sites far removed from the immediate scene of disaster. One of the most interesting and certainly most ironic aspects of these events is that even as a disaster site fades from view, preventive action and remedies may have widespread effects on other, distant landscapes. These remedial measures often outlive the memory of the disaster that spawned them. Rules and regulations to improve environmental safety almost always follow in the wake of accidental disasters: building codes are revised, inspection procedures are modified, and buildings and equipment are fitted with new safety devices. If the new codes cannot be met, buildings are demolished and equipment is retired from service.

The Iroquois fire resulted in building-code changes throughout the United States. New regulations adopted in cities across the nation demanded reinforced asbestos or metal fire curtains, emergency lighting systems, flame-resistant stage sets, automatic sprinklers and quick-opening vents above stages, broad aisles, fire extinguishers, and fire alarms. Furthermore stagehands and ushers were required to undergo training, unlike the Iroquois staff, who had never been mustered for fire drills. A regular schedule of inspections was also enforced. Indeed, in the wake of the Iroquois disaster, all Chicago theaters were closed until they could be reinspected, except for one theater whose owners demonstrated that they had met the city's building codes. These precautions, implemented long ago, have been demonstrably effective. There has never been a repeat of the Iroquois disaster in an American theater. Destructive fires have occurred since then, but not for the same reasons.

The *Eastland* disaster may not have led immediately to far-ranging changes in maritime safety, but it was part of a series of ship disasters that brought regulations into the twentieth century. Between 1904 and 1915, when travel by ship was as important as travel by air is today, thousands of lives were lost on the *Titanic, Empress of Ireland, General Slocum,* and *Eastland.* Hundreds of other lives were lost in major maritime disasters dating back to the 1890s. Most of these accidents claimed more lives than are lost in all but the largest air disasters today. Just as today's air crashes often result in sweeping regulatory changes, this two-decade series of disasters resulted in safer passenger liners and excursion boats.

The sad corollary of this observation is that virtually every safety measure in effect today can at some point be traced to a disaster in the past. Some of these precautions have resulted in changes that are visible across broad areas of the landscape, particularly the built environment of cities. One of the distinguishing features of sections of many American urban areas is the masonry fabric of inner-city residential and commercial districts and the lightly built wooden texture of the suburbs. The presence of stone, brick, and concrete is the result of building codes adopted in the late nineteenth and early twentieth centuries in response to the threat of large-scale urban fires. Few people realize today how common and destructive these fires were, particularly in the nineteenth century. Although many people are aware of the Chicago Fire of 1871 and know that San Francisco burned after the earthquake of 1906, fewer people realize that almost every large American city experienced one and sometimes several major fires in the nineteenth century. Wood was the inexpensive building material of choice for cities until the late nineteenth century. When fires in Baltimore, New York, Chicago, Boston, Philadelphia, Salem, and elsewhere demonstrated how dangerous this choice could be, building codes were changed.

Natural disasters such as floods have had similar effects. Cities throughout the nation have implemented substantial flood-control measures that are everywhere evident in channelized rivers, levees, dams, and holding ponds. Almost all this "floodproofing" can be traced directly to particular damaging and fatal floods. Some of the mammoth dam-building projects of the Army Corps of Engineers and Bureau of Reclamation were responses to the same imperative. Few of the killer floods that helped to justify these projects are memorialized in public monuments like the ones in Johnstown, Pennsylvania. They nonetheless have had pronounced effects on the shaping of landscape far and wide. Earthquakes, hurricanes, tidal waves, and tornadoes are treated the same way. In their aftermath stress is almost always placed on finding ways of reducing damage and death in the future, not on building monuments to the victims. These events are memorialized in revised building codes and remedial measures that may shape the landscape dramatically but leave no special mark on the site of the tragedy. Even in the case of the hurricanes of 1875 and 1886 that forced the abandonment of Indianola, Texas, then one of the largest settlements and ports in the state, all that remains is a small historical marker to designate the site.

The environment sometimes bears no trace of such remedies, for example, the improvements that have increased the safety of airplanes, ships, trains, and automobiles. The Cleveland Clinic disaster mentioned previously helped to force the adoption of safety film over its flammable nitrate-based predecessor. Even though it had been available for some time, safety film did not come into its own until after the Cleveland Clinic fire and another disaster at a film distribution center in New York City, also in 1929. The Triangle Shirtwaist Factory fire in New York City in 1911 spurred passage of a wave of industrial safety laws.[10] Some remedial measures are slightly more apparent and can be seen in the environment—if one knows where to look. For many years I was puzzled by the outright ban on fireworks in some cities and the corresponding proliferation of fireworks stands along highways just outside the limits of many cities. I imagined that this resulted from remarkable foresight on the part of civic leaders to help keep fireworks out of the hands of minors and to prevent injuries on the Fourth of July. Although I was accurate to a point, I did not realize until later that fireworks caused some destructive urban fires around the turn of the century. These and individual accidents left 1,300 dead and 28,000 injured between 1902 and 1908 alone. One of the worst of these fires, which occurred at a store in Cleveland, Ohio, in 1908, led to that city's ban on the sale and possession of fireworks, the first of its kind. Washington, D.C., followed in 1909, and New York, Boston, Baltimore, Toledo, Chicago, and Kansas City did so in 1910.[11]

Other equally important, but less obvious, safety measures are embedded everywhere in the built environment for similar reasons. Illuminated exit signs, emergency lighting systems, outward-opening exit doors, sprinkler systems, and many other safety innovations rest on the sacrifice of countless lives. In some cases improvements have had to be made on improvements—battery backup for emergency lighting systems that otherwise failed with a building's main circuitry, reservoirs for sprinkler systems to supply water when internal plumbing fails, and standpipes inside buildings connected to external water mains for the same reason. In the Cocoanut Grove disaster discussed in the next chapter, many lives were lost when the nightclub's revolving doors jammed at the main entrance, leaving victims with no means of escape. The result is that all revolving doors in use today are flanked by exit doors opening outward, all because of one major disaster. These safety precautions may seem obvious to us today, but in truth, no one has ever had the foresight to anticipate all the dangers arising from natural hazards, new technologies, poor judgment, and human mistakes. Just when the general public thinks one problem is fixed, another accident strikes with tragic consequence. Nowhere is our trust more displaced than in coming to terms with the dangers of new technologies. For every "fireproof" theater or "unsinkable" ship, "accident-proof" airplane, or "safe" nuclear reactor, there is a disaster around the corner, but not necessarily for the reasons expected.

Some scholars maintain that industrialized, capitalist societies invoke the notion of accidents to explain away avoidable catastrophes. Their position is that many tragedies are explained away as "acts of God" when in fact they are the result of calculated decisions involving profit and loss. This is not solely an issue of companies circumventing existing safety regulations to save money. Automobiles such as the Chevrolet Corvair and Ford Pinto were put into production with known, remediable flaws that cost many lives. In the case of the Pinto, calculations by the automaker indicated that any future liability payments would probably cost less than fixing the flaw that caused some of these cars to explode when hit from behind. Going further, some critics would maintain that the *Exxon Valdez* oil spill in Alaska, the factory explosion at Bhopal, India, and countless other industrial disasters are not really "accidents" at all but rather the almost cynical application of "the bottom line" to questions of human life and safety. Such cynicism certainly plays a role in explaining many disasters, but equally disturbing is the almost boundless trust people place in science and technology, a trust then shattered by a humbling tragedy such as the space shuttle *Challenger* disaster of 1986. Human ingenuity has its limits, regardless of how responsibly people and corporations behave. No matter how carefully known risks and dangers are considered, an unanticipated contingency can prove fatal.

In picking up the pieces of these disasters, perhaps implementing a remedy is the best tribute to the sacrifice of the victims. Years ago little crosses were placed along roadsides where people died in accidents (Figure 5-11). Some particularly dangerous stretches came to resemble small cemeteries, with rows of crosses marking dozens of fatalities. These small mementos disappeared in the 1950s and 1960s,

Figure 5-11. A marker along 26th Street in Austin adjacent to the University of Texas campus, marking a traffic death in 1993. Such roadside markers were once fixtures of American roads but are no longer encouraged or even permitted along most thoroughfares.

however, as the interstate highway system spread across the nation. No room was set aside in these grand plans for tiny crosses, as if to say that highway safety was now under control. The remedy for a crash was a new guard rail, a wider shoulder, or a banked turn, not a small cross. Some might argue too that the disappearance of crosses means Americans have become inured to the dangers of their auto-borne life-styles and do not wish to be reminded of the cost as measured in an annual death toll of tens of thousands. In a very abstract way, however, the guard rail, shoulder, or banked turn is a memorial to these accidents, a small remembrance to the sacrifices of thousands. Not every disaster needs to be marked with a memorial to be remembered. The reminders become part of our lives in far more subtle ways as small souvenirs of loss. In effect blame is shared widely, and the individual accident site is allowed to regain its innocence. These innocent places gradually fade from view through rectification. Although they may be out of sight, they are not necessarily out of mind.

Chapter 6

The Mark of Shame

Shame can be a powerful motive to obliterate all reminders of tragedy and violence. In contrast to rectification, obliteration makes no attempt to set things right but tries instead to scour the landscape of all evidence of a shameful event. Obliteration is almost the inverse of sanctification. Sanctification occurs when a community seeks to memorialize a tragedy, remember an event, and honor its victims; obliteration stems from the wish to hide violence and forget tragedy. My first encounter with the power of shame came in 1983 when I moved to Austin to teach at the University of Texas. I had then only a faint memory of the mass murder that had occurred on campus in 1966. I was taken aback by the responses to my naive questions about the tragedy—I was interrupted in midsentence with an abrupt "don't ask" or "there's nothing to see." Occasionally my informants would lean closer, drop their voices to a whisper, and confide: "You know, I was there that day . . . ," "I know someone who knew Charles Whitman," or "There's still a bullet hole you can see over on the South Mall." These odd responses did not mean much to me then. Now, after visiting dozens of these murder sites, they do. Some tragedies and acts of violence are so shameful, so viciously or recklessly intentional, that they scar a place almost permanently. These are events so shocking that survivors will try to deny the memory by effacing all evidence and obliterating the site. No matter how hard survivors try, however, these shameful sites are not easily effaced or forgotten. As I have talked with survivors and the families of victims, I have watched people break down in tears as they tried to describe their anguish. Once tainted, these sites are difficult to cleanse of their horrible associations. Some are so terrible that I would never choose to revisit them.

I will deal with the University of Texas murders later, but I want to begin with an example from Waushara County, Wisconsin. There the outlines of the process of obliteration can be seen more clearly in the case of mass murderer Edward Gein. Until Gein was discovered, Waushara was a peaceful, almost anonymous county in Wisconsin's central heartland. As events unfolded in November 1957, Waushara County found itself caught in the glare of national attention. The story began on 16 November in the small town of Plainfield, in the northwest corner of the county, when Bernice Worden was reported missing from her hardware store.[1] Blood was found at the scene, leading to suspicions of murder. A search was organized, and within hours Gein was in custody and deputies were on their way to search his farm a few miles outside of town. As officers entered the woodshed attached to the house, they found Worden's decapitated body hanging upside down from the rafters, eviscerated and dressed as a hunting trophy— the first in a series of grim discoveries. Continuing into the night, the deputies found the house littered with human heads and skulls, bones, skin, and other human remains. Worden's heart was in a saucepan on the kitchen stove; her genitals were part of a collection of nine in a shoebox in a bedroom. As evidence of mass murder mounted, so too did the shock of the discoveries.

Gein had not simply butchered his victims; he had fashioned the remains into furnishings and decorations. Tanned human skin had been fashioned into chair covers, lampshades, and a knife sheath. Skulls were found atop bedposts and shaped into bowls. Gein had even made robes and masks of human skin. The remains explained several unsolved disappearances and murders in the Plainfield area and in other parts of the state. Authorities could not identify all that they found, however, and for good reason. The evidence confirmed Gein's subsequent confession that he gathered some of his trophies from graves in Plainfield—where, incidentally, some of my own relatives are buried— and from cemeteries in surrounding communities. His thefts may have outnumbered the murders, but authorities could summon little enthusiasm for confirming the confession. Townspeople opposed a comprehensive exhumation, and Gein's story was verified with a few recent graves; the rest were left undisturbed.

The crimes were in dramatic contrast to Gein's hitherto harmless reputation. Gein had lived in Plainfield for most of his fifty-one years and was known as a quiet, somewhat withdrawn man who lived alone on what remained of his family's farm. He worked around town as an occasional farmhand and handyman, exchanging favors and baby sitting for meals and cash. Nothing about the man had aroused suspicion, even though it was clear in retrospect that his crimes began many years before his capture. After his arrest Gein was declared insane and committed to the Central State Hospital in Waupan without facing trial. Ten years later Gein was ruled mentally fit and finally put on trial in 1968, but to little consequence. Gein lived out his life in Wisconsin mental institutions.

Gein's long incarceration did nothing to dissipate the sense of shame his crimes engendered. Plainfield was forced to come to terms with the fact that its most famous citizen was a mass murderer and necrophiliac. A real source of shame lay in the fact that Gein had been a productive and accepted member of the community. The town could not just disown him as an outsider and pass off responsibility. The only option they had was to distance themselves as much as possible from Gein and his crimes by effacing the most obvious reminders of the association, as if obliteration were exculpatory. The place of the strongest association and greatest notoriety was Gein's farmstead. Gein probably killed his victims in many different places, but he had dismembered and stored them on the farm. As soon as Gein was arrested, the farm began to draw a constant stream of sightseers from all over the state and nation. Visitors even burgled the farmhouse and held parties on the property; the sheriff had to post full-time guards.

When Gein's assets were put up for auction by his legal guardian in early 1958, rumors circulated that a bidder was planning to purchase Gein's house as a tourist attraction. Three days before the auction scheduled for 27 March, the house was set on fire and burned to the ground. No one was ever charged with arson, and no one seemed upset that the most immediate reminder of Gein was gone. The auction went ahead, and on 1 April the farm had new owners—from out-

Figure 6-1. The site of Edward Gein's farmstead near Plain-field, Wisconsin. The farm buildings were destroyed by arson in 1958. The land was planted as a pine plantation, divided, and sold.

Figure 6-2. Edward Gein's grave in Plainfield, Wisconsin. Some opposition arose to burying Gein with his family in one of the cemeteries he had violated. Nevertheless the grave has not attracted undue vandalism.

side the local area. Gein's other major assets—his 1938 pickup truck and 1949 car, vehicles he had used in his crimes—were also sold. The car was intended to become a sideshow attraction at county fairs, but it quickly disappeared from sight. The land was planted with pine for pulp. The 160-acre tract was later subdivided, and the parcels were sold individually (Figure 6-1).

The disposal of these reminders could not undo Gein's crimes, but it did help the community to distance itself from the murderer. Soon sightseers went away, and Plainfield returned to its routines. Apart from occasional bursts of renewed interest in Plainfield, as when Gein finally came to trial in 1968, the last issue the town faced was where to bury the murderer when he died in 1984. Gein's family plot in the Plainfield cemetery was the logical place, but the cemetery was one that he himself had raided. People objected to burying him so close to his victims, and there was the fear that Gein's grave, if marked, would attract vandals. Anonymous burial in a state cemetery was considered, but in the end he was buried at Plainfield; his grave has not attracted undue attention (Figure 6-2).

THE POWER OF SHAME

The obliteration of the Gein farmstead stands in contrast to the acts of sanctification and rectification discussed in previous chapters. Sanctification is a ritual process in which sacred sites are delimited and consecrated. The *ritual* aspect is critical insofar as prayers, eulogies, and dedications sanction grief and channel emotion toward the reaffirmation of community values. There is no comparable ritual of effacement for coming to terms with shameful events people wish to forget. Unlike some cultures, American society has no ritual of purification to cleanse people and places of the guilt and shame that arise from events such as mass murder. The paradox is that whereas proud moments of history, however violent, can be commemorated readily using existing ritual formulas, shameful episodes are difficult to eradicate. This paradox manifests itself in two ways.

First, obliteration is usually an improvised process unique to a specific context, as it was in Plainfield. The process does not conform to any widely sanctioned pattern. The ad hoc nature of obliteration is expressed in many ways, not the least of which is the fact that no one group is ever automatically assigned control of the process. In instances of sanctification, convention demands that those placed in charge of the ceremony either come from the upper tiers of community life or have been participants (veterans or victims) of the event commemorated. This is untrue of obliteration, in that police, government officials, and private citizens may take the initiative as the need—and opportunity—arises. In Plainfield obliteration of the Gein farmstead was the work of anonymous arsonists. We need not know the identities of the vandals to understand their motives.

Second, obliteration subverts the cathartic release of emotion that is so much a part of the ritual of sanctification. I made a point in Chapter 3 of stressing the cathartic, emotive power of monument building. The creation of memorials provides a focus for release from grief and guilt. Rituals of sanctification allow entire communities to come to terms with tragic events as they pay respect to the dead. The element of denial that lies at the heart of obliteration can block this process of bereavement, however. Survivors have difficulty honoring the dead when knowing how they died casts a sense of shame over the community. These conflicting emotions temper collective response. Survivors can take revenge on the murderer by destroying the person's home and property, but they cannot pay tribute to the victims without acknowledging the very association they are trying to deny. Survivors are caught between conflicting desires, both to efface and to memorialize. Such conflicts give rise to transformations of place and landscape that I am inclined to term "pathological." These are places abandoned, ignored, avoided, and vandalized to silence their past, although the efforts are generally unsuccessful.

Obliteration does bear a resemblance to the process of rectification. The essential difference between the two is the final outcome. Rectification involves setting things right at a tragedy site and returning the site to the way it was before the event. Rectification is typical after accidents caused by factors unrelated to the site of the disaster. The site is innocent of blame, and no sense of shame attaches to it. Obliteration, on the other hand, does alter landscape. In this case a tragedy site is not simply cleansed and returned to use but rather effaced altogether. If the site is ever reused, it will serve a different purpose—as Gein's farm was converted to a pine plantation. Perceptions of cause and blame are critical to understanding the different treatments accorded to obliterated sites and to rectified ones. If investigations reveal a clear cause for tragedy, rectification of the site is the rule. If the causes are unknown or unknowable, then obliteration may occur to counter the residual sense of shame that may remain attached to place.

The search for the cause of a mass murder parallels almost exactly the quest for explanation in the aftermath of accidental tragedies like those discussed in Chapters 3 and 5. Usually the killer's entire past is scrutinized for some clue to the tragedy, preferably a clue that clearly implicates the murderer *exclusively* and exculpates the community *completely*. Such singularly exculpatory evidence rarely surfaces following mass murder because the issue of sanity usually clouds discussion. Confusion results from the fact that whereas insanity can be accepted as an *immediate* cause of mass murder, it only begs the question of the *underlying* cause—the factors that drove the killer insane. These contributing factors almost always reflect badly on family and community. The judicial finding of insanity in Gein's case—although sufficient as regards the criminal justice system—moved the community no further toward understanding the genesis of Gein's illness. The people of Plainfield had no way of knowing whether they were in some way responsible for not recognizing the insanity soon enough to stop Gein or, worse yet, responsible for his insanity. An element of shock and shame is also involved in learning that a "terribly and terrifyingly normal" member of a community can commit such violence.[2] In the absence of a clear explanation, a community such as Plainfield suffers under a burden of guilt by association and may be driven to efface the most troublesome reminders of their shame. The only situations producing a slightly different outcome arise when the murderer is an outsider to the community. In that case, the crime can be interpreted more readily as a sort of tragic accident outside the control of the community. Rectification is possible in these cases, even sanctification, but the latter has occurred only in a small number of cases where a community wished to honor the victims.

A key point is that the obliteration process can never be completed. The absence of a sanctioned ritual means that the shameful connotations can never be completely effaced from place. According to the saying, silence speaks louder than words. When abandoned or effaced, these shamed places maintain an emphatic hold on attention, just the opposite of what was intended. Linguists have commented on the ambiguous role attributed to silence within human communication and have argued that, contrary to popular assumption, silence is more than the space between words.[3] Thomas Bruneau, for one, has made the point that silence is often a reaction to emotional tension—a response to dissonant comments, insults, and repressed feelings.[4] Instead of being a purely arbitrary element of speech, silence is closely regulated by sociocultural norms that define social status and position.[5] Going one step further, Bruneau indicates that "there are many places, objects, and events to which silence is the expected response. . . . Churches, courtrooms, schools, libraries, hospitals, funeral homes, battle sites, insane asylums, and prisons . . . are often places of silence."[6] Perhaps these obliterated sites are like pauses in speech—empty of sound but resonant with meaning—and just as hard to ignore.

The case of serial murderer John Wayne Gacy reinforces these points. Like Gein, Gacy began killing long before he was apprehended.[7]

By the time he was arrested in late 1978, he had killed over thirty men and boys. The motive for the murders was sexual: Gacy had intercourse with his victims, or raped them, before he tortured and killed them. Gacy was not the first homosexual serial killer to gain national attention. Only a few years before, in the early 1970s, a homosexual murder ring centered on Dean Corll (discussed below) was discovered in Houston. Unlike Corll and his allies, however, who committed their murders in a number of apartments and rented houses, with the victims being buried elsewhere, Gacy interred almost all his victims at home. Gacy was a freelance contractor and was able to use remodeling projects on his own home to disguise the burial of his victims—in the crawl space under his house, below the concrete floor of his garage, and beneath additions to the house and yard.

Police were stunned by the number of burials they found but had never suspected. Gacy had preyed largely on young runaways and prostitutes, whose disappearances were rarely reported or investigated. The first excavations centered on the crawl space under the house. So many burials were found that a decision was reached to cut through the floor for better access. As the search continued, additional flooring was removed, along with Gacy's possessions, his furniture, and—eventually—the house's water and sewage systems. Suspicions that Gacy buried the bodies elsewhere on his property led to excavation of the concrete slab floor of his garage. When a body was found there, it became clear that every square foot of Gacy's property would have to be checked, including areas of the driveway and patio that were covered with concrete. The search continued for three months.

The gradual demolition of the house did not go unnoticed by Gacy's lawyers and family. They objected to the way authorities were tearing up the property, but their objections were overruled in court. The house was a ruin by the time the police finished their search. The state's attorney petitioned for complete destruction of the house and its outbuildings as unsafe and hazardous, their foundations having been undercut during the search. Objections by Gacy's counsel and family failed to stay demolition, and the house was flattened within an hour of the last appeal. Even as a vacant lot, Gacy's graveyard continues to attract passersby and vandalism (Figure 6-3). Gacy was condemned to death for his crimes and executed in 1994. While in prison, Gacy took up painting as a hobby. After Gacy was executed, many of his

Figure 6-3. The site where John Wayne Gacy's house stood,
8213 W. Summerdale Avenue in Norwood Park Township,
a suburb of Chicago.

paintings were gathered and burned by families of his victims to provide some sort of vengeance and to ensure that none would be left as
souvenirs. The outcome here is not much different from what happened in Milwaukee after the arrest of mass murderer Jeffrey Dahmer
in 1991. The apartment building where he committed many of the
murders and dismembered his victims was torn down, and Dahmer
was killed in prison.[8]

OTHER SOURCES OF SHAME

Mass murder produces a strong sense of shame more consistently than
do other violent and tragic events, which is the reason I began with
Gein and Gacy, but it is by no means the only source. Before I return
to the subject of mass murder, I wish to consider several other events
that have led to obliteration, the first being the Cocoanut Grove fire of
1942 and the Beverly Hills Supper Club fire of 1977. No arsonist or

mass murderer was involved in these two fires; rather, the source of each tragedy was negligence on the part of builders, owners, and operators. Their actions had the effect of transforming minor misfortunes into major disasters with shameful ramifications.

Late in the night of 28 November 1942, Boston experienced one of the most devastating fires in U.S. history.[9] The fire consumed only a single building but claimed the lives of 490 people and injured hundreds more. This was the famous Cocoanut Grove fire, which struck one of Boston's most popular nightclubs on one of the busiest weekends of the year. The Cocoanut Grove had opened fifteen years earlier, and over the years under a succession of owners, it emerged as a major focus of Boston's nightlife. The cause of the fire that struck the tightly packed nightclub on a busy Saturday night was never clearly established, but it worked quickly. Within minutes of ignition in a basement lounge, the flames raced upward into the ground-floor foyer and dining area. Patrons had only a few minutes to react and few routes of escape. The club's single revolving door jammed under the first press of the fleeing crowd in the foyer; most of the other exits were locked or difficult to find. The fire department was at the scene in minutes, but the fire fighters were helpless for the first critical minutes when the fire kept the victims trapped inside. Ignited at about 10:15 P.M., the fire was under control by 11:00, having produced the most destruction in its first seven minutes. Apart from killing with smoke and flame, the blaze gassed victims with toxic fumes from the vaporized upholstery, although this aspect of the disaster was not understood until much later.

The Cocoanut Grove disaster was of wartime magnitude, and the outrage generated by the disaster was of national scale. The club had never been called to account for numerous violations of safety and fire regulations. The public turned with vengeance on those they felt were accountable: the owner of the nightclub; his staff, particularly a busboy who had been near the point of ignition; and public officials who had failed to cite the nightclub for safety violations. The club's owner, Barney Welansky, was tried and convicted of manslaughter and served three years before being pardoned and released shortly before his death. Other defendants were acquitted, including members of Welansky's family who had helped to run the club, the building's architect and builders, the city building inspector, the fire inspector, and a police captain who had been at the club on the night of the fire. The

Figure 6-4. A photograph of where Boston's Cocoanut Grove nightclub once stood. The disaster of 28 November 1942 was one of the most devastating fires in American history, claiming almost five hundred lives. The site was effaced, and no trace of the nightclub remains.

victims of the disaster gained almost nothing in civil cases filed against the owner—the Cocoanut Grove had been underinsured, and Welansky held few assets apart from the ruins of the club.

The shell of the Cocoanut Grove was left abandoned and vandalized during the period of the trials. It was then sold in early 1945 and demolished late that summer. No trace of the Cocoanut Grove remains, and subsequent development makes its site difficult even to find. The nightclub was located near Park Square, with its main entrance on Piedmont and the building extending to the corner of Shawmut Street and Broadway. The junction of Shawmut and Broadway has disappeared. The streets are now blocked by a multistory car park, and a portion of the building would now lie across the lobby of a large highrise hotel. A parking lot occupies the position where the main entrance of the Cocoanut Grove once stood (Figure 6-4). This was not just inadvertent, inevitable reuse. Not long after the fire, a new city statute was enacted: the name "Cocoanut Grove" was never again to be used on a public building in Boston.

The real sense of shame arose not just from the magnitude of the disaster but equally from the perception that it could have been prevented. Postfire investigations led to many changes in safety codes and inspection standards in Boston and elsewhere around the United States, but even a few simple precautions could have saved many lives at the Cocoanut Grove. The absence of those precautions resulted in a disaster caused by greed, negligence, and bad judgment that left a blemish of shame on Boston's civic reputation. Obliteration was the result—up to a point. The Cocoanut Grove fire did have one immediately noticeable effect on buildings all across the nation. Revolving doors installed in public buildings are now always flanked by conventional hinged doors opening outward—a subtle memorial to the carnage in the foyer of the Cocoanut Grove in 1942.

On 28 May 1977 fire struck a popular supper club in Southgate, Kentucky, just across the Ohio River from Cincinnati, claiming 165 lives.[10] The disaster began as a slow, smoldering electrical fire behind the walls or above the ceiling of a small reception room. By the time the fire was discovered at about 9:00 P.M., it was almost to the point of flashover. Evacuation began at about the same moment as a fireball burst from the small room into the large supper club complex. Hundreds of patrons were able to escape, but casualties mounted rapidly when the fire reached the Cabaret Room, the club's main showroom. The night's performance had just begun—before an audience far too large for the auditorium—when the first smoke was seen. By the time flames swept across the auditorium, it was too late to escape.

In the aftermath the public had difficulty believing that the fire was the result of factors other than greed, negligence, and incompetence. The inquiry made clear that the fire was not an act of God but rather a direct consequence of the way the supper club was built and operated by its owner. The owner had circumvented existing building and fire codes in building the complex. He had employed unqualified architects and electricians and in effect constructed the building to his own specifications at the lowest possible cost. The poorly trained and overworked building and fire inspectors who served the jurisdiction never noticed or demanded correction of the problems that made the building a firetrap. Furthermore the owner had no evacuation plan

Figure 6-5. The site of the Beverly Hills Supper Club in South-gate, Kentucky, just south of the Ohio River from Cincinnati, Ohio. The fire here on 28 May 1977 claimed 165 lives.

and never trained his staff in emergency procedures—both fatal problems on the night of the fire. His policy of overbooking the showroom meant that the auditorium was almost always occupied beyond the capacity of the emergency exits. No criminal complaints were filed against the owner or public officials, but the sense of shame was as powerful as in a mass murder. The remains of the supper club were destroyed, and the site has remained vacant for years (Figure 6-5).

PASSIVE VERSUS ACTIVE EFFACEMENT

The Salem witchcraft executions of 1692 offer a far different perspective on the power of shame to spur the obliteration of place: it can do so passively, over a long period of time. Scholars such as Paul Boyer and Stephen Nissenbaum have argued convincingly that the Salem witchcraft episode arose from social friction within a growing community rather than from supernatural causes.[11] At the time of the trials, a schism had developed between Salem Town and Salem Village, the town's rural agricultural hinterland. Residents of the two areas had been bickering for some time over closely entwined political and religious issues. Through careful study of family and friendship ties, Boyer and Nissenbaum demonstrated that when the witchcraft episode began, most of the accusers were in Salem Town, on one side of a social and geographical divide, and the accused were in Salem Village, on the other side. By the time this factional dispute was over, twenty people had been executed.

Within a short time of the trials, the scope of the injustice was realized. Accusations and confessions were withdrawn, and the evidence used to convict the witches was discredited. Belief in witchcraft and other supernatural powers had already been on the wane in New England; the Salem trials brought the whole business to an end.[12] Salem Village eventually broke away to become Danvers, and Salem Town went on to become one of New England's major seaports by the mid-eighteenth century. As a particularly shameful act of community strife, the witchcraft executions were allowed to fade from memory. As I mention in Chapter 1, few sites linked directly to the witchcraft trials can be found in today's Salem. The Witch House, built in 1642, was the home of the magistrate presiding at the trials and used for some of the pretrial examinations. The Rebecca Nurse house in Danvers was occupied by one of the victims before her arrest and execution. A determined visitor can locate the sites of other places associated with the witchcraft episode, but nothing remains to see. Visitors are more likely to stop at the Witch Museum, even though the site of the museum has no direct connection with the events of 1692, being no more than a multimedia theater housed in a disused church.

No evidence suggests that residents of Salem and Danvers ever went out of their way to efface the physical reminders of the witchcraft episodes; rather, they simply failed to preserve them. Salem's growth into a prosperous seaport altered the building fabric of the entire town. Sites associated with the witchcraft episode were not singled out for effacement; they simply changed with the rest. In Chapter 1 I quote David Lowenthal as saying "features . . . that reflect shame may be ignored or expunged from the landscape."[13] Expunction was employed in the cases I examine earlier in this chapter, whereas Salem's stigmatized sites seem to have been ignored. Active or passive, the results are

Figure 6-6. A 1905 photograph from Salem, Massachusetts, toward Gallows Hill. Nineteen victims of the 1692 witchcraft trials were hanged in this vicinity, but the exact location of the executions is unknown. Photograph 18502 courtesy of the Peabody Essex Museum, Salem, Massachusetts.

the same, and no one knows exactly where the victims of the witchcraft trials were executed. Firsthand reports note that the hangings took place on high ground west of Salem Town, along a low ridge broken by gaps and crevices, an area that became known as Witch Hill or Gallows Hill (Figure 6-6). No additional details about the exact execution or burial sites can be found in the documentary sources that have survived. Most speculation has been based therefore on relatively thin evidence. Charles Upham, the nineteenth century's most authoritative writer on Salem witchcraft, inferred that the hangings took place at the highest point along the ridge and proposed a memorial for that spot.[14] Sidney Perley's monograph of 1921 does a more thorough job and is as complete a study of the question as is likely to emerge, unless new documentary or archaeological evidence is uncovered.[15] Perley's analysis entailed the careful correlation of written recollections of the hangings, some based on hearsay and some recorded long after 1692. In contrast to Upham, Perley concluded that a lower rise at the base of Gallows Hill seemed the likelier location for the gallows. As to pinpointing the site of the executions, Perley chose to map a range of possible locations rather than attempt to pick one.

Passive or active, the obliteration of shame is never complete, and Salem is no exception. The town has never been able to live down its reputation as New England's "witch city," even though a lighter perspective prevails today. The profile of a stylized witch graces civic insignia, and Salem even appoints an "official" witch. The town has found that the allure of the witchcraft is a good foundation for a thriving tourist industry. The approach of the witchcraft tercentenary in 1992 brought all the issues of shame and remembrance back into the foreground of public debate. At issue was whether the town should commemorate the three-hundredth anniversary and, if so, how. Many wanted to let the anniversary pass unnoted or celebrated with a minimum of fanfare. As one writer to the *Salem Evening News* maintained, "To refer to Salem as 'witch city,' to use Halloween as a Chamber of Commerce promotion, to permit Miss Cabot [Salem's official witch] to play any role at all in any public event simply perpetuates the morbid silliness and, of course, continues the accusation that those poor victims were witches."[16] Another editorial took a different position:

> For the city to try to deny this historical legacy would not only be fruitless, but damaging. More than one million tourists come to Salem each year and while not every one is drawn by the image of the witch on the broomstick, most are.
>
> True, Salem has more to offer than the memory of a chilling historical episode, but in order for visitors to discover that, they have to come here—something they won't do if the witch image is put to rest.
>
> Recalling the witchcraft hysteria does not mean promoting witchcraft or devil worship. It is an historical exercise, an attempt to understand one of the most vivid and passionate periods in our history.
>
> The fact that there are those who cry "Witchcraft!" at the idea of commemorating the 1692 episode is perhaps a telling commentary on the fact that the wounds from that period in some ways have never fully healed.
>
> If it approaches its task responsibly, the Tercentenary Committee has an opportunity to promote a true understanding

of what actually happened in 1692 and why. Perhaps in the process the wounds will finally heal.[17]

This editorial expresses the argument that eventually swayed debate. Plans for a commemoration—not a celebration—went forward and stressed the value of seizing the opportunity of the tercentenary to take a serious look at the implications of the witchcraft episode. Memorials were dedicated in both Salem and Danvers. More important, lectures, workshops, and presentations were organized to focus attention on religious intolerance, wrongful persecution, and the development of the American justice system. These events would be more reminiscent of sanctification than of obliteration but for the fact that they occurred three hundred years after the fact. That a commemoration did take place raises the issue I want to address next: shameful events do not always end in obliteration.

THE ALTERNATIVE OF RECTIFICATION

Rectification is perhaps as common a response to shameful events as obliteration is. To consider the difference, I want to return to mass murder, to a case much like Gacy's but with a different outcome. The episode came to light with a police call on 8 August 1973; teenager Elmer Henley had just killed his friend Dean Corll in a house in Pasadena, Texas, on the edge of Houston.[18] Taken into custody, Henley confessed that in the span of three years, he, Corll, and David Brooks, another teenager, had killed at least twenty-seven boys in drunken, drugged orgies of rape, torture, and murder. Henley killed Corll only when he thought he was being set up as the next victim. On the evening of 8 August, Henley led police to a set of storage sheds in an isolated area of far southwestern Houston. Police found seventeen bodies buried beneath the gravel floor of Corll's boatshed. Ten other burials were uncovered later in places as far removed as the beaches of the Gulf of Mexico and along the shore of the Sam Rayburn Reservoir, far to the northeast of Houston. The murders were committed in a number of places around Houston and its suburbs because Corll rented and moved frequently, for obvious reasons. Only six of the boys were killed in the house where Corll himself died.

Apart from the boatshed, none of the sites stigmatized by the Houston trio seems to have attracted as much attention as Gacy's house

Figure 6-7. The boatshed in southwestern Houston where Corll, Henley, and Brooks buried many of their victims beneath the gravel floor of one of the storage lockers. This shed and the houses where the victims were killed were rectified rather than obliterated after the discovery of the crimes in August 1973.

did. Many of Corll's former landlords simply denied that he rented from them or that he committed murder on their property. The scouting I have done among Corll's many Houston addresses reveals no discernible change at any of them, even at the house where he died. The boatshed itself looks little different now than it did in newspaper photographs of twenty years ago, and there was no public outcry over its reuse (Figure 6-7). The places touched by Corll, Henley, and Brooks were treated like the sites of most ordinary homicides, that is, rectified. It was as if the sense of shame, by being spread among many sites, scarred no one place in particular. Corll was never really perceived as a member of neighborhoods where he killed; he was only a murderous interloper.

From what I can discern from my surveys of many other mass murder sites, rectification has occurred many times before the Houston tragedy and often since. The earliest site I considered was the "castle" of H. H. Holmes, one of the most notorious killers of the 1890s.[19] On his arrest in 1894, he confessed to twenty-seven murders;

Figure 6-8. The post office where "Holmes's Castle" once stood in Chicago, Illinois. Holmes was one of the major serial killers of nineteenth-century America. Many of his victims were killed and dismembered on this site in the 1890s.

police suspected more but proved fewer. Holmes had been preying most recently on young women visiting Chicago's Columbian Exposition by luring them to his three-story building on the South Side at 63d Street and Wallace, a combination store, hotel, and torture chamber. No trace of "Holmes's Castle" remains today, but it was not immediately obliterated in the aftermath of his discovery or execution in 1896. Evidence from city directories indicates that an assortment of businesses used the ground-floor retail space for many years, and the building was not demolished until the late 1930s. The land is now owned by the federal government, which opened a post office on the site in 1938 (Figure 6-8).

Not long after veteran Howard Unruh returned from World War II, he went on a rampage in his neighborhood in Camden, New Jersey, killing twelve and wounding five. The murders took place at the intersection of River Road and 32d Street on 6 September 1949. After almost fifty years, the site is recognizable, if a little worse for wear (Figure 6-9). The corner store above which Unruh lived with his

Figure 6-9. The street corner where Howard Unruh launched his attack on neighbors and passersby in September 1949 at the intersection of River Road and 32d Street in Camden, New Jersey. This recent photograph captures the corner in almost its 1949 appearance, although a bit more worn.

family still exists, as do most of the buildings in the immediate vicinity. I can find no evidence that effacement of the murder site was ever contemplated following Unruh's murders.

This outcome was repeated again on Chicago's South Side in 1966.[20] In the early morning hours of 15 July, Richard Speck broke into a townhouse at 2319 E. 100th Street and killed eight student nurses. The townhouse was one of a row stretching between Luella and Crandon Streets, of which three had been leased for dormitory space by the South Chicago Community Hospital. Eight students had been assigned to each of two units, with their housemother stationed in the third. After the murders the townhouse was reused as a residential property (Figure 6-10). It does retain some of its notoriety, however, even today. On my visit local residents knew where I was headed before I read the addresses on the doors.

Less than three weeks after the murders in Chicago, the United States was shocked again on 1 August 1966 by another, larger mass murder on the campus of the University of Texas at Austin. A student,

Figure 6-10. Speck murder site in Chicago, Illinois. The three units to the left were being used as temporary dormitories for nursing students from a nearby hospital. Speck attacked the nurses living in the unit at 2319 100th Street on a night in July 1966. The building remains in use.

Charles Whitman, fired on the campus from a barricaded position on the observation deck at the top of the university's central tower (Figure 6-11). In what would be the largest simultaneous mass murder in U.S. history until 1984, Whitman killed fourteen people before he was trapped and killed. The list of victims grew to sixteen when it was discovered that Whitman had killed both his wife and mother the night before his attack on the campus. None of the sites touched by Whitman's murder spree was ever effaced. I can find no evidence at all in contemporary accounts that obliteration was even considered. Whitman's sniper post was at the top of the tallest building on the University of Texas campus, one that served the university at that time as its main library and administration building. Following the murders the university cleaned and patched the damage caused by the shootings and reopened the observation deck about a year afterward. Some years later the deck was closed to the public because of the suicides it attracted.[21] Whitman murdered his mother in her apartment in a new

Figure 6-11. The Main Building of the University of Texas at Austin. Charles Whitman launched his assault on campus from a barricaded position on the observation deck just below the clock in August 1966. Obliteration of this campus landmark was never contemplated.

Figure 6-12. Destruction of the McDonald's restaurant in San Ysidro, California, in the wake of the mass murder of 18 July 1984. Photograph courtesy of the Bettmann Archive.

high-rise tower only blocks from campus, but no thought was given to destroying the building out of shame. The site was rectified, and the building has remained in residential use right up to the present. The rented house in south Austin where Whitman and his wife lived and where he murdered her was also used again.

Of these and the other sites I visited, I could find only two examples that could be said to have resulted in sanctification. On 18 July 1984 Whitman's record was surpassed at a McDonald's restaurant in San Ysidro, California, by James Huberty. During a seventy-five-minute attack Huberty killed twenty-one people and injured nineteen others before he was shot and killed by a police sharpshooter. Huberty's actions irretrievably altered attitudes toward the murder site. Within a week the restaurant was closed permanently, despite the money invested in cleaning and repairing the building just after the killings. Within three months the restaurant was demolished (Figure 6-12), and within six months the land was deeded to the city of San Diego for public use. At this point the San Ysidro site showed every sign of undergoing obliteration on a large scale. The Gein and Gacy episodes led to the destruction of entire buildings, but not on the same scale. In San Ysidro shame forced the local proprietor of the McDonald's restaurant and the McDonald's Corporation to relinquish a fully functioning restaurant and a valuable parcel of land. The murder was so at odds with the public image the restaurant chain sought to foster that it chose to abandon the site rather than face censure for keeping the outlet open. In deeding the land to San Diego (of which San Ysidro is a part), McDonald's specified only that the land not be used again commercially and that the site not make use of the McDonald's name. Within a year of the tragedy another McDonald's restaurant was built just a few blocks away from the original.

For the next five years attention focused on what to do with this stigmatized site. Two positions were advanced, one favoring any of a variety of public uses for the site that would in effect ignore the killings and the other inclined toward some sort of memorial to the victims. This outcome was unprecedented in the history of American mass murder, but it arose for very good reasons. The deaths at San Ysidro quickly came to be viewed as a grave loss to the local community, one whose victims should be remembered. San Ysidro, a small, largely Hispanic community across the border from Tijuana, lost many children in the killing. Furthermore Huberty was an outsider, a non-Hispanic who had recently moved to California from Ohio. The mass murder seemed more like an accident, a horrendous act of God befalling the community from outside. In this situation it seemed shameful *not* to do something to honor the victims.

Immediately after the restaurant was demolished, local residents anonymously erected a small shrine to the victims of the massacre (Figure 6-13) and planted flowers before the road leading past the site. For several years this small memorial was carefully tended, despite the city's repeated threats to remove the shrine to keep the parcel clear. As debate over the site continued, the city of San Diego sought some low-key way to dispose of the property. Every time the city tried to do so, strident objections were raised in San Ysidro. Feelings ran high locally that the future of the site had to involve some sort of community center that would itself be, or would include, a memorial to the twenty-one victims. A compromise was reached in the late 1980s: the site could be used by the local community college for a classroom build-

Figure 6-13. The site of the San Ysidro mass murder in the interim between demolition of the restaurant and erection of a new community building. The site remained in this condition for about five years.

ing. This was a small college that had served San Ysidro for many years from temporary space in the community. Now it was to have a permanent headquarters. A small area in front of the building was set aside for a memorial (Figures 6-14 and 6-15).

In the meantime the mass murder in San Ysidro was surpassed in number by another, this time at a cafeteria in Killeen, Texas, on 16 October 1991. After a good deal of debate within the community, the cafeteria was rectified and reopened. A small memorial was erected on the grounds of the community center, a couple of miles from the cafeteria. In a twist of meaning rare among such events, the reconstruction of the restaurant and the construction of the memorial became points of community pride. This was a truly unusual outcome insofar as residents seemed determined to prove that the attack would not make them live in shame. They wanted to demonstrate their town's ability to respond effectively and positively to the tragedy. The efforts to reopen the cafeteria and build a memorial became emblems of community spirit (Figure 6-16).

THE VARIABILITY OF RESPONSE

Shame is the motive force behind obliteration, and perhaps also behind rectification. But shame is not induced by every act of mass violence or gross negligence. Mass murder itself arises from many motives, and each major instance has an almost unique effect on place. Jack Levin and James Fox, for instance, distinguish three types of mass murder in terms of whether they are committed within families and among close friends, for profit or criminal expediency, or for psychosexual and sadistic reasons.[22] Killings that occur in a single outburst are called *simultaneous*, whereas those spread over longer periods are termed *serial*. Most of the cases I have introduced have been simultaneous events from Levin and Fox's third category—the most unusual and rare events. Still, my surveys indicate that simultaneous mass murders of any type have a greater potential to affect attitudes toward the crime scene, if only because the killings are concentrated in a single location. Serial murders, unless they involve multiple killings or burials at a single location, such as Gein's and Gacy's, are more likely to be treated in the manner of isolated homicides, meaning that the sites are rectified and forgotten. In essence the general principle is that the

Figure 6-14. The new education center on the site of the San Ysidro mass murder. A small memorial garden was planted in front of the building just after its completion to honor the victims of the attack. Photograph by Stuart Aitken and Mona Domosh.

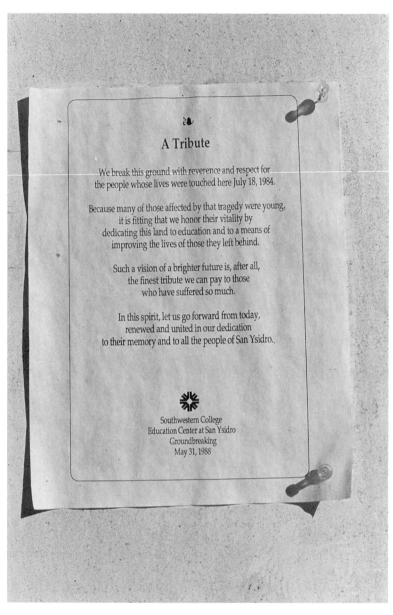

A Tribute

We break this ground with reverence and respect for
the people whose lives were touched here July 18, 1984.

Because many of those affected by that tragedy were young,
it is fitting that we honor their vitality by
dedicating this land to education and to a means of
improving the lives of those they left behind.

Such a vision of a brighter future is, after all,
the finest tribute we can pay to those
who have suffered so much.

In this spirit, let us go forward from today,
renewed and united in our dedication
to their memory and to all the people of San Ysidro.

Southwestern College
Education Center at San Ysidro
Groundbreaking
May 31, 1988

Figure 6-15. A sign pinned to the wall of Southwestern College in San Ysidro, California, as a tribute to the victims of the 1984 mass murder. Photograph by Stuart Aitken and Mona Domosh.

Figure 6-16. Memorial marker on the grounds of the Killeen community center honoring the victims of the mass murder of 1991. The restaurant where the murders took place was rectified and reopened. This memorial, like the one in San Ysidro, is an unusual outcome for mass murder. Here it seems to have been a way for the community to "get back" at the killer and claim some pride from a shameful event.

greater number of deaths at a given site, the more likely becomes its obliteration. Otherwise rectification is the more likely outcome.

This remains true regardless of the category into which the violence falls. Well over half of mass murders are of Levin and Fox's first type and arise in the family from interpersonal conflict or emotional distress. Most are simultaneous, and most result in rectification. Some do lead to effacement, however. Here it is possible to compare the house where Charles Whitman killed his wife the night before his attack on the University of Texas campus and one of the sites where George Banks killed most of his family in Wilkes-Barre, Pennsylvania, in September 1982. Both attacks involved members of the killers' families, but the house where Whitman murdered his wife was used again. The Banks massacre site was demolished within months of his crime. Whitman's attack on the University of Texas campus claimed more victims, but Banks's was the one effaced.

In dealing with criminal acts that result in mass murder—Levin and Fox's second category—the same general principle applies, although certain gang crimes, Mafia hits, and acts of terrorism are themselves quite capable of inducing a sense of shame. For the most part, however, rectification is the rule. The St. Valentine's Day Massacre in Chicago on 14 February 1929 is one of the legendary events in the history of organized crime in America.[23] Seven members of "Bugs" Moran's North Side gang were gunned down in a garage at 2122 N. Clark Street on Al Capone's orders. Even though the massacre left bullet scars on the rear wall of the garage, the building was returned to use after the killings. It remained in use for almost forty years before being demolished in 1967 to make way for new development (Figure 6-17). The infamous Union Station Massacre in Kansas City on 17 June 1933 claimed almost as many victims and again resulted in no major changes at the site.[24] In this episode "Pretty Boy" Floyd, Adam Richetti, and Vern Miller were attempting to free Frank Nash from arrest as he was being transported to Leavenworth Penitentiary. The gang bungled the rescue, killing Nash and four guards in the process. The immediate traces of the killings were removed, with the exception of a few bullet scars that could not be easily repaired.

After studying dozens of such episodes—mass murders, gangland hits, and even random violence—I do not think there is a way to pre-

Figure 6-17. The St. Valentine's Day Massacre site at 2122 North Clark Street in Chicago, Illinois. The shooting took place on 14 February 1929. The garage in which the attack took place was demolished in 1967.

dict exactly which will produce the greatest sense of shame and which will cross the line from rectification to obliteration. The factors are too complex to be arranged into a neat predictive algebra of response. Two "crimes of the century"—the Leopold-Loeb murder case of 1924 and the Manson murders of 1969—highlight this unpredictability of response.

The Leopold-Loeb murder case resulted in one of the most sensational criminal investigations and trials of the 1920s. Nathan Leopold and Richard Loeb were precocious young men from well-to-do Chicago families. Convinced of their own moral superiority and intellectual invincibility, the two decided to commit the "perfect" crime. On 21 May 1924 Leopold and Loeb kidnapped and killed Bobby Franks, a child from their own neighborhood, as he was on his way home from school. The killers' perfect crime unraveled quickly. Leopold dropped his glasses near Bobby Franks's body, and these quickly put the police on his track. By the time the pair came to trial, their lawyers, led by Clarence Darrow, were concerned less with defending the boys' innocence than with averting a death sentence. The two were sentenced to life in prison, where Loeb was murdered in 1936. Leopold was paroled in 1958, after thirty-three years in prison, and died in 1971.

Leopold and Loeb claimed only a single victim, yet their crime did have an effect on place. Within the social circles in which the Leopold, Loeb, and Franks families moved, the crime had tremendous repercussions. Richard Loeb's father was a millionaire vice-president of Sears and Roebuck. Leopold's father was almost as well off. To have their sons brutally murder a child known to both families was an unspeakable shame. Within weeks of the close of the trial, the Leopold family abandoned their home at 4754 South Greenwood Avenue; Leopold's two brothers changed their names. The house survived for a time but was eventually torn down to make way for new houses. Loeb's father was in ill health at the time of the murder and died just after Richard was sent to the penitentiary. Their mansion at 5017 South Ellis Avenue was immediately put up for sale. Through the years it had a number of owners but ended up as a rooming house before it was demolished in the 1970s (Figure 6-18). The Franks's mansion is the only one of the three homes that remains, at 5052 South Ellis Avenue, but the family moved away soon after the trial. Hal Higdon, writing about the Leopold and Loeb case in 1975, shows an unusual sensitivity to the fate of these places touched by the Franks murder. As he writes in the prologue of his book: "Fifty years later most of the scars are gone . . . all that remained was a bad memory, a very bad memory." [25]

Whereas the Franks murder was unusual in inducing such a strong sense of shame in the aftermath of a single death, the Manson murders of the 1960s are inexplicable for the opposite reason. [26] The murderers' predations had little effect on the places where they killed. In August 1969 Manson's followers murdered Sharon Tate and three of her house guests at a rented mansion far up Benedict Canyon in the Hollywood Hills along the northern edge of Beverly Hills. A fifth victim was a young friend of the estate's caretaker. The next night another group of Manson's followers—including Manson himself this time—traveled to the Silverlake district of Los Angeles far to the east and killed Leno and Rosemary LaBianca. The authorities did not connect the two crimes until November, but as the pieces came to-

Figure 6-18. The site where the Loeb mansion stood, 5017 South Ellis Avenue in the Kenwood neighborhood of Chicago, Illinois. No murder ever occurred here, but the shame engendered by Richard Loeb and Nathan Leopold's killing of Bobby Franks forced the family to move soon after the boys were tried and sentenced to prison in 1924.

gether, they developed into one of the most widely publicized cases of the twentieth century. Many people saw Manson and his followers as symbols of the violence of the entire decade. Nonetheless the estate Sharon Tate and Roman Polanski rented from Rudolph Altobelli at 10050 Cielo Drive, off Benedict Canyon Road, remained a private residence.[27] The LaBianca home at 3301 (now 3311) Waverly Drive has changed hands since the murders but remains intact. The murder sites were treated in the same fashion as the scenes of most homicides: they were rectified and reused. Despite the notoriety of the Manson murder case, it left no distinctive mark on the landscape.

THE PATHOLOGY OF PLACE

I have suggested that the process of obliteration is never really complete. No matter what ad hoc measures are improvised, shameful connotations can stain a place for long periods. These are events that *cannot* be forgotten but *should not* be remembered—obliteration is ineffective, but sanctification is inappropriate. The sites are held in a limbo of conflicting emotions; someone will object to what is done regardless of whether the site is marked, ignored, reused, or memorialized. In these cases shame interferes with the normal emotive bonds that develop between people and the environments in which they live, what geographers term *sense of place.*[28] These are the deep, positive bonds of comfort and well-being that people develop for environments they like and enjoy. People sometimes also experience a *sense of placelessness*—feelings of alienation, anomie, and even anxiety and fear—in situations where these strong positive bonds are missing.[29] Places touched by shame fall somewhere in between. They disrupt ordinary bonds of attachment and make it difficult to form new ones.

In a small number of unusual cases, shame can induce pronounced atypical and unhealthy attitudes toward place, ones I might go so far as to term pathological. I suspect that they are rooted in the way obliteration circumvents the normal process of bereavement. As I state in previous chapters, rituals of sanctification can serve as a focus for a cathartic release of emotion in the wake of tragedy and violence. The creation of memorials helps survivors come to terms with their loss and the meaning of their sacrifices. In instances of particularly shocking violence, survivors are compelled to forgo such rituals out of a sense of shame. In the absence of alternatives such as rituals of purification or atonement, people may be inclined to deny or suppress their grief or express it in unusual, perhaps less socially acceptable ways. Psychologists often argue that suppression leads nowhere, since it fails to resolve the tensions producing the discomfort. Eventually a person's or a community's grief will find expression, perhaps in episodes of anxiety or depression, although sometimes in positive ways. Nowadays teams of psychologists intervene routinely in communities struck by disaster for precisely this reason. Studies have suggested that survivors too often suppress their grief until long after the event and then vent their emotions in destructive ways. Immediate intervention seems to help survivors overcome their grief more readily and with less likelihood of negative consequences such as divorce, violence, and poor school performance. Among the events I discuss in this chapter, intervention is less common, sometimes even being rejected out of the very sense of shame it might remedy.

Emotional tension may instead be released in unusual or seemingly inappropriate ways. One of the psychiatrists involved in the Gein case became fascinated, for example, by the gallows humor inspired by the murderer's crimes. Gein jokes, riddles, puns, and rhymes proliferated, as they have after other unsavory mass murders, massacres, and other disasters. In concluding his study, George Arndt speculated that such humor served as a psychological defense, a way for people to confront their anxieties without actually admitting their fears, a view supported by other theorists right back to Freud.[30] The point is that laughter is a socially *appropriate* means of expressing socially *inappropriate* emotions. Some emotions—shock, sadness, and fear, perhaps— are simply not supposed to be expressed in public in some situations. Humor may be one of the only ways survivors have to release this tension when other outlets are blocked by shame.

Jokes are not the only outlet for responses to shameful and horrifying events. In modern American society, mass media and popular culture can serve as outlets for morbid curiosity and fear. Movies, television, newspaper, and magazine exposés, fiction and nonfiction books, and popular songs can all focus wide attention on shameful events yet simultaneously be condemned for being exploitive and in bad taste.[31] People can confront their anxieties and fears surreptitiously while denying their own furtive interest. This a key to understanding some of the success of popular novelists such as Robert Bloch. Bloch often weaves the thread of a real-life crime into his fiction. *American Gothic* is based loosely on the life and crimes of H. H. Holmes. Gein was the inspiration for Bloch's wildly popular *Psycho*. Alfred Hitchcock made the book into a movie that is now considered a classic of modern filmmaking, horror or otherwise. And *Psycho*, the movie, has since inspired further cinematic embellishments of Gein's grim life, including *The Texas Chainsaw Massacre*. When one murderer was asked her reason for shooting at children on a San Diego playground, she said only, "I don't like Mondays," now the title of a song recorded by the Boomtown Rats. Gacy's murders inspired the song *Another Kid in the Crawl*.

This rechanneling of emotion has consequences for place and landscape. Shameful places often become targets for vandals. Even after effacement, such sites may continue to attract such destructive attention. Gacy's empty lot in suburban Chicago still attracts carloads of visitors and the inevitable defacement, trash, and litter (Figure 6-3). Graffiti is not uncommon at other sites, and souvenir hunters can be a problem for nearby landholders who find that their property has become fair game for unwelcome collectors. So many people still ask for directions to Bonnie and Clyde's death site in rural Louisiana that Bienville Parish finally erected a marker. Ever since then visitors have been chipping away, shooting at, and scrawling graffiti on its surface (Figure 6-19). Authentic relics can attract high prices. The bricks scarred by the bullets of the St. Valentine's Day Massacre were sold at a profit when the garage was torn down. Charles Whitman's weapons and assault supplies were snapped up quickly at auction. Stigmatized places can attract and inspire other shameful events or violence, such as suicide, riots, or uprisings. As I mentioned about the University of Texas tragedy, the observation deck Whitman used for his assault high atop the university's central tower was reopened to the public about a year after the shootings. The university decided to close the observation deck permanently in 1974 to end a string of suicides that rekindled morbid public fascination with the site. The site of the Wounded Knee Massacre became the rallying point for the Sioux uprising of 1973, just as the Stonewall Inn became a focus for a whole series of riots and demonstrations. The man accused of the Oklahoma City bombing of 1995 traveled to Waco to visit the site of the Branch Davidian compound about whose destruction he was much incensed.

Finally, stigmatized places can become the subject of unusual stories and myths of the sort Jan Brunvand terms *urban legends*.[32] These are widely known stories and anecdotes that, although seemingly based on true events, are really fictitious. They are scary stories or accounts of strange happenings, often with an ironic twist. The most remarkable feature of these legends is that they can spread so rapidly—even across international and linguistic boundaries—and some are so commonplace as to be ubiquitous. Brunvand is concerned only with legends that fly free of reality, those he is unable to trace back to real-life events. Nevertheless real events can give birth to legends that are equally prevalent and just as long lived. The scenes of shocking events, as well as places indirectly associated with such events, often become the subjects of such legends. The infamous gangster John Dillinger was pursued and killed by FBI agents in Chicago on 23 July 1934. The next day's *Chicago Herald Examiner* carried the story "Scene of Death Made a Bazaar":

Figure 6-19. The death site of Bonnie and Clyde in Louisiana's Bienville Parish. Here the gangsters were ambushed in 1934 along a rural road on their way from one of their hideouts. The parish erected this marker much later to help visitors find the spot. The marker is badly chipped and vandalized. Visitors to Bonnie's grave in Dallas still leave flowers and remembrances.

"The spot" where John Dillinger was slain became a great bazaar yesterday, with gabby youngsters to tell you "eye-witness" stories for a coin and loud-mouthed men hawking handkerchiefs and bits of newspapers stained by the desperado's blood.

On the scene of Chicago's most famous "spot" in years gathered thousands of the curious, who proved eager bait for the scheming sidewalk spielers.[33]

The interesting point is that now—over sixty years later—people still point out the place where Dillinger died at the entrance to an alley just south of Chicago's Biograph Theater. No plaque marks the death site, but it has become a part of local lore and has been passed by word of mouth for well over half a century. Someday, when Chicago's depression-era gangsters come to be viewed as part of the city's "cultural heritage" and the gangsters themselves become the subject of high-brow history, Dillinger's death site may be marked. The point is that there are many places like the Dillinger death site that provide a foundation for oral legends. These may be sites of violence and tragedy, or they may be places associated indirectly with the characters and events implicated in the violence, such as places where a criminal was born, lived, arrested, or buried. These legends have much in common with the myths that grow up around heroic events and individuals, except that they are rarely committed to writing and are almost always transmitted furtively. The contrast is apparent in the fact that the tourist interested in important historical sites can buy a guidebook, whereas visitors must depend on informal help to find places like Bonnie Parker's grave (Dallas's Crown Hill Cemetery), Lee Harvey Oswald's grave (Fort Worth's Rose Hill Cemetery), or the site of the former Branch Davidian complex to the east of Waco, Texas.

Although the legends are different from the jokes and vandalism, they serve a somewhat similar defensive role. They allow people to come to terms with shameful events—and the fears and anxieties produced by such events—when other remedies are unavailable or thwarted by the power of shame. In these situations people may actually find it helpful to localize their fears to particular places. A generalized sense of anxiety can thus be isolated and confined. A diffuse sense of fear or foreboding may then be faced more directly at a single site. I do not have the evidence to confirm or disprove such conjectures here. More must be learned first about the relationship between the psychology of shame and the geography of everyday life.[34] It is almost inevitable that the necessary evidence will gradually become available. People are too often faced with events that force these issues into public view. In Waco, Texas, people are grappling with the meaning of the Branch Davidian tragedy of 1993 and what to do with the property. In Oklahoma City survivors of the 1995 terrorist bombing are trying to come to terms with their loss and the scene of the crime. The grief and shame engendered by events are hard to face. Memorials may help to heal the wounds of grief, but shameful reminders will be more difficult to efface. Their obliteration can never be complete.

Chapter 7

The Land-Shape of Memory and Tradition

Sanctification, designation, rectification, and obliteration are not necessarily final. Minor adjustments are common, and major changes not unusual, sometimes long after an event. In extreme cases obliterated sites may be rediscovered and venerated, and sanctified sites may be effaced. The motive for change is retrospective interpretation. Looking back, people reappraise an event's significance. The most interesting examples involve reshaping sites to mark historical points of origin that become emblems of local or regional identity. Recent historical scholarship has focused on how conceptions of the national past, patriotism, and regional identity evolve through time. Stories about the past that come to be accepted as objective, historical truth are better characterized as invented narratives—tales shaped and reshaped over time to meet the demands of contemporary society. This is not to maintain that "history" is merely myth and legend but rather to claim that facts and events are filtered, screened, and interpreted to make them seem more coherent and heroic than they might have been. Eric Hobsbawm and Terence Ranger call this the *invention of tradition.* They and their colleagues have charted how the rise of nationalism and national consciousness have been accompanied by the creation of traditions, myths, and legends that explain the past in terms of romantic or heroic struggles for sovereignty.[1] Other writers have applied the term *making histories* to this process by which nations and social groups come to anchor their sense of identity in the past or bond community in a sense of historical continuity.[2] The interesting thing is that landscape is involved intimately in the emergence of such historical traditions. Not only do these traditions become inscribed on the landscape in the form of memorials and monuments, but in many cases the condition of the sites themselves precipitates debate over what will be commemorated as part of these traditions.

In this chapter I consider the powerful influence that the invention of tradition has had on the American landscape and the way that sites of violence and tragedy have been woven into these traditions. I consider three cases to illustrate different aspects of the process. The memorialization of places associated with the Texas Revolution of 1836 shows how state and regional identity emerge over time. I then consider Chicago's civic identity from the standpoint of how the Fort Dearborn Massacre of 1812 and Great Fire of 1871 have been woven into the city's myth of origins. Finally, sites marking the westward flight of the Mormons from New York to Utah will illustrate how religious identity can come to be anchored in place. These examples set the stage for the next chapter, where I turn my attention to the emergence of U.S. national identity and the way that historical traditions have been inscribed on landscape.

REMEMBERING TEXAS

Today in the state of Texas, hundreds of monuments and memorials pay tribute to the revolution of 1836 and the creation of the Republic of Texas. Perhaps no state has been so lavish in celebrating its origins or so preoccupied with them. Legends, histories, and textbooks all stress the outnumbered Texans' heroic struggle against the tyranny of Mexican dictatorship. The sites of all the major battles have been amply marked and these days attract thousands of visitors each year. The Alamo—"shrine to Texas liberty"—is one of the largest tourist attractions in San Antonio and the state. On special occasions presidents of the United States have made special visits to these sites to pay tribute to the sacrifices made for freedom. Nonetheless nowhere is there a better example of how fact and myth mix to shape a landscape into a heroic representation of a historical tradition. The sites of revolutionary battles have grown in direct proportion to the stories and legends that have developed around them.

There are actually few elements of the Texas Revolution that seem capable of inspiring the historical epic into which they have been woven.[3] The Texans acted from mixed motives, some of which were far less than heroic by any standard, past or present. The first Anglo settlers had moved to the new territory at the generosity of a Mexican government seeking to colonize a vast frontier. By moving into the territory, they agreed to abide by the terms of their invitation: free land in exchange for allegiance to Mexico. The Anglo settlers became Mexican citizens and agreed to abide by the constitution and laws of that nation—including conversion to Roman Catholicism and, at times, a prohibition on slavery. These laws were lightly enforced, and the Mexican government was so anxious to promote settlement that the colonists were offered concessions unavailable to native citizens, including exemption from taxes, military service, customs duties, and mandatory church tithes.[4] In retrospect it seems that most of the new settlers intended to abide by these terms. For a small minority, dissembling allegiance was simply an easy means of claiming vast tracts of land. Almost everyone in Texas and across the borders to the north and south realized that the territory lay directly in the path of American westward ambitions. Tension was growing between the United States and Mexico even as the first Anglo settlers arrived. These tensions increased as Mexico entered a period of political turbulence in the 1820s after it gained its independence from Spain. It seemed likely that sooner or later Mexico would have to pass this territory to the United States, and as the political climate in Mexico changed radically through the 1820s and 1830s, some settlers became intent on spurring this conveyance to take place as rapidly as possible.

The Texans were not wholly ungrateful guests, but they did recognize themselves as different from other Mexicans not only politically and territorially but, more and more as time passed, culturally as well. The resulting conflict was as much a clash of cultures along a vast, sparsely settled, and lightly defended frontier as it was a question of immediate political and territorial aims. Misperceptions stemming from cultural difference were prevalent on both sides as Texans misinterpreted the decisions of the Mexican government and Mexican leaders miscalculated the loyalties and intentions of the Texans. In this atmosphere action and reaction amplified rather than dampened tensions. In particular, Mexican actions in the early 1830s intended to bring government policy toward Texas in line with that exerted elsewhere in Mexico, including the introduction of taxation, customs, and a military presence, were interpreted by the Texans as meddlesome interference and infringement of rights. The situation deteriorated for a number of years before resulting in open conflict. The turning point was reached not long after the popular general Antonio López de Santa Anna assumed control of the government in 1834. Santa Anna was at first perceived as sympathetic to special treatment of Texas, to letting the Anglo settlers hold sway on the frontier. Within a year he turned toward making sure Texans followed Mexican policy to the letter of the law, no matter how these changed from month to month and day to day. The Texans saw that their claims to new territory, as well as their investments in their claims, could be sustained or dismissed at the whim of a distant central government. If the Texans did not submit, however, Santa Anna was prepared simply to drive them out of Mexico.

The Texans' loyalties were divided, even when violence finally arrived. The Texans did not renounce their citizenship and even flew the Mexican flag as they first marched to battle. Nevertheless they were rallying to the Mexico of 1829, when states' rights were more firmly assured under the constitution, not the Mexico that had evolved in the 1830s. Years of confusion and political ambiguity finally resolved around defending Texas from "invasion" from the south. There were few heroic moments in the fighting. Three major massacres—at the Alamo, Goliad, and San Jacinto—punctuated a series of minor skirmishes. The Texans were so weak in numbers and munitions that they had to rally soldiers of fortune and supplies from the United States. When the fighting was over, Texans held to the fiction of maintaining an independent republic for almost ten years before joining the Union, a period just long enough to establish control over the republic's land resources and sustain the illusion that statehood was only an afterthought of revolution.

Interpreted in this unflattering light, the Texas Revolution was another complex and fatal clash of cultures precipitating one of the greatest land grabs in American history. It was inspired in no small measure by the settlers' unbridled self-interest, their distaste for Mexican culture and Catholicism, and the certain desire to transplant their way of life—including slavery—in the new territory. This was to be accomplished by any means necessary, even if it entailed enlisting soldiers of fortune and even mercenaries from the United States to reinforce the small Texan forces. These are the facts that have gradually been transformed into the story of a heroic quest for liberty and a crusade for freedom from dictatorship. Not only have the rough edges been smoothed from the story, but the heroic elements of the tale have grown in almost inverse proportion to the facts. The less appealing motives of the settlers were played down, and their sacrifices were played up. The more times the story was told, the more consistent it became in weaving the settlers mixed motives into a coherent program of grievances. Given the scale of the transformation involved, it is no accident that many decades had to pass before the story was fleshed out in heroic detail. The process itself is recorded in the Texas landscape at the sites associated with the Texas Revolution, most of which have since been sanctified. In some cases the sites themselves seem to have had a hand in precipitating reappraisal and interpretation.

The sites of greatest interest are the Alamo, Goliad, and San Jacinto, the key battles of the revolution. All occurred during the brief period of hostilities between November 1835 and April 1836 that marked the climax of the longer period of rising tension between Texas and Mexico. The first true challenge to Mexico was in Gonzales on 2 October 1835 when the citizens of this small town refused to give up a cannon to Mexican troops. A declaration of causes and grievances was issued on 7 November, followed on 5 December by the Texans' laying siege to Mexican forces at San Antonio (Béxar) and taking the Alamo in vicious house-to-house fighting ending on 9 December. After a brief pause to allow the factions to regroup and reorganize, fighting resumed in February when the Alamo was again besieged, but this time by additional Mexican troops brought north to subdue the rebellion and force the Anglos out of Texas. The siege was joined on 23 February 1836 and lasted just long enough for the Texans to declare independence at Washington-on-the-Brazos on 2 March. By this point the fate of the Alamo's defenders was sealed. Unreinforced, their garrison broke under the force of a Mexican assault on 6 March, with the loss of all troops. Not far away, at the abandoned Goliad mission, were the Texan troops who could have aided their comrades at the Alamo but failed to respond. Finally led away from Goliad to regroup with troops under the command of Sam Houston at Victoria, this force was trapped by Mexican troops at the Coleto Creek battlefield only a few miles from Goliad on 19 March. Under the command of James Fannin the troops surrendered, were returned to Goliad in captivity, and executed on 27 March. Only a handful of the Texans survived. Following the brief panic—the Runaway Scrape—ensuing from these dramatic massacres, the fortunes of the Texans turned at San Jacinto, not far from present-day Houston. In an attack on 21 April the Texans surprised and overwhelmed the Mexicans during their afternoon siesta, slaughtering hundreds of troops as they tried to flee or surrender. Santa Anna surrendered on the battlefield. Texas independence was ensured by treaty in May 1836 but not completely conceded until the Treaty of Guadalupe Hidalgo in 1848. By that time Texas had already been admitted to statehood.

In turning to the history of these sites since the revolution, one is left with the distinct impression that the motives for sanctification were often as mixed as those that inspired the revolution and were only gradually reconciled one to another. The rallying cry "Remember the Alamo, Remember Goliad" was heard at San Jacinto, and certainly vengeance was on the minds of the Texan troops as they flailed away beyond the point of any tactical necessity at the trapped Mexican troops. Vengeance is a motive for obliteration, however, not sanctification. At first there was little to commend the sanctification—or even conservation—of any of the battlefield sites. Two massacres and a sneak attack were unexceptional candidates for mythmaking and legend building. As soon as Santa Anna surrendered and the land was conceded to the Texans, the sites of the fighting fell from view. At the Alamo, where the dead had been burned by the Mexicans, it took almost a year for the Texans to find time to bury the remaining ashes and bones, which they did on 25 February 1837. At Goliad the Texans had been consigned to a common, mass grave, unmarked and barely covered with enough earth to keep out animals. Apart from a small graveyard at San Jacinto for some of the Texan dead, this battlefield too returned to obscurity. This remained the situation for all three battlefields for most of their first fifty years.

Significantly the first efforts toward sanctification of the sites were by veterans on behalf of their fallen comrades.[5] Between 1856 and 1881 funds were raised to erect a grave marker at the San Jacinto burial ground, and in 1883 the Texas Veterans Association was finally able to raise enough money to purchase the cemetery (Figure 7-1).

Figure 7-1. The San Jacinto burial ground. Only a handful of Texan troops died in the battle and were buried here. Between 1856 and 1881 veterans raised funds for a grave marker and eventually purchased the cemetery in 1883. The 1880s marked the first concerted effort to commemorate the battlefields, and activity increased substantially through the 1930s. The San Jacinto battlefield is now encompassed by a large state park.

Although a modest step, the purchase of the San Jacinto graveyard sig-naled a rising tide of interest in the battlefields in the 1880s, coinciding with the fiftieth anniversary of the revolution. A marker was erected at the Coleto Creek battlefield where Colonel Fannin's troops had sur-rendered in advance of their execution at Goliad (Figure 7-2). A similar marker in honor of Colonel Fannin was dedicated in Goliad proper in 1885 (Figure 7-3), although the burial site outside of town near the abandoned presidio remained unsanctified. Little had changed there apart from the rocks that local residents had piled on the mass grave from the 1850s onward.

The Alamo site in San Antonio saw many changes up to the 1880s, but none focused on its sanctification. The Catholic Church retained ownership of the abandoned mission compound but had no interest in restoring the site. The compound lay in ruins until 1847, when the U.S. Army rented it from the Catholic Church to use as an armory, a role the structure held until 1877, with an interlude of Con-federate occupancy during the Civil War. When the Army gave up its lease, the Catholic Church rented the space for commercial use. The upwelling of interest in the battle sites in the 1880s led San Antonio to purchase the small Alamo chapel in 1883, although the city had no immediate plans for its use. The Catholic Church sold the remainder of the compound to commercial interests in 1885 (Figure 7-4).

Only after the turn of the century did major changes begin to take place at any of the sites. In 1905 the state intervened at the Alamo and purchased the privately held portions of the compound, although there seemed to be little enthusiasm within state government to transform the site into a park or shrine. Instead the rights to use and maintain the site were passed to the Daughters of the Republic of Texas, a pa-triotic group formed in the late nineteenth century. At San Jacinto the Texas Veterans Association had expanded their holdings and activi-ties and marked key battlefield sites in 1897. In 1907 the entire park was placed under the jurisdiction of the San Jacinto Park Commis-sion, thus like the Alamo moving from private to public ownership. The Daughters of the Republic of Texas replaced the veterans associ-ation's plaques with substantial granite markers in 1910.

These modest efforts at conservation dating to the 1880s were ful-filled in the centennial decade of the 1930s. No other state in the Union has much to compare with the outpouring of commemorative activity

Figure 7-2. The Coleto Creek battlefield, where Fannin's retreat from his fortified position at Goliad was thwarted by Mexican troops on 19 March 1836. The Texan force surrendered the following day, and the men were marched back to Goliad, where they were confined in the Presidio until their execution on 27 March.

leading up to the Texas centennial of 1936. All three battlefields were transformed, as were hundreds of other sites throughout the state, eventually encompassing virtually every location associated in any way whatsoever with the state's past and significant citizens. The centennial celebration was over ten years in the making, beginning with lobbying as early as 1923 by the Advertising Clubs of Texas. Work proceeded slowly at first but picked up pace in the 1930s. With Texas in the midst of the Great Depression and with the promise of New Deal funding on the horizon, the centennial seemed like a good opportunity to boost the economy a bit through tourism and public works projects. A temporary centennial commission was created in 1931 to begin laying plans, lobbying for funds, and drafting enabling legislation. In envisioning the centennial, the president of the commission wrote:

> It will be far more than a mammoth modern exposition,
> whose buildings are models of architecture, in brick and stone,

Figure 7-3. Fannin Monument in Goliad. This was one of the first monuments raised—in the 1880s—to the heroes and events of the Texas Revolution.

housing triumphs of invention and miracles of science and the riches of Texas soil and sun.

It will testify that Texans are not unworthy of the incomparable heritage left to them by martyrs and patriots, dying and ready to die, that Texas might become an Anglo-Saxon commonwealth.

It will commemorate the sacrifices of the plain pioneer men and women who first treked [*sic*] the unpeopled wilds, with ax and plow and rifle and spelling book and Bible, to lay the mudsills of civilization.

It will lift our eyes to the hilltops of our history, whence cometh our help above bog and fog, for taller thinking and nobler living.[6]

Materials promoting the centennial were composed in the same high-flying rhetoric: "For variety of incident, flavor of adventure, lessons of

Figure 7-4. The Alamo in 1898. At this time the state of Texas owned the chapel visible in the upper right of the photo, but the remainder of the site was held privately. A major portion of the site was occupied by the Hugo and Schmeltzer store. The original compound defended by the Texans in 1836 extended into the foreground, encompassing the present-day Alamo Plaza and other surrounding properties. Photograph courtesy of the San Antonio Conservation Society.

endurance, patriotism and valor, heroic achievements in the crisis of battle and splendid triumphs . . . the history of Texas is unequaled."[7] From this point of view the Alamo became the "scene of the most heroic sacrifice in American history—without parallel in world history," and Goliad became "a desperate battle" that "so inflamed Texans that the battle cry of San Jacinto, 'Remember the Alamo, Remember Goliad' was invincible."[8] With a certain sense of modesty San Jacinto was termed only "the sixteenth decisive battle of world history." The rhetorical latitude of these claims is understandable in the light of their promotional motive, but by the 1930s they were relatively unexceptional in their hyperbole. By the time of the centennial Texas history had been smoothed and shaped effectively in all manner of literature and popular media. Historical scholarship, biography, textbooks, popular fiction, and movies all had the effect of accentuating the positive connotations of Texas history and muting the negative ones. The process involved simplifying the historical record to omit troublesome detail and shaping what remained into a wide range of myths and legends.[9] By extending the peaks and bridging the troughs, Texas history became a curve arching ever upward toward progress, liberty, and freedom. The battle for the Alamo was a choice of "victory or death" rather than an issue of the justifiability of holding a tactically ineffective position. The sacrifice of troops at Goliad become a rallying cry rather than a question of poor judgment and leadership or, as the marker at the Coleto Creek battlefield maintains, of "Victims of treachery's brutal stroke, they died to break the tyrant's yoke." The mixed motives that inspired the revolution became an unequivocal struggle against the tyranny of dictatorship. The issues of slavery and Catholicism disappeared entirely.

When the official centennial commission was legislated into being in 1934, it had well-developed plans to mark key historical sites all across the state, but most particularly those associated with the revolution. Funds earmarked for the work included over $3 million in state funds and an equal sum from the federal government supplied through the United States Texas Centennial Commission (created by the U.S. Congress in 1935 to work in tandem with the state commission). The San Jacinto battlefield was transformed substantially by the investment of approximately $1.5 million in roads, landscaping, utilities, and most significantly the erection of the tallest concrete memorial ever built (Figures 7-5 and 7-6). The memorial is a massive 570-foot tower, crowned by the star of Texas and visible for miles. The Alamo received a $250,000 face-lift, including a new sixty-foot memorial developing the theme of the "spirit of sacrifice" (Figure 7-7), its inscription reading, "They chose never to surrender nor retreat, these brave hearts with flag still proudly waving perished in the flames of immortality that their high sacrifice might lead to the founding of this Texas." The mass grave at Goliad finally received a marker, too (Figure 7-8).

Some of the projects undertaken were too large to complete in time for the centennial celebrations but were finished over the next several years. Many other projects benefited from the largess of both centennial commissions. Apart from the San Jacinto memorial, the largest project was the State of Texas Building on the grounds of the Centennial Central Exposition in Dallas (at what is now the State

Figure 7-5. A view across the San Jacinto battlefield looking from the scene of the greatest carnage toward the centennial memorial. It was here, in the foreground, that Texan troops trapped and slaughtered Mexican troops caught in the surprise attack of 21 April 1836.

Fairgrounds). Partial funding was provided for historical and natural history museums in Alpine, Austin, Canyon, Corpus Christi, El Paso, Huntsville, Gonzales, Lubbock, and San Antonio. The final report on the commissions' work issued in 1938 is a truly impressive catalog listing hundreds of community centers, restorations, park improvements, statues, monuments, historical markers, grave markers, and highway markers funded entirely or at least partially with public funds.[10] By the time the commissions had finished their work, all the battle sites had been sanctified in large public ceremonies. More important, the narrative tradition of Texas history had been impressed on the landscape in monumental form as tangible myths and durable legends.

Despite the uniformly bold claims of centennial promoters, not all sites received equal billing. Goliad continued to lag behind the others.[11] The Goliad State Historical Park was created in 1931, but the Coleto Creek battlefield gained little architectural garnish at the centennial, and the massacre site received the smallest memorial. No

Figure 7-6. The San Jacinto Memorial, built for the Texas centennial of 1936, although not completed until 1939. Built at a cost of almost $1.5 million, the tower rises 570 feet above the battlefield and is topped with Texas's "lone star." The base of the tower contains a museum and visitor center.

Figure 7-7. The "Spirit of Sacrifice" memorial raised for the Texas Centennial of 1936 in Alamo Plaza. The inscription reads, "They chose never to surrender nor retreat, these brave hearts with flag still proudly waving perished in the flames of immortality that their high sacrifice might lead to the founding of this Texas."

Figure 7-8. Goliad burial site. After Fannin's troops were executed, their bodies were burned and dumped here in a common grave. Local residents did mark the grave with stones during the nineteenth century, but the site was in such poor condition in the 1920s that animals were scattering bones about the site. The monument dates to the centennial of 1936.

matter how much the historical record was polished to reflect all the sites in a positive light, Goliad remained shadowed by Fannin's surrender. Here Texan troops gave up, unlike the Alamo, where they fought to their deaths, or San Jacinto, where they achieved victory against overwhelming odds. At Goliad they surrendered and by so doing exposed themselves to massacre (since Santa Anna had decreed that all non-Texans captured fighting would be executed). However recast, the story lacked the heroic resonance of the Alamo and San Jacinto. Texans did not have to die at the Alamo. They could have retreated and regrouped, but once they made the decision to stay, they died fighting. At Goliad the Texans again held a strategically insignificant position, they had failed to move to the aid of their comrades at the Alamo, and when the time came, they were not even able to make a success of their retreat. For these reasons Goliad is the most equivocal of the battle sites and—consequently—the last to be marked. The burial site was in such poor condition by the late 1920s that local residents rediscovered it only because burrowing animals were carrying bone fragments to the surface. The 1936 memorial redressed this situation, but very modestly. Other changes have been made since the centennial—reconstruction of the mission compound beginning in 1937 and excavation and restoration of the presidio compound in the 1960s—but Goliad remains somewhat of an outcast, occupying a dark corner in the pantheon of battle sites.

It would be unfair to portray Texas's myth of origins as entirely one-sided. The inscription on the base of the San Jacinto monument notes: "The early policies of Mexico toward her Texas colonists had been extremely liberal. Large grants of land were made to them, and no taxes or duties imposed. The relationship between the Anglo-Americans and Mexicans was cordial. But, following a series of revolutions begun in 1829, unscrupulous rulers successively seized power in Mexico. Their unjust acts and despotic decrees led to the revolution in Texas." The inscription credits the generosity of the original grants, and certainly Santa Anna's rise to power soured the situation, but the inscription quickly glosses over the unjust acts and despotic decrees. A number of colonists were indeed arrested unjustly in the prerevolutionary period, but nothing is made of the issues—such as slavery, politics, and religion—that were fundamental sources of friction. This verbal sleight of phrase extends to other aspects of the revolution. The Texans' massacre of Mexicans at San Jacinto is not overlooked but is relegated instead to a mere four words in the inscription: "The slaughter was appalling, victory complete, and Texas free!" The fact that noncitizens had come to Texas as *illegal immigrants* to fight is transformed into a virtue: "Citizens of Texas and immigrant soldiers in the army of Texas at San Jacinto were natives of Alabama, Arkansas, Connecticut, Georgia, Illinois, Indiana, Kentucky, Louisiana, Maine, Maryland, Massachusetts, Michigan, Mississippi, Missouri, New Hampshire, New York, North Carolina, Ohio, Pennsylvania, Rhode Island, South Carolina, Tennessee, Texas, Vermont, Virginia, Austria, Canada, England, France, Germany, Ireland, Italy, Mexico, Poland, Portugal and Scotland." These were not mercenaries but *immigrant soldiers*, whose appearance demonstrates not so much the universality of greed but the virtue of unity of purpose within a frontier community. In this case the ends justified the means, and the victors' trophy was enormous: "Measured by its results, San Jacinto was one of the decisive battles of the world. The freedom of Texas from Mexico won here led to annexation and to the Mexican War, resulting in the acquisition by the United States of the states of Texas, New Mexico, Arizona, Nevada, California, Utah and parts of Colorado, Wyoming, Kansas and Oklahoma. Almost one-third of the present area of the American nation, nearly a million square miles of territory, changed sovereignty."

Here then is a story of Texas inscribed in stone, marked in the soil, and sanctified in the landscape. The story is not wrong, only misleading. A complex drama of great nuance has been reduced to a simplified morality play pitting good against evil. The virtue is that, in this form, the story fits ever so neatly into a broader mythologized vision of the American past with parallels neatly drawn between the Texas Revolution and the American Revolution, between Texas's frontier immigrants and America's huddled masses, between Texan valor and American patriotism. It is this vision of Texas as a microcosm of the nation that was shaped in the period of the centennial.

This vision of Texas history took a century to emerge, but it has changed little since. From the centennial to the present, the only noticeable changes have been modest amplifications and adjustments of the story and its monumental landscape. The sanctity of some of the sites has been reinforced over the years by the construction of additional monuments and memorials. That is, once sanctified, the sites have attracted additional memorials. This process of symbolic accretion is most noticeable at the San Jacinto battlefield, where the dread-nought-class battleship USS *Texas* was retired and placed on perma-nent display in 1948. Its dock was aligned with the park's memorial tower (Figure 7-9). Following the Vietnam War, a POW-MIA memo-rial was also constructed on the grounds of the San Jacinto memorial. In effect the battlefield has become a repository for other memorials that help to reinforce its status as a meaningful place.

Over the years it also became apparent that the early rhetoric of Texas history devoted little attention to the true range of social groups that built the state. The president of the Texas centennial commission probably meant what he wrote when he stated, "Texans are not unworthy of the incomparable heritage left to them by martyrs and patriots, dying and ready to die, that Texas might become an *Anglo-Saxon commonwealth* [italics added]."[12] Although this sentiment is not far from the truth, a more accurate picture of the Texas patriots has emerged in recent decades, one that credits the contributions of non-Anglo fighters and supporters. Many Hispanic citizens were also will-ing to revolt against Santa Anna and the Republic of Mexico, and their contribution to the cause of the revolution was substantial. Revised plaques, new histories, and recent tourist brochures now almost in-evitably make special mention of Mexican Texans who participated in the revolution. These include individuals such as Colonel Juan Seguín, who delivered the funeral address (in Castilian) at the burial of the Alamo heroes on 25 February 1837, and Don Francisco Ruiz, who signed the Texas Declaration of Independence on 2 March 1836. More recently credit has also been extended to African Americans who fought for the Texans, some of whom died at the Alamo and Goliad or helped to lead the charge at San Jacinto. The irony, of course, is that free African Americans such as these were banned by the new Repub-lic of Texas once the revolution was over. Credit here was slow to ar-rive. The first marker to recognize their contributions as a group was raised in 1994 in Austin, just south of the state capitol grounds, by the Texas African American Heritage Organization (Figure 7-10).[13]

Controversy over the sites still arises periodically, particularly the Alamo because of its worldwide fame and its location in the center of one of the nation's largest cities. For many years some Texans have been attempting to have the state take back control of the Alamo from the Daughters of the Republic of Texas. The state owns the land but

Figure 7-9. The battleship USS *Texas* on display at the San
Jacinto battlefield. This was the last of the dreadnought-class
battleships and served in both world wars. It was moored
here as a memorial in 1948. It is not uncommon for memorials such as the San Jacinto battlefield to serve as the focus
for additional commemorative activity. Such sites, once sanctified, begin to attract other memorials of local, regional, and
national significance through a process of accretion. Just out
of view in this photograph is a memorial to POWs and MIAs
of the Vietnam War.

Figure 7-10. A plaque in Austin honoring African Americans in the Texas Revolution. This tribute was erected in 1994. It was sited not adjacent to the major monuments to the revolution on the grounds of the state capitol but a block away, in a small park. The dome of the capitol building can be seen in the distance.

Figure 7-11. The Alamo today. Visitors to the chapel are asked to maintain a respectful silence as they pass through this "shrine of Texas liberty." The entire complex is now owned by the state of Texas but is maintained and operated by the Daughters of the Republic of Texas.

has allowed the group to control it since 1905. The Daughters of the Republic of Texas receive no state or federal funds for their work but do earn income from sales to tourists that does not pass to the state. It rankles many that this organization—with its closed membership—should be allowed to maintain the Alamo and in a sense profit from property owned by the citizens of Texas.[14] The other sites are managed by the Texas Department of Parks and Wildlife, and it is conceivable that the Alamo will eventually be passed to this department. The site clearly remains special in the popular imagination as a "shrine of Texas liberty"—as the Daughters of the Republic of Texas depict it—or simply as a point of statewide pride (Figure 7-11). Visitors are asked to remove their hats as they enter the shrine, and silence is enforced rigorously by guards. When rock-music star Ozzy Osbourne urinated on the Alamo in 1982, he was not just convicted of public indecency but banned from performing again in San Antonio until he made a public apology and a $10,000 donation to the Daughters of the Republic of Texas, which he did in 1992.[15] Finally, the state of

Texas, after all these years, is still lobbying for the return of the only Texas battle flag that survived the fall of the Alamo, even though the Mexican government continues to resist such efforts for equally patriotic reasons.

These events are of minor, almost anecdotal consequence today, but they give some sense of the way Texas history has been shaped, smoothed, and impressed on landscape. There seems to be little doubt, given the forces at work in North America in the nineteenth century, that Mexico and the United States would eventually have come to blows over Texas. Even had the circumstances been slightly different, the outcome would probably have been the same. The United States was expanding rapidly toward a large, but sparsely occupied salient of the Mexican frontier during a time of political turmoil in the southern nation. The entire episode is really a classic example of contact and conflict between two very different cultures. In such contests one side may gain a prize, as did the Texans, but abstract notions of right and wrong can be applied only with difficulty, and neither culture really wins. The result is simply a new balance of power. The United States had even been willing to buy the entire territory before the revolution, but this option was unworkable in the context of Mexican politics of the period. When the territory finally changed hands, its cost was denominated in lives rather than dollars. Such a complex and ambiguous parable was of little use to either side in the aftermath of the conflict. To rally its citizens, a new republic needs heroes who have died for a noble cause, not simply cultural misunderstandings, and reasons for independence that set it apart from its past. For Texans, this involved simplifying the story and shaping it into a heroic struggle for a just cause. Only modest changes were then required to cast the entire story in the mold of American history: rugged frontier settlers casting off the yoke of tyranny under the banner of "victory or death."

Four Stars for Chicago

Not only states but cities commemorate their pasts in landscape and civic symbols. From the standpoint of the commemoration of tragedy, perhaps no American city is as interesting as Chicago. Arrayed in the center of its municipal flag are four red stars, each meant to represent a formative event in the city's history. Two mark the city's great expositions: the World's Columbian Exposition of 1893 and the Century of

Progress of 1933. The other pair mark far less auspicious events: Fort Dearborn, destroyed in a massacre in 1812, and the Chicago Fire of 1871. The juxtaposition of stars symbolizing such disparate events is startling. The expositions are a natural source of civic pride whose inclusion is unsurprising. The Fort Dearborn Massacre and Chicago Fire are different and at first glance seem to be unlikely points of civic pride. Fort Dearborn was the first white settlement on the site of the city. It was burned and most of its inhabitants killed by Native Americans during the War of 1812. Settlers returned to the site later to found the city of Chicago in 1837. The fire of 1871 was one of the most destructive of the dozens of major conflagrations that plagued the flammable wooden cities of nineteenth-century America. The fire claimed relatively few lives, but the property destruction was enormous and exposed many inadequacies of Chicago's municipal government.

One would hardly expect civic pride to revolve around either event, the first being a significant tragedy in the settlement of the West and the second constituting a major embarrassment involving poor building practices and inadequate fire protection. Yet today both are viewed in a far different light. The Fort Dearborn Massacre is taken to indicate Chicago's resilience in the face of adversity, and the Great Fire is seen as a symbol of the city's ability to overcome obstacles and rise phoenixlike from the ashes of its misfortunes. Indeed the image of the phoenix was quickly adopted as a symbol of the city after the Great Fire and has been used ever since. The transformation of these events from misfortunes to symbols of civic virtue and strength is reflected in the way they have been memorialized and marked in the landscape.[16]

Of the two, the Chicago Fire was the easier to cast in a positive, heroic light. It was symbolized with one of the two original stars on the city's first civic flag, adopted in 1917, an honor Fort Dearborn did not share until 1939. Furthermore the fire was *designated* an important event only a few years after it occurred—in 1880, when a historical plaque was affixed to the façade of the building that stood on the site of the fire's origin. Although a small stone tablet was placed on the original site of Fort Dearborn in the same year, the events of 1812 were not marked in a substantial way until later, and the first tablet was lost. The fire was, of course, the more dramatic and immediate of the two events.[17] More important, the Great Fire had a direct effect on the city's prosperity that was clear within a few years. Alarmists claimed that in the wake of the fire, Chicago would never recover and would surrender its key role in the midwestern economy to its principal competitor, St. Louis. These worries proved to be unfounded. Chicago's recovery was stunning, even by today's standards, and the regrowth was so rapid that it actually strengthened Chicago's advantage over St. Louis. The business opportunities presented by the fire attracted labor and capital to Chicago at a tremendous rate and produced a building and industrial boom. The fire had other positive consequences, for it forced reform on the city government and resulted in the modernization of the police and fire departments.[18] Indirectly the fire set the stage for the tremendous efflorescence of Chicago school architecture from the 1880s into the early twentieth century. The fire transformed both the fabric and the government of the city into their modern forms. As the inscription beneath one public sculpture entitled *Regeneration* proclaims from a pylon of the Michigan Avenue Bridge: "The Great Fire of October, Eighteen Hundred and Seventy-One Devastated the City. From its Ashes the People of Chicago Caused a New and Greater City to Rise, Imbued with That Indomitable Spirit and Energy by Which They Have Ever Been Guided."

The Great Fire gave the city a fresh start almost totally unencumbered by shame or dishonor. By October 1872, only a year after the fire, work was underway on a fire monument no doubt inspired by London's monument to that city's Great Fire of 1666. The column was to be built in part from debris from the fire. Work continued for five years, but the column was never completed, and the remains were destroyed in 1882. This is not to say that interest in the fire had waned entirely. Interest in the origin of the fire—the O'Leary barn on the South Side—had always remained strong, and ironically most of the O'Leary property, apart from the barn, survived the fire. The O'Learys, who had lived in somewhat forced seclusion since the fire, gave up the property in 1879. When a new house was completed in 1880, the Chicago Historical Society obtained permission to affix a marble tablet to its façade designating that "the Great Chicago Fire of 1871 Originated Here and Extended to Lincoln Park" (Figure 7-12). The tablet was replaced with a bronze plaque during the centennial celebrations of 1937 and remained until the house was demolished in the 1950s during the site's most remarkable transformation.

By the early 1950s plans were in motion for the construction of what became the Dan Ryan Expressway. The DeKoven Street prop-

Figure 7-12. The site of the origin of the Chicago Fire in the late nineteenth century. This building was built on the former O'Leary property in 1880. The plaque, added by the Chicago Historical Society, notes simply that "The Great Chicago Fire of 1871 Originated Here and Extended to Lincoln Park." Photograph ICHi-14487 by William T. Barnum courtesy of the Chicago Historical Society.

erty lay in an area adjoining the expressway route, a zone that was to be completely redeveloped for new commercial and industrial use. The property was purchased by the Chicago Land Clearance Commission in 1954, and a private company was allowed to demolish the house in 1955 by burning it down as a test of some sample building materials. During this period, completely by coincidence, the Chicago Fire Department was scouting new sites for a station in the redeveloped zone, as well as for a new training academy. The prospect of claiming the O'Leary property for the fire department proved to be irresistible, and in 1959 construction began on a new fire academy that included the original house site as a fire memorial (Figure 7-13). This was an altogether fitting choice because the Great Fire of 1871 was seen by this time as a turning point for the fire department, not at all as a shameful failure. A local sculptor was commissioned to design *Pillar of Fire* in memory of all those who died in the Great Fire. The sculpture was unveiled and the site sanctified in October 1961, ninety years after the fire.

Chicago's fire memorial numbers among America's most ironic tragedy sites but in some respects counts as no more than an afterthought. Long before *Pillar of Fire* Chicago had a ready-made monument: the city's waterworks, including the famous water tower, which were among the tiny handful of buildings in the burned district that survived the Great Fire almost unscathed. Again, a certain irony is implicit in this de facto memorial, since the failure of the water system (when the roof of the pump house collapsed) allowed the Great Fire to sweep north to its final burnout in Lincoln Park. Nonetheless no attempt has ever been made to demolish these buildings on North Michigan Avenue, even though their functional life had long since passed. Their association with the Great Fire has been too strong.

Fort Dearborn and the massacre of 1812 took far longer to be shaped into a viable part of the civic past; the star representing the massacre was the last added to Chicago's flag, although the event predates all the others so commemorated. This event suffers from two disadvantages: the fort and massacre were relatively inconsequential to Chicago's later development, and the massacre was difficult to interpret in an unabashedly heroic light. The site's only obvious claim to fame is that it came first. Built in 1803, Fort Dearborn was one of the garrisons positioned within the territory of the just completed Louisiana Purchase. It was occupied uneventfully until 1812, when advances by the British in Michigan and the stirring of Native American tribes against further white settlement arose as threats. On 9 August the commander of Fort Dearborn was ordered to dispose of public property, evacuate the garrison, and move his troops and settlers to Detroit for safety.[19] At first safe passage seemed possible, since a number of the Native American leaders and fighters surrounding the fort were on generally peaceful terms with the garrison. Others were less so, however, and were angered when the garrison destroyed its excess ammunition, extra muskets, and surplus liquor rather than disburse them. When the evacuation began on the morning of 15 August, the soldiers and settlers were attacked a mile and a half south of the fort by an over-

Figure 7-13. The Fire Memorial at the Chicago Fire Academy. The academy opened here in 1961 at the exact site of the start of the Great Fire. The irony of the selection is tempered by the fact that the Great Fire came to be seen as a key turning point leading to the creation of the city's modern fire-fighting force rather than its darkest moment.

whelming force. After a brief fight in which almost forty soldiers were killed, the remainder of the party surrendered. The attackers were not generous victors, and only about thirty-six of the approximately ninety-three people who left the fort survived the day. The fort was burned the next day, and the captives were distributed among the victorious tribes. Neither side achieved anything of significance or pride. There was nothing heroic or decisive about the evacuation. It was poorly planned, timed, and executed, and the hostile Native Americans pursued the retreating whites largely out of anger at the destruction of supplies they had expected to obtain. The only bright spot in the tragedy was that the killing of soldiers, women, and children had not been wholly indiscriminate. Timely intervention by sympathetic warriors saved many lives during the fighting and protected them in captivity until they were repatriated.

For the next four years the site remained in ruins. When the fort was regarrisoned in 1816, all traces of the original fort were effaced. Between then and the 1830s, when the property was assumed by the city of Chicago, the fort was twice again evacuated, but without loss of life. After the Black Hawk War of 1832, Chicago was never again threatened by attack and began to grow into a city. From the standpoint of this later development, the first Fort Dearborn and the massacre were little more than footnotes—one of dozens of such minor bloody encounters in the western territories during the eighteenth and nineteenth centuries. Even the second Fort Dearborn was of little consequence to the budding city. Most of the structure was either demolished in 1857 or caught in the Great Fire, with only a few logs surviving to be contributed to the World's Columbian Exposition of 1893. This situation changed only gradually with a first act of designation in 1880: a marble tablet noting the site of the forts was placed on a building that had been built on the site and remained in place until 1919, when the building was demolished. When planning for the Columbian Exposition began, some hope arose that a replica of the fort would be built on the fairgrounds. Although this hope did not materialize, 1893 saw the appearance of the massacre's first influential champion, the wealthy industrialist George M. Pullman.

Sites of violence are often set on the path to sanctification through the work of individuals. These are often humble citizens, such as Osborn H. Oldroyd, who held so tenaciously to the Petersen House, where Abraham Lincoln died, but members of the elite—such as Pullman—can often set sanctification in motion more rapidly. In Pullman's words the statue was to honor "the struggles and sacrifices of those who laid the foundation of the greatness of this City and State" (Figure 7-14).[20] The memorial was given to the Chicago Historical Society and positioned near the "Massacre Tree," where tradition held that the killings took place, a site that coincidentally was adjacent to Pullman's fashionable South Side mansion at 18th Street and Calumet. The statue is rich in nuance, for it attempts to depict the sacrifice and heroism of the defenders represented by a child and the garrison's surgeon about to die at the base of the group, along with a "good Indian" defending a woman against a mortal blow. The real beauty of Pullman's statue was that it cast the entire episode as part of an appealing story, one that made the massacre an important formative event with sacrifice and heroism all round.

After 1893 the Fort Dearborn Massacre was framed as the birth of Chicago and gradually received increasing public attention and support, particularly among the city's elite. This was a period in which most American cities were engaged in rivalries expressed in monumental new urban designs, grand expositions, and massive public buildings. The massacre became a conveniently heroic anchor point for civic history. When a massive new bridge was planned to cross the Chicago River at Michigan Avenue, at the exact site of the original Fort Dearborn, this story was retold in a bas-relief titled *Defense* and dedicated in 1928 (Figure 7-15). The caption read: "Fort Dearborn stood almost on this spot. After an heroic defense in 1812, the garrison, together with women and children was forced to evacuate the fort. Led forth by Captain Wells they were brutally massacred by the Indians. They will be cherished as martyrs in our early history." When a world fair came again to Chicago in 1933, a replica of Fort Dearborn was this time constructed for the exposition. After a tremendous amount of lobbying and discussion, Fort Dearborn finally received a star in the municipal flag in 1939. Technically the star represents Fort Dearborn itself, not the massacre, but the citation alluded directly to the events of 1812 in which the "gallant men" of the fort "afforded protection to the pioneers of the region and upheld the sovereignty of the United States until peace came to the old Northwest Frontier." In many respects the Fort Dearborn Massacre had been recast in the same mold as the Great Fire. Both events expressed Chicago's "I will" spirit and the city's ability to thrive in the face of adversity.

Figure 7-14. The statue commemorating the Fort Dearborn Massacre commissioned by George Pullman and donated to the Chicago Historical Society. The statue was dedicated in 1893 and remained at this site until 1931. The decline of the neighborhood and vandalism prompted the society to move the monument indoors to their headquarters in Lincoln Park. Photograph ICHi-03334 courtesy of the Chicago Historical Society.

Figure 7-15. The site of Fort Dearborn today. The outlines of the original fort have been marked in the surrounding pavement. A commemorative relief entitled *Defense* can be seen in the distance on the pylon of the Michigan Avenue Bridge.

Modest changes have been made to the Fort Dearborn and massacre sites since the 1930s, but none of them changed the meaning of either site. Pullman's statue was moved away from the massacre site and indoors to the Chicago Historical Society in 1931. Wealthy residents had moved away from the mansion district where the statue had been sited. During the district's transformation to largely commercial use, the statue had been vandalized at 18th Street and Prairie Avenue (Figure 7-16). For its protection, it was moved away and replaced with a plaque on the side of one of the new businesses. Since the 1930s the district has gone through a second transformation and is now the site of the Prairie Avenue Historical District, which encompasses a few of the mansions left from the nineteenth century and includes a few other historic buildings moved from other parts of the city. It is not inconceivable that the Pullman statue will someday be returned to its original site as the area stabilizes.

The site of Fort Dearborn is better marked now than ever. A number of buildings have occupied the site since the second fort was destroyed in 1857. Although the site has not been designated continuously since the first historical plaque was posted in 1880, it seems to have been ignored for only a short period between 1919, when the first plaque was lost, and 1928, when a memorial statuary group was added to the new Michigan Avenue Bridge. At the time when the star for Fort Dearborn was added to the municipal flag, plans were put forward to mark the site differently, including renaming the Michigan Avenue Bridge and some of the surrounding streets. Not all the recommendations were enacted, but the outlines of the fort are now indicated in the pavement, and the site became an official historical landmark in the early 1970s. When Chicago inventoried all its official historical sites in the 1980s, the Fort Dearborn site, along with the site of the origin of the Great Fire and the surviving water tower, were among the seventy-seven then recognized. They had become firmly established in the city's pantheon of the great places and remain so today.

THE MORMON FLIGHT INTO THE WILDERNESS

At the time of Joseph Smith's first revelations, few people outside his circle could have imagined how successful his church would become.[21] Beginning with a handful of followers, Smith forged a religion that has

Figure 7-16. The site of the Fort Dearborn Massacre, about a mile and a half south of the original fort at 18th Street and Prairie Avenue. Only a small plaque marks the site today, but this may change with the emergence of the neighboring Prairie Avenue Historical District.

emerged in the twentieth century as one of the fastest growing in America, and its missionaries are meeting with equal success in other parts of the world. The Mormon church is the most successful of the dozens of religious separatist and utopian communities founded in or transplanted to the United States during the nineteenth century. Other such communities have survived and prospered, but none quite so spectacularly as the Mormons. With a reported membership of about 7.7 million in 1990, the Mormon church is a dominant force not only in Utah and surrounding states but increasingly in communities throughout the entire nation. Major temples have been established outside Utah and the western states, as well as overseas. Yet the success of the modern church was won at the price of early hardships. The heartland of the Mormon church lies in Utah because Smith's followers had to flee from persecution in the East. They chose Utah as a destination in the 1840s because at that time the land lay outside the territory of the United States, and they felt they would be able to protect themselves from non-Mormons—"Gentiles," the Mormons called them. The Great Basin of Utah did offer substantial protection, but it could not completely isolate them from the tide of frontier settlement. When their land was annexed by the United States and as Gentiles moved westward across their territory, tension often returned. Nonetheless, by the time Brigham Young led his followers into the Great Basin, they had triumphed over the worst of the persecutions. The story of how the sites of this persecution came to be marked in the twentieth century is an interesting study in how a religious group comes to commemorate and mark its heritage retrospectively in the landscape.

From the time of Smith's first visions in the late 1820s until the time of his followers' arrival in Utah, the Mormons were in almost constant conflict with their neighbors. Smith was living in Palmyra in upstate New York at the time of his first visions, a resident of what has come to be known as the "Burned Over District." An area of great religious fervor and ferment in the early nineteenth century, the Burned Over District was home to untold numbers of revivalists, millennialists, preachers, and prophets. Smith's visions led him to Hill Cumorah, outside Palmyra, where, he claimed, he found the last remaining testament of a great vanished civilization—golden tablets inscribed by the ancient prophet Mormon with the history of the Nephites. Unable to read the ancient script, Smith was assisted by the angel Moroni in translating this Book of Mormon into English. It became one of the principal scriptures of Smith's new religion, although the tablets were removed from earth by Moroni when their translation was complete. The book told an amazing story of how a small group of Israelites came to the New World in about 600 B.C. and founded a new civilization. The civilization grew and prospered but was eventually consumed by conflict and war until nothing remained but the tablets. Smith had been chosen to restore this civilization's church and, in effect, its continuity with Old Testament scripture. Later Smith would assert for his church continuity with New Testament scripture and the ministry of Jesus Christ. He saw his personal mission in life as the reestablishment of the precepts of the Christian church lost in the centuries since Christ's ministry. Smith claimed that his followers were "saints" of a new age rededicated to the lessons of Old and New Testament theology. Founded in 1830 in Fayette, New York, Smith's sect eventually adopted the name "Church of Jesus Christ of Latter-day Saints."

Smith began quickly to attract converts. Many other prophets and seers were active in the Burned Over District in the 1820s and 1830s, and initially there was little to distinguish Smith's followers from these other millenarian and revivalist groups apart from Smith's claim to possess this new testament, the Book of Mormon. The appeal grew as Smith was able to articulate additional and continuing visions that resonated with the spirit of the times. His Latter-day Saints claimed that his teachings enjoyed continuity with both Old and New Testament traditions, that Christ had indeed revisited the earth and fulfilled the prophesies of the millenarian groups, that his followers were a chosen people divinely anointed to restore the true church, and that his followers had a special mission to separate themselves from Gentile society and prepare for Christ's final return. From these earliest days of the church right up to the present, Mormons proved to be effective missionaries and proselytizers and sought out converts far and wide. By the early 1840s, for instance, Mormon missionaries in Britain were particularly successful in recruiting hundreds of followers who were attracted not only to Smith and his theology but also to the prospect of moving to the United States to begin new lives.

Smith believed in the necessity of the "gathering" of his Latter-day Saints, of his followers' banding together and withdrawing from secular society. It was this gathering that, perhaps more than any other single factor, began to attract attention from and friction with outsiders. Compared to those of other religious splinter groups in upstate New York at the time, Smith's beliefs were not so wildly extreme as to be rejected out of hand. As the Mormons gathered, however, their numbers began to cause problems. By concentrating in small towns, they became threatening for religious, economic, and political reasons. Their numbers were sufficient to overrun most small communities, and because the Mormons saw themselves as special, as selected for a special mission, they increasingly rejected—and were rejected by—their neighbors. Rather than stay in upstate New York, where tensions were already mounting, Smith decided to move his small group. From Fayette, Smith and his followers began their slow journey westward, propelled both by their desire to separate themselves from society and by the hostility of this society. Smith died at the hands of a mob in Carthage, Illinois, before his followers made the decision to move to Utah.

The group's first stop was Kirtland, Ohio, in 1831, where Smith managed to convert an entire congregation of a different faith. He and his followers built on this success and maintained a presence in Kirtland until 1838, long enough to build their first temple. Almost from the time of his arrival at Kirtland, Smith was considering a move still farther west. He believed that the original site of the Garden of Eden lay in western Missouri and that this "Land of Zion" would make an ideal site for the gathering. He dispatched followers to scout and settle this new territory in Jackson County on the far western border of Missouri, in the vicinity of present-day Kansas City and Independence. Following the Mormons' arrival, tensions arose for the same reasons as before. Now not only were Mormons the focus of attacks in Ohio (Smith was tarred and feathered there in March of 1832), but they came under mob attack in Missouri as well. During the summer of 1833 mobs destroyed the offices of a Mormon newspaper in Independence. By November the Mormons had to flee north across the Missouri River into Clay County. By the summer of 1836 the Latter-day Saints were asked to leave Clay County, so they moved north and east into Caldwell County. Smith and many other followers joined the other Mormons here in 1838 after Kirtland began to disintegrate. Guerrilla warfare broke out between Mormons and non-Mormons almost as soon as Smith arrived. Seventeen Mormons were killed in October 1838, and in the following month, Smith and many other leaders were arrested and the principal Mormon settlement at Far West was looted. That winter and spring the remaining Mormons were forced out of Missouri altogether, into Iowa and Illinois.

In April 1839 Smith and his leaders were allowed to escape from jail and leave Missouri. Smith quickly found another site for the gathering in a small Illinois town on the Mississippi River he renamed Nauvoo. Chartered in late 1840, Nauvoo quickly became the focus for the Mormon gathering. In addition to attracting the Mormons spread around Ohio, Illinois, and Iowa, Nauvoo welcomed new members recruited by missionaries in Britain. Total church membership reached about 30,000 at this time, helping Nauvoo to become the largest city in Illinois, as well as the most important settlement the Mormons founded until they reached Salt Lake City years later. Here the church began to solidify its organization and theology. Basing his work on a continuing series of visions and revelations, Smith began to develop additional rites and rituals, design a major temple, and further articulate the church's hierarchy of leadership. Between 1841 and 1844 Nauvoo was one of the most prosperous settlements in the West and consisted of well-built wood-frame and brick homes and businesses.[22]

The success of Nauvoo became the reason for its fall. Nauvoo's size meant that Smith held tremendous political influence in the state. Since he insisted that the Mormons vote together as a bloc, he was able to hold state politicians hostage to his demands—and his demands grew after each concession. Smith was the prophet and leader of his church, but now he also served as mayor of Nauvoo. Non-Mormons felt not only unwelcome but threatened by his usurpation of power. The situation worsened as Smith assumed additional police and military power.

His forced exodus had made Smith adamant that his group be able to defend itself against outside society. When he won a charter for Nauvoo, he was granted special concessions by the governor: he became the leader of his own militia, the Nauvoo Legion, reporting solely to the governor. Smith became a threatening figure in western Illinois, where non-Mormons already resented his political influence. He was now the sole religious, political, civic, and military leader in an area where his followers outnumbered all other groups. The separation of powers and the division of church and state no longer held true in Nauvoo. Conflict between the Mormons and non-Mormons was inevitable, and crop burnings, harassment, and sniping increased.

In June 1844 Smith finally stepped past the point of good judgment. Affronted by anti-Mormon articles published by a small newspaper in Nauvoo, Smith had the staff arrested and the press destroyed. State officials intervened and Smith was arrested. He and three other Mormon leaders were taken to Carthage, the county seat, for arraignment. Before Smith was brought to trial, a mob overran the jail and killed him and his brother on 27 June.

Smith's death was a crisis for his followers, but unlike other small religious groups that have disbanded on losing their leader, the Mormons persevered. The church did split after Smith's murder over the questions of succession and leadership, however. Smith was only thirty-eight when he died and had not clearly specified how leadership was to devolve on his death, whether through his family or to fellow leaders. One group maintained that leadership should pass to Smith's son and through his family. This contingent eventually became the Reorganized Church of Jesus Christ of Latter Day Saints. By far the largest share of Mormons accepted the notion that leadership should pass through the existing church hierarchy to Brigham Young. Under Young's leadership this contingent came to accept the idea that they would have to abandon Nauvoo and move further west. To free themselves from Gentile society they would move completely out of United States territory into the wilderness of the Rocky Mountains. Neither group left Nauvoo immediately. Before his group left, Young insisted that the Mormons complete the Nauvoo temple. Smith had claimed that certain blessings would be bestowed on his followers only if they completed their temple at Nauvoo. With determination the community completed the massive temple, a building that dwarfed all others on the western frontier. The community had no sooner consecrated the new temple in 1845 than its members began to pack for their journey west. The first wagon train left Nauvoo for Utah during February 1846. The first group reached the Great Basin in July 1847. Significantly Joseph Smith's wife and family remained behind. The Reorganized Church of Jesus Christ of Latter Day Saints eventually established its headquarters in Independence, Missouri, closer to where Smith envisioned the site of his Zion.

As the Mormons left Nauvoo, most of the land was sold to another group of utopian colonists, the Icarians. The Icarians, a much smaller group, stayed on in Nauvoo for many years before disbanding. Before the end of the nineteenth century, Nauvoo had shrunk to a tiny rural village. Some of the original Mormon and Icarian buildings remained, but most were abandoned. The massive temple had been used by the Icarians for a short time, but it burned in 1848, and the ruins were razed in 1850. By the turn of the century very little evidence of the Mormon exodus remained anywhere along the route from New York to Illinois, Missouri, and beyond. Both branches of the church were preoccupied with far weightier issues than the memory of their flight from persecution.

For Brigham Young and his followers, the flight to the wilderness of Utah did not end their problems with Gentile society or the federal government. Young had the idea of creating the independent enclave of Deseret, but the territory the Mormons claimed unfortunately lay in the path of American territorial expansion. Furthermore Mormon land lay astride some of the major trails into and across the West. The

Mormons were simply not strong enough to resist these incursions. All through the late nineteenth century, the church tried to sustain its domination of the intermountain West in the face of federal force. For a period Utah was even occupied by federal troops. Over decades, as Utah became a territory and then a state, the Mormon leaders made concessions to the federal government; for instance, in 1890 they abandoned their group's practice of polygamy. These compromises left the Mormons with perhaps less power than they originally intended to claim but still with substantial control of the economic, social, political, and cultural life of a large territory centered on Salt Lake City.

The church was also tremendously successful, despite the political concessions it was forced to make. More important for a separatist group such as theirs, the Mormons survived the passing of the first generation of converts and leaders. By the time of Brigham Young's death in 1877, the leadership was firmly in control and the rules of succession clearly defined. As the evidence of success grew, so too did the impulse to celebrate the accomplishments of the church and its members. As is to be expected, this impulse extended backward in time to the Mormon exodus from the East. The Mormons were quick to grasp that there is no better way to highlight achievement than to look back on the hardships endured to reach success. Even as they moved westward, they recognized the figurative significance of having been forced by Gentile society into the *wilderness* of the continent. What better way to reinforce this biblical allusion than to mark the route of the exodus? Jumping ahead to the present day, virtually every site from Hill Cumorah to Nauvoo to the Great Basin has been reclaimed by one or both of the major Mormon churches. The two actually compete for land at some of these sites. Today's visitor to Nauvoo, for instance, will be welcomed by not one but two major visitors' centers—one run by the Reorganized Church out of Independence and the second by the larger Salt Lake City faction. As in Texas and Chicago, however, this reclamation of sites happened over an extended period and long after the first settlers had passed.

The fact remains that marking the sites of their exodus made sense only after the Mormons had achieved a measure of success. Just as in Texas and Chicago, time had to pass before the Mormons could establish themselves as a stable and viable community with the affluence and interest to mark historical traditions in the landscape. This is not to say that the Mormons were not overly preoccupied with history—

they were, from the very start of the movement. Smith and his followers were infused with a sense of historical destiny by the nature of their scriptures. In seeing their movement as restoring Old and New Testament traditions, they could not help but become preoccupied from an early stage with documenting their own history. Theirs was a mission that almost demanded to be chronicled in scriptural detail, and it was. Even before he formed his church, Joseph Smith had had a revelation that "there shall be a record kept," and by 1831 he already had a church historian "to write and keep a regular history."[23] Smith even began to work on a monumental history of his life in 1839.

This early history was little more than a chronicle of events and people, even after the move to Utah. Mormon historiography remained rooted in this tradition, whose purpose was to validate the religion, win converts, and defend the church from outsiders. As historian James Allen has noted:

> The earlier generation of Mormon historians had been the first creators of the Mormon past; as such it was their task to lay out the major outlines, to develop the major images of the past appropriate for church manuals, and to build and support the faith of church members, to tie them to their foundations. Much of what they wrote was necessarily defensive in nature, for much, if not most, of what had been written about church history by non-Mormons consisted of bitter and often brutal attacks upon the church and its founders. Not unlike their scholarly successors, these early church historians selected their historical evidence carefully, with the honest intent of meeting the needs of the church as they perceived them in their time.[24]

From these foundations it was easy to expand Mormon history to epic proportions. The Mormon experience resonated with the themes of biblical sacrifice and frontier heroism—the flight from persecution, escape to the wilderness, and creation of a new life on the frontier. By the 1870s and afterward, these themes were woven into Mormon history and biography. Some aspects of the Mormon past took on a heroic, larger-than-life quality, but this was not the only way in which its rough edges were smoothed.[25] By repositioning the Mormon past squarely within the currents of American history, historians could gradually reinterpret it to fit archetypally "American" themes. By drawing parallels with other groups that came to America to flee religious persecution, the Mormons could frame their past in quintessentially American terms as the pursuit and defense of religious freedom. Their success in Utah allowed them to draw on another archetypal theme of American history, that of hearty, frontier pioneers carving a future out of the wilderness. This thematic reinterpretation was no simple task, for it involved turning some early Mormon history on end. The unique qualities of Mormonism—the origins of its scriptures and the importance of the gathering—had to be played down. The very reason for the flight to Utah—to escape the U.S. government and create an independent religious state—had also to be glossed over. Finally, it was useful to shade over the fact that Joseph Smith and his Latter-day Saints had in many ways induced their own persecution, not just on religious grounds, but also for some important political, economic, and military reasons. The key to this transformation, as it extended over many decades, was to normalize Mormon history, to take the tale of an unusual religion that rejected and was rejected by nineteenth century society and make it into an all-American story. One result was that the grand historical epics celebrating and defending Mormon difference appeared relatively early—in the first fifty or hundred years. Since the mid-twentieth century the normalization of Mormon history has resulted in a significant change of focus, with work now concentrating on the social and economic history of the Mormon community and such topics as immigration from Britain, the church's missionary activities, agriculture and industry, political history, and the institutions of church welfare and charity. These are all topics that fit squarely within contemporary currents of American western and regional history, the Mormons becoming one of many groups that helped to win the West.[26]

Before this somewhat idealized past could be inscribed on landscape, much time had to pass to smooth the rough edges of Mormon history. Time also had to pass before the community was sufficiently large and well established to undertake the project of marking its past. The church was quite conscious of its anniversaries—the jubilee of 1880 was widely celebrated among the Utah community—but no attempt was made to commemorate the sites of early Mormonism in the East. The community itself was still quite small, with about 160,000 members, and the church was still preoccupied with consolidating its position in the Great Basin and resolving its differences with the federal government. The church had few resources to spare for the sort of monument building sometimes inspired by major anniversaries. The community was struggling instead to complete a chain of major temples it had planned for Logan, Salt Lake City, Manti, and St. George, and only the St. George temple was completed by 1880. These building projects came to fruition in the 1880s and 1890s, as did attempts to resolve tensions with the federal government. The last major stumbling block to statehood—polygamy—was renounced in 1890, and Utah was admitted to the Union in 1896.

By the time of the 1930 centennial, the Mormon church and community were in a far better position to commemorate their past, but this still did not extend to the early Mormon sites. Some individual Mormons returned to these sites to purchase property, and some land at Nauvoo had been retained by Joseph Smith's heirs, but no major plans existed for commemorating the early Mormon settlements. This situation began to change slowly through the 1950s, 1960s, and 1970s. Both the Church of Jesus Christ of Latter-day Saints in Salt Lake City and the Reorganized Church of Jesus Christ of Latter Day Saints in Independence began to acquire properties for restoration. The Salt Lake City church opened a large visitors' center at Nauvoo in 1971, and the Independence church has a slightly smaller center nearby. The process of restoration has continued unabated ever since. Homes and shops that were abandoned in the nineteenth century have been restored and, in some cases, reconstructed to their 1840s form (Figure 7-17). The past two decades in particular have seen Nauvoo converted into a sort of frontier Williamsburg. There is even mention of someday rebuilding the Nauvoo temple.

The old Carthage jail where Joseph Smith and his brother Hyrum were killed has also been purchased and restored (Figure 7-18). Other sites have been acquired and commemorated in recent times, including the Kirtland temple in Ohio and Hill Cumorah in New York. In many respects the commemoration of these sites has followed the pattern of Texas and Chicago, only expressed over a longer period of time. What took place in Texas and Chicago after fifty or a hundred years took an extra fifty years for the Mormons. After all, they faced additional hurdles, being a relatively small society far removed from the sites of their early settlements and preoccupied with far more pressing economic and political problems during their first hundred years. During this period Mormon society spent much of its time on the defensive against both real and imagined threats to its domination

Figure 7-17. Mansion House in Nauvoo, Illinois, viewed from the Joseph Smith homestead on the banks of the Mississippi River. Houses and businesses from the 1830s and 1840s have been restored in the twentieth century by the Church of Jesus Christ of Latter-day Saints (based in Salt Lake City) and by the Reorganized Church of Jesus Christ of Latter Day Saints (based in Independence, Missouri). Both churches maintain visitors' centers in Nauvoo.

of the Great Basin. One should not overlook that Joseph Smith's family buried him secretly after the 1844 assassination and kept the location of the grave site to themselves until 1928 (Figure 7-19). This fear of desecration speaks to the entire Mormon community's defensiveness toward outsiders, which continued well into the twentieth century.

Even if it takes 150 years, the process of marking a historical tradition in the landscape remains the same. Perhaps this point is reinforced by the creation in 1978 of the Mormon Pioneer Historic Trail by the National Park Service. In 1968 the National Park Service was authorized to establish two national scenic trails in the Appalachian and Pacific coast mountains. When the National Trails Systems Act was amended in 1978 to include trails of historical interest, the Mormon route from Nauvoo to Salt Lake City was the first one marked. This meant that by the time of the Mormon sesquicentennial, the path of the exodus had been commemorated, as well as all the individual sites associated with the church's early history.[27] The entire course of Mormon history has been embossed on landscape.

Figure 7-18. The jail in Carthage, Illinois, where Joseph Smith and his brother Hyrum were assassinated in 1844. The property has been acquired and restored by the Church of Jesus Christ of Latter-day Saints and is open to the public.

Smoothing the rough edges of Mormon history meant not only Americanizing its central themes but also playing down events that could blur the neat outlines of this story of a quest for religious freedom on the frontier. The event that always held the potential to subvert the normalization of Mormon history was the Mountain Meadows Massacre of 1857. In the period during which tensions between the Mormon community of the Great Basin and the federal government reached a peak, Mormon settlers in southeastern Utah assisted by Native Americans massacred an entire wagon train of immigrants on its way to California. The approximately 120 settlers who lost their lives in this massacre outnumbered all the Mormons who died at the hands of Gentiles along the entire path of the exodus from New York. The massacre of the Fancher party has long been the most shameful event in Mormon history. The cover-up was so successful that no one was prosecuted for the crimes until twenty years later, and then only a single Mormon leader was convicted and executed. The church maintained its silence well into the twentieth century, and the first true study of the massacre did not appear until 1950. Even then its author, Juanita Brooks, felt compelled to preface the study with a sort of apologia for her investigation of this darker side of Mormon history.[28] The Mormon reticence concerning the documentary and historical record was just as plainly evident at the site of the massacre itself.

Fate could not have orchestrated a worse moment for the encounter between the Fancher party and the Mormons of the Great Basin. The immigrants arrived during a period of rising antagonism between the Mormons and the federal government. Indeed the Mormons were already anticipating war and making preparations. The Fancher party, like many of their predecessors, were also unpleasant guests. Non-Mormon wagon trains were arriving in the Great Basin in increasing numbers, often traveling south from Salt Lake City to St. George through the heart of the Mormon homeland on their way to California. Friction between immigrants and Mormons was always a problem, particularly over water, grazing, and food for the trains. The Fancher party, larger than most and with members who were particularly disrespectful of the Mormons, inspired even greater resentment. The church leadership soon forbade the Mormons even to trade with the Fancher party for necessities. After making its way south during the summer, the party was obliged to camp and recuper-

Figure 7-19. Joseph Smith's tomb to the side of his original homestead in Nauvoo, Illinois, overlooking the Mississippi River. Smith was reburied here in 1928. Until then his grave had been hidden to safeguard it from potential defacement.

ate for a time in a high mountain meadow before heading into the desert country of Nevada and California.

While the Fancher party was camped, Mormon leaders conspired with loyal Native Americans to have them stage a raid on the bivouac. After a temporarily successful defense, the immigrants found themselves pinned down on open ground for several days waiting for the siege to be lifted—they thought—by the Mormons or perhaps other white settlers in the area. Acting with duplicity, the Mormon leaders visited the besieged party and offered to lead them away from their attackers if the immigrants would surrender their weapons. This accomplished, the immigrants were slaughtered—by both Mormons and Indians—as they were led away from their encampment. Only a few children survived the massacre to be adopted, for a time, by Mormon families. The cover-up began immediately, since it was clear that news of the massacre would spur intervention by the federal government and a military occupation of the Mormon territory. On this point the cover-up had little effect, because hostilities were by then so far advanced that military occupation was almost inevitable, and federal troops moved into the territory in the winter and spring of 1857–1858. The cover-up did succeed in obscuring the role played in the massacre by high Mormon leaders, particularly Brigham Young, and delaying for twenty years the punishment of lower-level Mormon leader John D. Lee, who was in immediate command of the raid. To this day the most sensitive issues surrounding the massacre remain the extent of Young's complicity in the massacre and whether Lee was scapegoated by the Mormon leadership to protect Young and the church.

Given the shameful and harmful political, social, and religious connotations of the massacre, it is no surprise to learn that the cover-up extended also to landscape. Just as was done with the stigmata considered in the previous chapter, the Mormons sought to obliterate all evidence of the massacre. Although the bodies of the immigrants were left for a period after the massacre to give the appearance of an Indian massacre, most of their bodies were eventually buried in a mass grave—in the defensive pit the immigrants had themselves dug to protect themselves after the first attack and during the siege. When John Lee was finally condemned to die for his part in the massacre, he was returned to Mountain Meadows to be shot. After Lee's execution the site faded into obscurity for the remainder of the nineteenth century.

The site remained unmarked until 1932, when, with the approval of Mormon officials, the Pioneer Trails and Landmarks Association erected a low stone wall around the mass grave and a small commemorative tablet (Figure 7-20). Road signs were positioned nearby to help visitors find the out-of-the-way memorial. In the 1960s the Mormon church purchased the site and removed the road markers, so that although it was possible to visit the site, it was difficult to find. The road signs were returned in the 1980s, and in 1990 a major new memorial was erected overlooking the valley in which the massacre took place. This monument was funded largely by the families of the immigrants slain in 1857 and pays tribute to their sacrifice (Figure 7-21). In this case almost eighty years had to pass before the site was recovered from its obliteration, and another fifty years before a true memorial was erected. In this case a site once obliterated was, after almost 130 years, sanctified. This change mirrors almost exactly the transformation of

Figure 7-20. The mass grave of the victims of the 1857 Mountain Meadows Massacre. The victims were buried in a defensive trench they themselves had dug to protect their wagon train after the first attack. The wall and plaque were added in 1932 by the Pioneer Trails and Landmarks Association. The site is in southwestern Utah, about midway between St. George and Enterprise.

Mormon history from the story of a militant religious separatist group into a tale of a stalwart frontier society that helped to win the West.

TRADITIONS MADE TANGIBLE

Several points emerge from the comparison of these sites in Texas, Chicago, and along the path of the Mormons to Utah. First, the inscription of tradition in landscape requires a lengthy period of time lasting in most cases between 50 and 150 years. When major commemorative activity begins, it often coincides with important anniversaries such as jubilees and centennials. Few states, cities, or religious movements dwell on their origins during their first fifty years. Only with

Figure 7-21. The memorial to the victims of the Mountain Meadows Massacre raised in 1990 by the state of Utah and descendants of families on both sides of the massacre. The memorial is positioned on a slope above the meadow with a view across the entire valley. The names of the victims of the massacre are inscribed on the memorial.

success does the appeal of marking the past grow, particularly around centennials. The delay allows time for the past to be filtered. Tragedies can be transformed into coherent and cohesive heroic epics. Equivocal and ambiguous events can be positioned in a positive light.

Second, most sites that are eventually commemorated usually go through a lengthy process of canonization. Most are rectified or obliterated in the immediate aftermath and then designated and eventually sanctified. Designation is a critical step; a site is granted a sort of *probationary* status. Sanctification then proceeds in the absence of objections. No one social group or stratum can be credited for all the work. Sometimes sanctification is instigated by individuals, sometimes by groups, and these vary widely in status. Grass-roots efforts by local citizens are just as successful as those instigated by elite or wealthy members of a community. The key to success really revolves around rallying support within a larger community. Without a relatively broad base of support, sanctification will not succeed.

Third, the individuals most consistently involved in commemoration are survivors or veterans of the event. At San Jacinto veterans of the battle were the first to return to claim the graveyard, to mark the tombs of their fallen comrades, and to ask that they themselves be buried nearby. The first markers to the Great Chicago Fire were raised by people who remembered its devastation. If any commemoration takes place within the first fifty years of an event, it is most often led by survivors or veterans. This type of commemorative fervor reaches a peak about fifty years after an event—just as the last of the immediate witnesses are reaching the ends of their lives and have the resources and interest needed to create a lasting memorial to their experiences. Sometimes survivors and veterans need to die before reinterpretation takes place, especially after equivocal events. Particularly in the case of the Mormon past, and to a lesser extent with respect to Texas's, the reshaping of the complex strands of historical fact into heroic epics would have been exceedingly difficult immediately following the events themselves. The Mormon flight from religious persecution was not a one-sided story, but it could be portrayed as such once the antagonists were dead. The complex clash of cultures manifested in the Texas Revolution was also easier to simplify once the last survivors were gone.

Finally, these local and regional traditions were built on themes that were evolving almost simultaneously around the interpretation of the American national past. Parallels were drawn between the American Revolution and the Texas Revolution, between the American struggle against adversity and Chicago's rise from the ashes of Fort Dearborn and the Great Fire, and between American frontier heroism and the Mormon quest for refuge. By the time of the centennial of 1876, a sort of national mythology had already evolved around key events and virtues such as the struggle against tyranny, the American spirit, and the frontier ethic. These themes could be folded into local and regional history and used to shape relatively minor events into major features of a grander pageant of history. Yet the influence runs both ways. To the extent that the American past helped to validate local and regional traditions, these local traditions sometimes helped to reinforce and occasionally spurred national commemoration. The next chapter takes up how the American national past has been inscribed on landscape.

Chapter 8

Stigmata of National Identity

Traditions have been inscribed on the national landscape just as they have on Texas, Chicago, and the Mormon Trail. Shrines and monuments now mark the entire course of nation building from first settlement to the present. Most of these memorials took many years to develop, and their transformation into emblems of national identity is my concern in this chapter.[1] I concentrate on just a few sites that highlight the key elements of the process. Hundreds of other sites have been enshrined with patriotic fervor, but these are often only variations on common themes of sacrifice, valor, and perseverance. By selecting three, I can spare space to reflect on another, more interesting dynamic—the arrangement of shrines into grander, cosmographical representations of America's origins and past.

COSMOGRAPHY, CIVIL RELIGION, AND THE INSCRIPTION OF TRADITION

Over two decades ago Paul Wheatley drew attention to the role of cosmographical principles in the design of ancient cities.[2] These cities, particularly those of classical China, were designed as celestial archetypes—models of the cosmos—intended to balance and coordinate the terrestrial and celestial forces that were thought to guide human conduct. The cities and landscapes so designed were inscribed to represent a civilization's entire worldview in tangible, symbolic form.

These were, of course, civilizations in which virtually all members shared a common worldview. In jumping to modern secular societies, comparable cosmological principles are far more difficult to discern. Some writers, such as Donald Horne, have argued that such symbolism is manifest implicitly in the monuments, memorials, and museums of Europe's capital cities, but Horne's is a highly informal and impressionistic account.[3] Others have examined the close relationships between nationalistic ideology and public architecture.[4]

The crux of the problem is that modern secular societies lack the explicit, homogeneous belief systems that act as templates for cosmographical design. The populations of most early civilizations were bound by a common ancestry, way of life, and religion that together defined human beings' place in the cosmos. As sociologist Emile Durkheim argued almost a century ago, these were societies guided by canons of what he termed "mechanical solidarity." Social cohesion was based on common ideas and widely held beliefs shared among virtually all members of a given society.[5] For Durkheim, modern societies achieve cohesion through principles of "organic solidarity," that is, solidarity based on institutionalized, but consensual economic, political, and legal relationships—contracts, voluntary affiliations, rights, obligations, and the like—that serve to accommodate individual differences. Durkheim did not believe that the rise of modern societies subverted the social foundations of religion or destroyed cosmological conceptions of humanity's place in the universe. His point—that of a structuralist—was that these beliefs are expressed in different ways as societies move from mechanical to organic solidarity. Belief systems did not disappear but only took on different representations in modern society. I maintain in addition that some modern societies harbor—indeed, cherish—certain vestigial artifacts of earlier cosmological representations. In the Western world these atavistic tendencies derive in part from continued reliance on traditions of architecture and planning devolving from the classical principles of the Hellenistic and Roman worlds and the Gothic principles of the medieval period.[6]

Apart from these vestigial symbols, cosmo-national principles have helped to shape the cities and landscapes of modern societies such as the United States. The trick is knowing what to look for. Rather than search for ceremonial centers that serve as celestial archetypes in modern societies, one looks instead for sites that represent secular archetypes. Such sites do not outline a cosmo-magical myth of origins but rather celebrate and uphold the values and institutions of a secular cosmos and profane worldview. These shrines celebrate the covenant of nationalism in the landscape.

Aid in assessing these nationalistic representations can be found in the concept of "civil religion": all the socioreligious values invested in the maintenance of a secular state. This concept can be traced back to Rousseau, but it has proved to be useful more recently in discussions of the American historical experience. As employed by scholars such as Robert Bellah and Catherine Albanese, the concept of civil religion suggests that, although a society may renounce religion as a scaffolding for national identity, comparable sentiments emerge in support of the social contract and celebrate the virtues of patriotism and civil obedience.[7] As Albanese writes of the Revolutionary War: "Reading the language and watching the extraordinarily heightened ritual behavior of the American Revolution suggest that the inner drum to which the patriots marched was a general mythic consciousness. This fundamental orientation led them to appropriate their past as a sacred tale of origins and amalgamate it to their present, thereby creating a new sacral myth of origins out of the very events of the Revolution."[8] Writers of the Revolutionary War era were not unaware of the issues involved, as is evident in the following extract Albanese draws from a work by Joseph Galloway published in 1780: "The fundamental and general laws of every society are the lessons of instruction by which the subject is daily taught his duty and obedience to the State. It is the uniformity of these lessons, flowing from the same system of consistent polity, which forms the same habits, manners, and political opinions throughout the society, fixes the national attachment, and leads the people to look up to one system of government for their safety and happiness, and to act in concert on all occasions to maintain and defend it."[9] In her exposition Albanese adds that, in discussing civil religion, she is "referring to various perceptions of the world, to the conceptual and emotional concomitants of these perceptions, to their expression in language and behavior, and finally their reinternalization as objective realities after they have been projected onto the world as word and action."[10]

This description of "historical consciousness" is far removed from a chronology of dates and events and closer to the "invention of tradition" and "making of history" that I discuss in the previous chapter.[11] The idea is that historical consciousness is less a matter of objective reality than it is a retrospective invention conditioned by the ideological imperatives of contemporary society.[12] This idea has been valuable to scholars such as Michael Kammen, Patricia Limerick, and Richard Slotkin, who have explored the strength, prevalence, and malleability of these perceptions and myths.[13] Civil religion as an ideological system can be expected to guide forcefully the invention of these interpretive traditions. A few geographers have considered this issue, but two questions bear further investigation.[14] First, how are the canons of civil religion cosmographically projected onto landscape? Second, how does the invention of tradition influence the shaping of landscape through time?

Rather than survey all the manifestations of America's civil religion in landscape, I will revisit and amplify three issues that I touch on briefly in previous chapters. They are the delay inherent in the creation and projection of sacral myth on landscape, the federal government's role in creating and maintaining national shrines, and the extensive debates sometimes involved in matching the meaning of shrines to the creed of civil religion. I examine these points in the context of three events: the Boston Massacre, John Brown's raid on Harpers Ferry, and Pearl Harbor. Each of these events is seen to mark the opening of a period of war that for Americans began on their own soil. The Boston Massacre of 1770 was not the first direct confrontation between American and British troops, but it was the first act of violence of the Revolutionary War era. John Brown's raid at Harpers Ferry in 1859 anticipated the violence that would erupt two years later at Fort Sumter to begin the Civil War. Finally, Japan's surprise attack on Pearl Harbor in 1941 precipitated America's entry into World War II. These are stigmata of American identity that have come to be interpreted as signal sacrifices to the cause of freedom and liberty.

The Boston Massacre and the
Slow Expression of Sacral Myth

Catherine Albanese was concerned with the origins of civil religion in the Revolutionary War period, and indeed a tie can be found between the patriots' "sacral myth of origins" and that myth's projection onto sites touched by the War of Independence. One of the most important aspects of this process of projection was the long delay between events and their enshrinements. This process can be seen at work in the story of the Boston Massacre of 5 March 1770, the first act of violence of the Revolutionary War period. Three years passed before the Boston Tea Party of 16 December 1773, and another two before the first battle-field encounters between British troops and the American militia in April 1775 and the Battle of Bunker Hill and siege of Boston in June of that year.

The massacre took place at the Boston Custom House when a mob turned violent. A crowd hurling angry words at British sentries switched to stones, ice, and coal. As the taunting reached its peak, the troops fired into the crowd, killing five and wounding seven. The massacre, also known as the "Battle of King Street," became a rallying point for the Revolution and during the war was commemorated annually with orations and memorial services.[15]

The public 5 March ceremonies ended in 1783, the year of the signing of the Paris peace accord that brought the war to a close formally on 3 September. The annual ceremony was moved to 4 July to commemorate the signing of the Declaration of Independence in 1776. It is of symbolic significance that 4 July was selected as the day to celebrate the birth of the United States, for in 1783 Americans had three days from which to choose: 5 March, 4 July, and 3 September. In the course of events, 4 July proved to be a more apt date for the expression of patriotic sentiments. The events of 5 March carried the negative connotation of being an incitement to violence, and whereas 3 September symbolized a bilateral action requiring British consent, 4 July signified a unilateral decision by Americans.

This change of dates was reflected at the massacre site itself. Discussion of marking it immediately after the events of 1770 came to nothing, and the site drifted into obscurity. Energy was invested instead in memorializing battlefield sites such as Bunker Hill, and even there nothing happened for many decades. By the time of America's centennial in 1876—measured, tellingly, from 4 July 1776 rather than 5 March 1770—private initiatives had succeeded in marking many, but not all, of the sites associated with Revolutionary War battles. Nevertheless the centennial saw the beginning of a gradual change of attitude toward the Boston Massacre. Broadly speaking, the centennial helped to convince Americans that their experiment in democracy had succeeded. With a century of "history" to celebrate, Americans began to mark the sites of events judged to be important to this record of success, although not all at once. Several decades were

Figure 8-1. The site of the Boston Massacre marker in State Street. The riot of 5 March 1770 occurred here in front of the Custom House. The massacre was celebrated during the revolutionary period with the same zeal now reserved for the Fourth of July. The site was not marked formally until 1886, when the stonework visible in the pavement at the center of the photograph was added.

required for the development of this heightened awareness of histori-cal consciousness. It seems to have reached a particular peak toward the end of the nineteenth century.

The Boston Massacre site was first marked a decade after the cen-tennial when, in 1886, the first president of the Bostonian Society pre-sented a design to the Boston street commissioners that was approved and built within the year. The Bostonian Society, founded in 1881, was one of a growing number of private organizations dedicated to lo-cal history. The wheel-shaped granite marker, about ten feet in diam-eter, was laid flush with the pavement of State Street (formerly King Street). The hub of the wheel was claimed to rest on the exact spot where Crispus Attucks shed the first blood of the massacre. Spokes ex-tended from the hub, one for each of the original thirteen colonies (Figures 8-1 and 8-2). Within a year Boston was contemplating a more substantial monument, a statue eventually raised in 1888 on the com-mon depicting "Free America" and honoring the five massacre vic-

Figure 8-2. Closeup of the Boston Massacre marker. The hub of the wheel is said to rest where the first blood of the Revolutionary War was shed by Crispus Attucks, a black man. There is one spoke for each of the original thirteen colonies.

tims. The plan met with considerable resistance. Even though no less an authority than John Adams had referred to the massacre as the start of the Revolution, others were displeased to trace the birth of their nation to a riot in which a black man—Crispus Attucks—was the first casualty.[16] The massacre and its victims did not match their heroic image of the Revolution, but the memorial was completed over these objections (Figure 8-3).

As the present era unfolded, an interesting change in the Boston Massacre site took place, its incorporation into a more encompassing system of shrines administered by the federal government. Today the site and monument are but two stops along Boston's Freedom Trail. As blazed by the National Park Service in the twentieth century, the trail leads from the Boston Common past sights including Paul Revere's house and Old North Church before crossing the Charles River to the Bunker Hill monument and the USS *Constitution* in Charlestown. From there the pilgrim can travel to Lexington and Concord to

Figure 8-3. The monument commemorating the massacre, built in 1888, is located several blocks from the site of the attack, on the Boston Common. Considerable controversy surrounded the erection of this memorial because, by the late nineteenth century, some people viewed the massacre as a less than heroic start to the "glorious" Revolution.

view another set of memorials. The creation of Boston's Freedom Trail is only one instance of the consolidation of such shrines into a broader cosmographical representation during the late nineteenth and early twentieth centuries. The individual sites were enshrined independently but, through time, grouped into a single constellation united around the "story" of the Revolutionary War. These sacred sites were not acquired systematically or all at once. The federal government did not really become involved until the twentieth century. Until then the individual shrines were maintained independently of one another by local authorities and private citizens. Each was pressed on reluctant federal officials by an isolated upwelling of popular support for a particular shrine or because a crisis threatened a site's sanctity. The federal government was initially unequipped to administer these sites. Some were given to the Department of the Interior; others, largely battlefields, to the Department of War and the army. During the New Deal the National Park Service's mandate was expanded to encompass many historical sites like these, particularly Civil War battlefields in other parts of the nation. The idea of shaping the sites into a "Freedom Trail" came later. Although the job of shrine keeping is far removed from the park service's original mandate—to guard America's great natural wonders, as begun in 1872 at Yellowstone—there is a certain logic in the decision as it evolved over several decades. The National Park Service became the agency best equipped to maintain the nation's shrines, both those dedicated to its natural wonders and those that highlighted the progress of nationhood.

HARPERS FERRY AND THE CREATION OF A LANDSCAPE RELIQUARY

The National Park Service took an even more active role at Harpers Ferry, West Virginia, the Civil War counterpart of the Boston Massacre. The years preceding the Civil War had witnessed sporadic violence in the western territories over the issue of slavery. The Missouri Compromise, which defined the limits of slavery as new states entered the Union, had already led to sectional friction between the slaveholding states of the South and the free states of the North. Yet the scope of John Brown's plan dwarfed all previous incidents. Brown planned to steal weapons from the U.S. armory at Harpers Ferry to arm a general slave insurrection. The raid of 16–18 October 1859 failed, but it unequivocally raised the specter of war between North and South.

It was no accident that, in the aftermath of the raid, attention focused on Harpers Ferry and the fate of what became known as "John Brown's Fort."[17] The fort was the armory's fire engine and guard house and, coincidentally, the building into which Brown and his men retreated before being captured by U.S. marines led, all too prophetically, by Robert E. Lee. During the Civil War the strategic importance of Harpers Ferry, its armory, and its railroad lines brought fighting to the valley on several occasions.[18] By the end of the war the fort was one of the few armory buildings left intact, although souvenir hunters vandalized it badly. The U.S. government decided to give up most of its property at Harpers Ferry in 1869, including the armory ruins. In a curious turn of events, however, the federal government reappeared at Harpers Ferry a century later. Acting through the National Park Service, the government reclaimed the fort and much of Harpers Ferry itself. This story includes an interesting lesson in how a site, once abandoned, may be reclaimed as a national shrine.

After one false start in 1869, the fort passed into private hands. It remained at its original site as a tourist attraction for many years, thanks to the help of the Baltimore and Ohio Railroad, which welcomed the extra riders on its route through the valley. The fort began to assume a life of its own in 1892 as a symbol of John Brown's raid. Promoters purchased the building and moved it to Chicago to display at the Columbian Exposition. When the fort was removed from Harpers Ferry, a small marker was erected at its original site, although the land itself was purchased by the Baltimore and Ohio Railroad to improve the grade of the tracks leading to its Potomac River bridge (Figure 8-4). Unfortunately the company that moved the fort to the Columbian Exposition failed, and the fort was left stranded in Chicago. Only the hard work of private benefactors succeeded in bringing the fort back to Harpers Ferry. By then the original site was owned by the Baltimore and Ohio Railroad, and although the company had left the fort's marker in place, there was no longer room for the wandering shrine. From its return to Harpers Ferry in 1895 until 1910, the fort was displayed instead on a local farm. Change came in 1909 when Storer College, a postwar school for African Americans that housed its students in former armory buildings, acquired the building and had it

Figure 8-4. The site where John Brown's Fort originally stood. After the fort was moved to Chicago for the Columbian Exposition of 1893, the Baltimore and Ohio Railroad purchased the original site to improve the grade of its track. Even though the site had been disturbed, this marker was placed adjacent to the tracks to mark the original position of the fort.

Figure 8-5. John Brown's Fort at Harpers Ferry, West Virginia, in 1986. At the time of Brown's raid on the Harpers Ferry armory in 1859, this building was the factory's guardhouse and fire engine shed. At that time the fort was located on a site at the right edge of the photograph, on land now owned by the Baltimore and Ohio Railroad. Most of the buildings in this photograph, including the fort, are owned and maintained by the National Park Service.

moved to its campus on the bluff above Harpers Ferry. There the fort remained until 1968, when the National Park Service moved it closer to its original site (Figure 8-5).

The fate of the fort and the fort's site may seem to be different from that of the Boston Massacre site, but two parallels exist. First, both sites required about a century to be transformed into shrines of national identity. Once again sacral myth was projected onto landscape, but only after considerable delay. Second, canonization of both sites depended first on private initiative and only later on federal action. The parallels are made stronger by the most recent episode in the fort's history—the acquisition of much of Harpers Ferry by the National Park Service beginning in the 1950s. Harpers Ferry never quite recaptured the vitality of its antebellum days. The loss of the armory was a blow to the city's economy, but more important, the town's location at the confluence of the Potomac and Shenandoah Rivers exposed it to severe, recurrent floods. Devastating inundations in the late nineteenth and early twentieth centuries led to the town's gradual abandonment. Storer College remained longer than many other institutions did, but it too closed in 1955.

As Harpers Ferry was abandoned, the federal government, encouraged by the state of West Virginia, began to take an interest in the town. Following the enactment of enabling legislation in Washington in 1944, West Virginia began to buy land at Harpers Ferry and deed it to the federal government. The first major parcel was passed to the National Park Service in 1954, and more land was added in the 1960s, including the Storer College campus and John Brown's Fort. The park service used the fort as part of its headquarters until 1968, when the fort was moved downslope to a position close to the original site. The park service restored the fort in the late 1970s, and someday, should the railroad property become available, the fort may be repositioned on its original site. In the interim Harpers Ferry will remain a "government" town, largely owned and maintained by the National Park Service as a symbol of an important episode in the nation's history.

Harpers Ferry, like the Boston Massacre, was a somewhat inauspicious symbol of America's heroic past. Recast ever so slightly, it could be seen as a guerrilla action led by terrorists. Nonetheless today Harpers Ferry is tied inextricably to the saga of the Civil War, a story that has been projected onto landscape in many other places, such as those I discuss in Chapter 4. The site of every major wartime engagement between the North and South has been enshrined.[19] Fort Sumter, for instance, the site of the first real engagement of the war on 12–14 April 1861, was acquired by the National Park Service in 1948, when the military abandoned it as an obsolete coastal defense. Although Fort Sumter simply changed hands between two government agencies, most battle sites had to be purchased from private citizens. This was not a task that the federal government was immediately willing to assume. The government had of necessity purchased private land during the Civil War for national cemeteries at major battlefields, but these were modest purchases compared to the battlefields that were gradually being enshrined. The lobbying for commemoration moved up from veterans and people who lived on or near the properties, not from the federal level down. Yearly encampments by veterans on battlefields where they fought led annually to fresh crops of memorial tablets and statuary.[20] Southerners were at first more reticent in marking battlefields and in some cases less able to afford the statuary. By the mid-twentieth century, however, the Southern states had dedicated some of the largest and most impressive monuments, even on battlefields where they lost.[21]

The most interesting facet of this monument building, like that stemming from the Revolutionary War, was the federal government's assumption of this work, largely done by the National Park Service from the 1930s onward.[22] Previously battlefield property donated to or purchased by the government had been passed to the War Department and army to be maintained as national military parks. In justifying each new acquisition, significance had to be found in each battle so enshrined. Whereas the war itself had been a confusion of campaigns and battles, with some occurring—like Gettysburg—almost by accident, the events were now ranked by importance and ordered within an interpretive chronology. Nowadays it is possible to point to Harpers Ferry as the prelude to war, Fort Sumter as the war's actual beginning, Appomatox Courthouse as its end, and Washington's Ford Theatre as the tragic coda of the conflict. The midpoint of the Civil War was localized to Gettysburg and the High Water Mark Monument, where Pickett's Charge ended in defeat for Southern troops on 3 July 1863. All these sites are now administered by the National Park Service, which as the nation's shrine keeper has created more than a landscape cosmography. It has assembled a collection of memorials and sacred artifacts, including John Brown's fort, which is as close to being a reliquary as can be sanctioned by the "theology" of civil religion.

Pearl Harbor and the Question of Meaning

By the mid-twentieth century Americans had enshrined a wide variety of sites that outlined the nation's origins and history, among other themes, but the explicit symbolic associations of these sites remained at best diffuse and sometimes contradictory. If efforts to enlist public support for shrine making were to succeed, the meaning of some sites had to be modulated, and often substantially attenuated, to appeal to as broad a constituency as possible. The South could, for instance, hardly be expected to support public battlefield memorials if they stressed the Confederacy's defeat or the injustices of slavery. Instead proponents usually assumed the middle ground and appealed for support by stressing heroic qualities displayed by soldiers on both sides of the conflict. Events such as the Boston Massacre and John Brown's raid at Harpers Ferry were more difficult to interpret, however, because if read too closely, they seemed to support a citizen's right to lead armed insurrections against the government. Instead of broadcasting such radical messages, most shrines had their meanings modulated to give them a popular flavor that stresses themes designed to appeal to the greatest number of people and alienate the fewest. This process of modulation and attenuation can be observed in efforts to build a memorial at Pearl Harbor in the wake of the Japanese surprise attack of 7 December 1941, which brought the United States into World War II.

The meaning of the Pearl Harbor attack may seem less equivocal than that of either the Boston Massacre or Harpers Ferry, but in fact the connotations are just as complex.[23] After all, Pearl Harbor was an unambiguous defeat for the United States. The strong feelings of embarrassment, shame, and outrage at having a major military base caught completely by surprise were amplified by claims of deception and calls for revenge. Nonetheless it was not these highly charged emotional issues that led eventually to a memorial but rather calls to honor the victims of the attack.

The idea of a memorial for the victims was first voiced early in the war but not acted on for years. One key reason for the delay was that Pearl Harbor remained an active naval base, and the demands of security made the site inappropriate for a public memorial. More to the point, the navy owned Pearl Harbor and exerted primary control over memorials on the base. The navy was not eager to commemorate such a resounding defeat. It managed to repair and return to service all but three of the ships damaged in the 7 December attack, but such quick work hardly compensated for being caught by surprise. Given these circumstances alone, a monument at Pearl Harbor would have been unlikely. The problem was that the navy could not overlook honoring its casualties, and sadly the bodies of over a thousand sailors lay trapped in the wreckage of the USS *Arizona*. It was the sinking of the USS *Arizona* that produced almost half the attack's fatalities, and as a de facto tomb for its crew, the wreckage drew attention to itself as a natural focus for memorialization that the navy could not ignore. After the attack the USS *Arizona* had been stripped of as much usable equipment as possible, but large portions of the wreck had to be left in place. During and after the war it was the poor condition of the wreckage, which was seen as a tomb unbefitting its dead, that drew attention to the need for a proper memorial.

Given this situation, it was no coincidence that the first efforts to mark the site were undertaken by the navy and intended to pay tribute to the dead of the USS *Arizona* and the casualties of the Pearl Harbor attack in general. In 1950 the commander of the Pacific fleet had a flagstaff affixed to the wreckage so a U.S. flag could be flown daily. Five years later the Navy Club placed a stone marker on Ford Island near the wreck of the *Arizona* and dedicated the memorial to all American servicemen who died in the Pearl Harbor attack. Further work was stymied by a number of bureaucratic hurdles, as well as a lack of money. The navy's mandate encompassed the authority neither to build a monument nor to accept private donations for such a project. Besides, the issue of opening an active-duty base to the general public ran across the grain of navy practice. Beyond these bureaucratic roadblocks stood the problem of defining—however tentatively—the reasons for building a monument. Without a well-defined objective acceptable to the navy, supporters of a memorial had little chance of solving any of the other problems.

As it turned out, a compromise was reached that stressed honoring the dead and avoided addressing some of the collateral issues. During the planning period a number of ad hoc interpretations were proposed to console one or more of the monument's constituencies, and the number of constituencies had grown considerably since the war. Among the groups now taking an interest in the memorial were the navy, naval veterans, veterans of other armed services, the territory (and later state) of Hawaii, the civilian survivors of those killed in the attack, the general public both in Hawaii and on the mainland, and one or two commissions assigned the task of marking key wartime battles.

For the U.S. Navy, honoring the dead was the only really acceptable reason for building a memorial. Even then, the navy faced the issue of whether the memorial should honor only the crew of the USS *Arizona*, all the casualties it suffered on 7 December, or all naval personnel killed in the Pacific theater of war. By making the terms of the memorial as inclusive as possible, higher levels of support could be expected within the navy and among its veterans. Solely as a naval memorial, the project would be less capable of attracting supporters from the other armed services. Veterans of other services were, in turn, more likely to be supportive if the memorial alluded to all American casualties. On the other hand, a purely military memorial in distant Pearl Harbor was not likely to garner the widespread popular and financial support such an ambitious project would require.

As the efforts progressed, the task of enlisting support for the USS *Arizona* memorial became particularly complex; some of the legal hurdles had to be resolved by Congress.[24] When Hawaii's territorial delegate to Congress made his case, he stressed repeatedly the need to honor the dead. He wisely drew attention to the fact that sailors from all across the United States died on the USS *Arizona* so as to gain the support of other members of Congress. This strategy further broadened support for a memorial by stirring interest among a much larger constituency on the mainland.

Despite the stress laid on honoring the dead, it was never possible to ignore completely the collateral meanings of the Pearl Harbor attack. War memorials are often highly equivocal because a fine line separates the glorification of war from the celebration of peace. The competing meanings of the Pearl Harbor attack were even more involved. When it became known that U.S. officials had received—and ignored—warning of the attack, the fact was fast woven into the fabric of 1950s McCarthyism. In this sinister light Pearl Harbor symbolized the threat of subversion from within the military and among high government officials. A related theme was that of military preparedness and the view that a memorial would help remind Americans never again to be caught unprepared for war—a homily perfect for the cold war. These militaristic interpretations were countered by the theme of peace and a desire to remind visitors of the destructiveness of war. The architect who designed the memorial, Alfred Preis, developed a more complex conception of the meaning of the Pearl Harbor attack.[25] Preis saw the United States as a nation inclined toward pacifism, a country that always had to be provoked to war. In Preis's view America had the potential to turn the tide of any war to victory, but the price of victory would always be a first defeat like Pearl Harbor; it was a necessary sacrifice to America's ideals. An interpretation as sophisticated as Preis's was of little use to more pragmatic supporters of the memorial.

Interpretations of the attack were also shaped by the ups and downs of postwar Japanese American relationships. As Roger Dingman has pointed out, these changes were often registered on the anniversaries of Pearl Harbor.[26] For many years the message "Never Again!" was stressed. As Japan came to be viewed as an ally against communism in East Asia, the anniversary of the attack was all but ignored. Recent friction between Japan and the United States over economic and trade issues has turned Pearl Harbor back into a controversial site. The fiftieth anniversary celebration aroused strong feelings and resulted in accusations and recriminations being hurled both ways across the Pacific. Any sense of reconciliation was lost in a struggle over differing views of the meaning of Pearl Harbor and World War II.

The federal legislation that eventually made a success of private and military efforts to build the memorial refrained from such complex interpretations. Public Law 87-201 of 1961, which provided the balance of the funds needed to complete the memorial, specified that "such memorial and museum shall be maintained in honor and in commemoration of the members of the Armed Forces of the United States who gave their lives to their country during the attack on Pearl Harbor, Hawaii, on December 7, 1941." As if to reinforce this point, the monument was dedicated in 1962 not on 7 December but on Memorial Day, a holiday already set aside for honoring America's war dead. Located offshore at the USS *Arizona*'s final berth, the completed memorial bridges the beam of the wreckage without actually touching the hull (Figure 8-6). The navy was to maintain the memorial and provide shuttle boats to transport visitors to the memorial's dock.

The National Park Service, as expected, did enter the Pearl Harbor story, but not until the late 1960s, when calls were heard for a visitor center at the shuttle boat landing. The previously undeveloped landing was now overburdened by tourist-pilgrims. Proposals suggested that the memorial be placed under the care of the National Park Service at the same time. A decade was required to solve the problem of raising funds for the visitor center and achieving an administrative compromise between the navy and National Park Service. In the end the navy was given the money to build the center through a military appropriations bill. On completion of the center in 1980, the navy passed its maintenance to the park service. The navy relinquished neither title to the property nor rights to operate the shuttle boat service. Debate over the visitor center was more concerned with promoting tourism than it was with discussing the memorial's meaning any further. The navy seems to have been persuaded to back the project as a means of enhancing its image in the post-Vietnam era. Clearly it took

Figure 8-6. The USS *Arizona* Memorial off Ford Island in Pearl Harbor, Hawaii. The sinking of the *Arizona* on 7 December 1941 claimed 1,117 of its crew—almost half the American losses of the surprise attack—and left many entombed in the wreckage. A proper memorial to the sailors of the *Arizona* and the other casualties of the attack was the subject of years of discussion as the "meaning" of the Pearl Harbor attack was debated. The present memorial was dedicated on Memorial Day 1962 but was preceded by other, smaller monuments and remembrances. The structure was designed to straddle the wreck of the *Arizona* without actually touching the hull. Photograph courtesy of UPI / Corbis-Bettmann Archive.

far less time to create a shrine at Pearl Harbor than it did in Boston and Harpers Ferry. Experience made it easier for Americans to decide which events fit their myth of origins and how best to mark them. More than the other sites do, however, Pearl Harbor shows how the meaning of America's civil shrines has to be modified to meet the demands of varying constituencies.

SELECTIVITY, HIERARCHY, AND PRACTICE

The sites discussed above illustrate only three of the many issues bearing on the interpretation of the cosmography of America's civil religion: the delay, the role of the National Park Service, and the problem of negotiating the meaning of civil shrines in a secular society. Selectivity, hierarchy, and practice are three other issues I consider important.

The first relates to a point I have stressed in this chapter and the previous one—few sites gain the support needed to transform them into local or regional, much less national shrines. The selectivity of this process produces a highly filtered view of the past. The Boston Massacre, Harpers Ferry, and Pearl Harbor were commemorated because they could be molded into a heroic view of the national past. The ones that succeed are those that, in Galloway's words of 1780, lead "the people to look up to one system of government for their safety and happiness, and to act in concert on all occasions to maintain and defend it." These are sites that affirm a sense of patriotism, uphold community values, and honor sacrifices made for nation and community. Not all these sites involve tragedy and violence. The sites on which I dwell in this book are only a subset of the many places and landscapes that have been inscribed with these patriotic messages. Violent and nonviolent, tragic and nontragic, all have been shaped selectively to reflect positively on the nation and the national past.

The corollary is that many major episodes of tragedy and violence remain unmarked because they conflict with or contradict this message. These events, which I term the "shadowed past" in the next chapter, are particularly interesting to explore. Some are so shameful that it is nearly impossible to cast any positive light on them, such as the history of slavery and the genocide practiced against Native Americans for centuries. Others are not marked because two or more groups are in conflict over the interpretation of an event. The commemoration of the Vietnam War and of sites relating to antiwar protest are examples of controversial events that have pitted a number of constituencies against one another; so too have the events of the civil rights movement and even the internment of Japanese Americans during World War II. Finally, some events are unmarked simply because there has not been time to fit them into the nation's lore of the past. Their meanings are presently unresolved, but the sites may eventually be sanctified when an interpretive solution is found. The labor movement has all the heroic elements needed to be absorbed into the saga of American history but remains poorly marked. I think more of these will gradually be enshrined; it is a matter more of time than of meaning. I address these cases of conflicting and unresolved meaning in greater detail in the next chapter.

Second, the sites commemorated nationally are usually closely related to those sanctified closer to home. As I argue in the previous chapter, various interest groups, cities, and states have created shrines and maintain them with the same care as the National Park Service gives to those in its charge. Chicago and Texas are merely two examples. Virtually every city and state has made an effort to designate significant events and sanctify the sites of the most important. These local and state monuments make the interpretation of the cosmography of America's civil religion far more interesting. Instead of being expressed in a single system of shrines, America's myths of origin have assumed a complex hierarchical form supported by local, state, regional, and national agencies. The task of creating and maintaining shrines is occasionally shared by agencies arrayed at more than one of these hierarchical levels. The marking of Texas's state shrines was, for instance, assisted by the National Park Service (and the Civilian Conservation Corps) during the depression years of the 1930s. The Mormon Trail was already a fixture of the lore of the Church of Jesus Christ of Latter-day Saints when the federal government and National Park Service began to develop it further as one of the important pioneer trails to the West. This hierarchy also appears to outline, in a general way, the usual steps in the process of canonization and enshrinement. Sanctification is almost always initiated by private citizens working at the local level and only later assumed by state or federal agencies.

When I speak of hierarchy, I am referring both to sponsorship and to the actual arrangement of these shrines in cityscapes and landscapes. During the late nineteenth and early twentieth centuries, just as Americans were beginning to mark their origins and accomplishments in monumental style, so too were they ambitiously redesigning their cities and capitals to grand new plans. Cities such as St. Louis and Indianapolis developed new civic spaces around war memorials, and capital cities around the nation were embellished with shrines and memorials (Figure 8-7). The precedents for these symbolic tableaux were, of course, L'Enfant's plan for Washington, as well as Chicago's Columbian Exposition of 1893. The highly stylized plan of radiating avenues and vistas of the former and the monumental beaux arts plan of the latter shaped the vision of the city planners all across America.

Figure 8-7. Looking east across St. Louis's Memorial Plaza to the Civil Courts Building. This is a late example of the sort of monumental redesign of civic complexes that was popular among American cities in the late nineteenth and early twentieth centuries. St. Louis's was begun in 1923 but is flanked to the left by the massive Soldier's Memorial.

These designs lent themselves to symbolic embellishment that then evolved new meaning. L'Enfant's plan in particular permitted the creation of a spatial hierarchy of memorials and monuments through their relationships to the different quadrants and axes of the plan and their relative proximity to different branches of government. The Washington Monument, honoring the nation's founding father, was positioned at a focal point of the plan, where the axis drawn west from the capitol intersects another drawn almost perpendicular, north to the White House (Figure 8-8). This, in turn, created a strong axial alignment along the Mall that was extended further west by the addition of the Lincoln Memorial in 1922. This memorial not only elevated Lincoln almost to Washington's status but also carried the vista along the Mall all the way across the Potomac to the Arlington National Cemetery, one of the national cemeteries created during the Civil War (Fig-

Figure 8-8. The alignment of the Washington Monument and Lincoln Memorial in Washington, D.C. L'Enfant's plan for Washington provided many axial and radial alignments that have been used to position major monuments, public shrines, and government buildings such as the Washington Monument. This monument has in turn been used as a point of spatial and symbolic alignment for other monuments built since its completion in 1885. From Edward F. Concklin, *The Lincoln Memorial in Washington* (Washington: GPO, 1927), 54.

ure 8-9).[27] Subsequent additions have taken advantage of these points of orientation. For example, when a grave site for President Kennedy was selected in Arlington Cemetery in 1963, it was positioned to align with the Lincoln Memorial and the White House. The design specifications for the Vietnam Veterans Memorial required it to fit in a site between the Washington and Lincoln memorials. The final design met this criterion by joining its two sides at an oblique angle so that the axes of the memorial pointed to these neighboring monuments.

As they have developed a hierarchy of symbols, Americans have also gained a tremendous amount of experience in shrine making. Practice and regular rehearsal have established a repertory of national symbols, increased the speed with which sites are marked, bequeathed a set of services and rituals of commemoration, and created a hierarchical system of sacred sites within which others could be placed. The

Figure 8-9. A vista from the front lawn of the Arlington House in Arlington National Cemetery over President Kennedy's grave to the Lincoln Memorial and beyond. The White House is just out of view to the left. The alignment was intended. Arlington evolved as a cemetery for the nation's heroes over many decades, in a gradual process similar to the development of many national shrines. It began much differently, being established as a graveyard on Robert E. Lee's estate after he abandoned the United States for the Confederacy at the start of the Civil War.

effects of such experience can be seen again in the aftermath of President Kennedy's assassination. A state funeral was arranged in a mere three days based on precedents dating back to Abraham Lincoln's assassination in 1865 and, still further, to George Washington's funeral in 1799. Arlington National Cemetery was selected for the grave, confirming this cemetery's growing reputation as an especially sacred burial ground for national heroes. The grave site was aligned, as described above, with the White House and Lincoln Memorial, and an eternal flame was chosen as the centerpiece of the grave marker.

Such prompt commemoration was not always the case. For decades after independence, Americans had difficulty choosing emblems for their nation and ways to commemorate great events and heroes. They wished to resist the trappings of monarchy and hesitated to memorialize presidents and patriots in the same imperial styles. This was the same problem the French would face after the revolution of 1789.[28] Both the Americans and French wished to symbolize a break from the past and explored a wide range of "rational" emblems befitting their Enlightenment philosophies. Almost inevitably, Egyptian, Greek, and Roman prototypes slipped into this mix of symbols: obelisks, pyramids, columns, rotundas, cenotaphs, and temples. Americans gradually acquiesced to some of these, particularly in the nineteenth century, when the glories of their accomplishments seemed to demand a grander style of commemoration than the austere Enlightenment prototypes with which they had experimented. By the nineteenth century Americans were using most of the conventional European funereal emblems in their monuments to fallen heroes, embellished with a few homegrown symbols.

Once Americans had sanctified a few sites with memorials, they had places to put more. In Chapter 7 I draw attention to this process of accretion in Texas at the sites of some of the events of the revolution of 1836. Once set apart as sacred ground, the Alamo and San Jacinto battlefields proved to be very attractive as sites for other memorials. These were memorials not to the Texas Revolution but to other events that demonstrated the sacrifice and determination of Texans in others' wars and tragedies. Other public spaces, such as the grounds of capitol buildings, serve the same function. In Austin, on the grounds of the Texas capitol, monuments to the revolution of 1836 and the Civil War vie with other tributes, such as one to volunteer fire fighters (Figure 8-10). This latter monument pays tribute to fire fighters who have

Figure 8-10. The fire fighters memorial on the grounds of the state capitol in Austin, Texas. Public spaces such as this one attract memorials through a process of accretion. Each addition highlights sacrifices made on behalf of the state and its people.

given their lives in disasters all across the state (including the Texas City explosion discussed in Chapter 3). The capitol, as the centerpiece of state government, provides an excellent backdrop to memorials celebrating sacrifices made on behalf of the state and its people. The same thing has happened in Washington, D.C. The original Vietnam Veterans Memorial has attracted two other statuary groups, one of soldiers and the other honoring the women who served in the war. Now a Korean War Veterans Memorial has been dedicated on the Mall, to the east of the Lincoln Memorial and across the reflecting pool from the Vietnam memorial.[29] Finally, after all these years, some groups are contemplating substantial monuments to American sacrifices in World Wars I and II in the nation's capital. They point out that the United States Holocaust Memorial Museum is the only monumental building in the District of Columbia dedicated to the events of those wars, and it can hardly be considered a tribute to American "victory."[30] The only other well-known reminder of World War II is the U.S. Marines' Iwo Jima monument on the edge of Arlington Cemetery, and this statue is somewhat out of the public eye in its present location.

Patriotic ceremony has evolved at the same pace as national shrines and symbols have. Through the nineteenth century and into the twentieth, Americans learned how to respond to adversity in unselfconscious ways. They learned how best to pay tribute to their fallen heroes, how to honor the sacrifices of their war dead, and how to sanctify the sites of great community tragedies. By the time of the Korean and Vietnam Wars, Americans could draw on precedents for war memorials dating back to the Revolutionary War and including the Mexican-American War, Civil War, Spanish-American War, and World Wars I and II. As a consequence, memorials to the two world wars arose quickly in communities all across the nation, perhaps apart from Washington, D.C. Great controversy surrounded commemoration of Vietnam, as I note in the next chapter, but there was never really any doubt that the nation's losses in that conflict would be honored.

This experience with shrine creation was also expressed in small ways. After the loss of the space shuttle *Challenger* in 1986, calls for a memorial were almost instantaneous. Even in cases confined to individual communities, responses are just as fast. In Killeen after a mass murder in 1991, a small memorial was quickly erected to honor the victims. A memorial garden is already being proposed for the site of the Alfred Murrah Federal Building in Oklahoma, which was bombed in 1995. These are sites that would not have been marked even two decades ago, say, at the time of the University of Wisconsin antiwar bombing of 1970 (discussed in the next chapter). Now, however, there seems to be a consensus that such tributes are fitting and proper and help communities overcome their grief, as I discuss in Chapter 3. Overall Americans are much more effusive in marking events of tragedy and violence than they once were—and they recognize what to do in these situations. The paradox is that the 1990s have seen the first discussions I can identify advocating a reduction in support for national commemorative efforts. Congressional efforts to trim the national budget have targeted agencies such as the National Park Service that are vitally important to this effort. It is far too soon to know what will happen in the long run. It would be ironic if efforts to balance the federal budget had the effect of trimming support for these many memorials to the national past. These parks and memorials are among the most powerful national symbols Americans have created and engender a sense of community and shared sacrifice sought by many groups in contemporary society.

Irrespective of such future decisions, America's civil religion has already left a lasting imprint on the American landscape. Shrines dedicated both to events and to individuals celebrate the values of heroism, valor, loyalty, and patriotism. Together these shrines outline a carefully filtered vision of the national past and present a heroic vision of American history. Yet these shrines are more than simply passive projections of sacral myth. In many of the cases examined in this chapter and elsewhere in this book, the act of enshrinement forces people to grapple with the meaning of the past in ways they might otherwise avoid. For Catherine Albanese, a historian, and Emile Durkheim, a sociologist, society itself defines the symbols of collective life. To these writers, landscape can be no more than one more representation of a preexisting, preformed social cosmos. But this is to overlook the interplay of landscape and place in defining these symbols. Landscape is more than a passive reflection of a nation's civil religion and symbolic totems. Landscape is the expressive medium, a forum for debate, within which these social values can be discussed actively and realized symbolically. Moreover the debate never ends. As I argue in the next chapter, many sites are still shadowed by their pasts, their fates as yet undecided.

Chapter 9

Invisible and Shadowed Pasts

Tragedy sites that have been shaped to represent local, regional, and national traditions present a selective view of the past. They are sanctified to highlight points of origin and great accomplishments and to celebrate the lives of heroes and the sacrifices ordinary people have made for city, state, and nation. These are exceptional places; the vast majority of sites touched by tragedy and violence fade from view after being rectified or obliterated. Yet among these invisible, unmarked sites are some that seem to meet all the prerequisites for sanctification but remain unmemorialized. Some of these will eventually be rediscovered, but their current, unmarked status is not merely a matter of oversight. Their invisibility can be traced to issues of unresolved meaning and to conflicts over memory. Some have yet to be fitted into an encompassing interpretive scaffolding; the traditions that will guide their shaping await invention or are now emerging. Other sites face a greater obstacle. They can be sanctified only at the expense of other sites that have already been consecrated to local, regional, and national historical traditions. In these cases it is an issue not of creating a new tradition but rather of altering existing traditions enough to make room for new meanings. This is of particular relevance to the marking of African American and Native American history in the United States. To stress the heroic aspects of the struggles over slavery and the suppression of Native American cultures is to question other traditions that have already been marked in landscape. Once consecrated, sites do not always give way easily to revision.

As I address these issues of unresolved meaning and conflicting memories in this chapter, I cannot avoid discussing the extent to which the shaping and reshaping of place reflect broadly held social attitudes toward violence and tragedy. This will be the final question I raise in this book. My answer relies as much on what is invisible in the American landscape as on what is visible. The invisibility of so many events of tragedy and violence seems to indicate a tolerance or acceptance of such events as fundamental elements of American life. These events are so common and so ordinary that they go unremarked—and unmarked. Visibility, on the other hand, arises from an inclination to see virtue in violence and tragedy. These are events that are celebrated as fundamental to the national past and national "character." This dual tendency—sometimes to ignore, sometimes to celebrate—provides an indication of highly equivocal attitudes toward violence and tragedy in American society. Violence and tragedy have helped to cement the bonds of community and nationhood that unite Americans around shared traditions and a common vision of history. Nevertheless the creation of such traditions inevitably divides the nation into winners and losers, victors and victims. That violence and tragedy can both bind and divide is an irony that casts an unusual shadow over American history and the American landscape.

UNRESOLVED MEANING

Throughout the United States there are many sites I classify as "in process." They seem headed for designation or sanctification, but somewhere along the path progress is slowed, stalled, or becomes unsteady. Sometimes this reversal stems from unexpected issues that complicate debate about an event's significance and take additional time to resolve. In other situations such sites await the development of interpretive traditions within which they can be assessed, framed, and promoted. Until these more encompassing traditions are carefully defined and widely accepted, the sites remain in limbo. This changes only as they are gradually linked to—and interpreted within—a broader vision of local, regional, or national history. Among these sites are those associated with the struggles of American labor, a variety of legal injustices, and protests against the Vietnam War.

Martyrs without Memorials:
The Rise of American Labor

Tucked away in odd corners of the United States are small markers testifying to the sacrifices ordinary Americans made to gain rights as workers within an industrializing society. The clash between labor and capital was as violent in the United States as it was in any other nation coming to terms with the rapid economic changes of the nineteenth and early twentieth centuries. Strikes, riots, and massacres punctuated this period at regular intervals as workers sought the right to pool and negotiate the terms of their labor, just as industrialists could already bargain with capital. This was an unequal fight in almost every instance. Industrialists were able to mobilize their tremendous resources—and usually those of the local police and government—to suppress any attempt to win profit and power for the workers. In retrospect the success of the American labor movement is remarkable given the forces arrayed against it from the mid-nineteenth century onward. Rights that modern workers take for granted were won at a high price in struggles as heroic as any in American history. The movement is replete with martyrs and heroes, myths and legends, but nowhere in the United States are these marked by anything more than modest local memorials. A national holiday is dedicated to labor, but the movement itself has never been inscribed on a grand scale in the American landscape. Not a single national park is dedicated to the cause of labor or to its heroes and martyrs.

At the local level these sites vary greatly in the manner and extent of their marking. Some are sanctified and others designated, but perhaps just as many have been rectified and even obliterated. The small memorial at the site of the Lattimer Mines Massacre marks where sheriff's deputies killed nineteen miners and wounded forty in 1897 during a strike in eastern Pennsylvania's anthracite fields (Figure 9-1). This sort of sanctification is rare, even on a small scale, but it has occurred after a few other events of violence, such as the strikes at Ludlow, Colorado, and Homestead, Pennsylvania. The small plaque affixed to the façade of the building where the Triangle Shirtwaist Factory fire

Figure 9-1. Site of the Lattimer Mines Massacre of 1897 in the coal fields of Pennsylvania. Striking miners were marching along the road to the left when sheriff's deputies fired on them. This memorial was erected in 1972 by the United Labor Council of Lower Luzerne and Carbon Counties, AFL-CIO, and the United Mine Workers of America. It is one of relatively few memorials that can be traced to the violent suppression of American labor.

claimed 146 sweatshop seamstresses in 1911 is an example of designation (Figure 9-2).[1] These small memorials and markers are almost invariably funded locally, by union shops and families of the victims, rather than by national organizations. Even then rectification is by far the most common outcome. Most instances of labor-related violence are difficult to locate today because the sites received no special attention and were built over and reused (Figures 9-3 and 9-4). Industrialists controlled some sites and blocked commemorative efforts, as when the memorial to the martyrs of the Haymarket Riot was forced outside Chicago. Even after discounting such resistance, however, there is little evidence that these many sites are being shaped to reflect broader "invented" traditions of labor history.

The issue here is one of unresolved meaning—what to make of a struggle that was instrumental in shaping elements of contemporary

Figure 9-2. The site of the Triangle Shirtwaist Factory fire of
1911 in New York City. The fire in a crowded sweatshop in
the upper stories of the building claimed the lives of almost
150 seamstresses. The small plaque visible on the corner column of the building marks the site and was placed there by
the International Ladies' Garment Worker's Union.

Figure 9-3. Derelict hop kilns on the Durst Ranch on the edge of Wheatland, California. In August 1913 a riot broke out here over conditions in the migrant labor camp, claiming victims on both sides of the conflict. Like most events in the history of the American labor movement, this one remains unmarked.

American society but has gradually faded from view. The significance of individual events is clear in retrospect, so that such events are often marked in landscape, but these local memorials have yet to be assembled into an encompassing national representation of the travail of labor. A number of reasons lie behind the difficulty in resolving this meaning and the tardiness of efforts to sanctify sites at the national level, efforts that emerged only in the 1990s.

One aspect of the problem is that the United States itself has yet to come to terms with some elements of its past. The labor movement, like the industrialization and economic change of which it was part, has not yet been framed in the same scaffolding as the Revolutionary and Civil Wars and frontier settlement, and as a result, few nationally sanctioned shrines mark the course of industrialization. The Lowell National Historical Park in Massachusetts, authorized in 1978, is perhaps the most ambitious of these and marks the rise of the early water-powered New England textile industry. The only other labor-related

Figure 9-4. Site of the "Memorial Day Massacre" in Chicago during the Little Steel strike of 1937. Strikers marching across this field toward the gates of a Republic Steel Company plant were met by police. In the ensuing struggle ten protesters were mortally wounded. No marker designates this as one of the last major violent strikes in the long history of the American labor movement.

national sites mark either the rise or consequences of particular technological achievements—the early iron industry at Hopewell Furnace in Pennsylvania, railroad and canal transportation at Chesapeake and Ohio Canal National Historical Park in Maryland and Allegheny Portage National Historical Site in Pennsylvania, or the inventors themselves at Edison National Historical Site in New Jersey or the Wright Brothers National Memorial in North Carolina. This is not a large number of sites to mark such dramatic changes in American life, and they tend to frame the process in terms of technologies and inventors. On the other hand, of course, broader social and economic forces in which these fit are difficult to portray in landscape, apart from perhaps conserving entire company towns and industrial complexes such as Lowell's.

The emphasis on inventors such as Edison and the Wright brothers is not unexpected in a secular society such as the United States, where the celebration of great leaders and heroes serves as a binding tie of community. The industrialists and financiers of the nineteenth century were not at all shy in trying to assume a similar role for themselves. The American landscape of today owes much to the self-aggrandizing philanthropy of industrial magnates such as Rockefeller, Mellon, Frick, Carnegie, and Pullman. Not only did they fund or endow innumerable schools, libraries, universities, museums, and galleries, but their work shaped entire communities both at the factory gate and in the wealthy enclaves they established to escape the urban conditions they helped to create. The success of these endeavors means that the American landscape is presently shaped to reflect industrialization in a relatively positive light, that is, from the perspective of the industrialists who came out ahead. The period of peak industrialization when the great vertically integrated monopolies and oligopolies took shape is known as the "Gilded Age." It celebrated the victors of the war between industrialists and workers rather than the vanquished.

This bias in favor of the victors of the industrial revolution can hardly be viewed today as a barrier to celebrating the progress of the American labor movement. The great industrialists who were the generals in the war on labor are long since dead, and the self-interest of their heirs has long since waned. Perhaps an additional problem to widespread sanctification lies not in the opposition but in the cause itself. The events of the labor movement are more difficult to frame as a coherent whole than is, say, the progress of first colonization or the sweep of westward frontier settlement. Many of the most important battles fought for the cause of labor were deeply rooted in their immediate situations and did not produce substantial rewards outside those contexts, or at least not until a long time afterward. The struggles of labor were much divided by industry, occupation, and region. Steelworkers in Pennsylvania, coal miners in the Appalachian Mountains, hardrock miners in the mountain West, seamen and dockworkers on the coasts, sweatshop seamstresses in New York, agricultural laborers in California, and railroad workers all across the United States differed by class, ethnicity, immigrant status, and pure self-interest. One of the most difficult aspects of the entire labor movement was to rally such varied constituencies around a common cause, to get workers to see their immediate fight as part of a larger struggle. All the while the industrialists were trying to use these same points of difference to shatter consensus and divide emerging nationwide federations. The result is a history of fits and starts, of precedents and setbacks, of a movement lurching from one crisis to another, trying to wrestle change out of adversity. This sort of story does not yield readily to grand, unified interpretations, to the sort of tradition building considered in previous chapters. It would be a mistake, though, to maintain that the history of labor has yet to be written.

Even in the nineteenth century, writers could fathom the significance of key events such as the succession of rail strikes, the Haymarket Riot, and the Homestead and Pullman strikes. These were of national importance at the time and were assessed accordingly. Other events of perhaps only local importance were being recognized more widely from World War I onward as labor achieved substantial political power and a lasting national organization and as major scholarly histories of the labor movement began to appear.[2] The movement as a whole has many rough edges, the smoothing and shaping of which is already well along. The cause of labor has not always been a blameless, unalloyed struggle for justice. In instances such as the Herrin Massacre in the southern coalfields of Illinois in 1922, immigrant strikebreakers were among those massacred.[3] None of the strikers was ever sentenced for the killings. Chinese immigrants were the target in the Rock Springs Massacre in the coalfields of Wyoming in 1885.[4] During its history the labor movement has been influenced at times by strong nativist, anti-immigrant, and antiblack sentiments that would be embarrassing if emphasized today.

Nonetheless the unsavory episodes and ideologies of the labor movement's distant past are by no means insurmountable obstacles to tradition building. Perhaps a more important factor is that in the twentieth century, just as the labor movement was reaching the point when it could look back on its heritage to celebrate centennials and mark its past, it began to decline in numbers and influence. In 1955 labor unions represented 17.7 million members, or 24.4 percent of all American workers. Membership peaked in 1978 at 21.8 million, but this constituted only 19.7 percent of American workers. By 1988 membership had fallen below 1955 levels and included only 16.8 percent of the work force. Although this trend is disputed, it does seem clear that the pattern was set as long ago as the 1950s rather than in the political climate of the 1970s and 1980s. Furthermore no single factor accounts for these changes. Changing economic conditions and government policies seem just as important as the offensives against unions mounted by a new generation of capitalists.[5] The important issue here is not the likelihood that this trend will continue but rather the timing of these changes—they come at a point when most movements would begin to reshape the landscape to celebrate their past. For the labor movement, with many sites almost begging to be commemorated, the process has stalled.

I think that the process of commemorating labor's past will receive increasing attention in coming years. First, it would be inaccurate to maintain that the process of commemorating all sites has abated entirely. In the past several decades several centennials of significant moments in labor history have been celebrated locally, such as the Haymarket Riot in Chicago and the Homestead strike in Pittsburgh. Perhaps more important, over the next several decades some of these sites are going to come to national attention because they are on the verge of disappearing. Many Civil War battlefields were pressed into federal ownership by veterans and their families when the land itself was threatened by alternative development. The idea was to preserve the battlefields as memorials to the sacrifices of the soldiers. Some of the "battlefields" of the labor movement are now coming up for grabs, and similar lobbying is likely to take place—to conserve them as memorials to the sacrifices of ordinary working-class Americans.

Johnstown, Pennsylvania, has already begun investing in developing itself as a labor heritage site. Not far away the Homestead works along the Monongahela River near Pittsburgh may be another moving in this direction. Here was one of the largest and most significant steelmaking complexes not just in the United States but in the world.[6] The complex exists no more. The blast furnaces and mills were closed gradually during the 1980s, and the site was recently cleared of almost every structure built there in a history stretching back over a hundred years (Figure 9-5). The fate of this site is still in debate. The Steel Industry Heritage Task Force is pushing to have the site declared a national historical landmark. Others are pushing to have the site commercially redeveloped to provide jobs for a badly depressed local economy. Of course, even if the site is conserved, little evidence remains of the steel complex itself or of the vibrant community that once thrived outside its gates. Regardless of the outcome, some sort of national recognition is likely to come to Homestead. If so, it will be a natural progression of commemoration. A memorial was raised at Homestead to the strike of 1892. Now, after a hundred years, it is likely to achieve national sanction.

Figure 9-5. The remains of the steel mills of Homestead, Pennsylvania, once one of the nation's largest steel plants and the site of the famous strike of 1892. Plans to commemorate the site are now in debate, but little is left to conserve.

There is other evidence that the labor movement is just now arriving at the point where its past can be marked in landscape. Recent reports before both the Senate and House of Representatives have called for studies of nationally significant places in American labor history as a first step toward having the National Park Service establish some new historical landmarks. As was noted in the House report:

> In 1935 the Historic Sites Act established the National Historic Landmarks program, which seeks to identify and commemorate sites of national significance. Since that time, 1,967 sites have been designated as National Historic Landmarks. The National Park Service has a "thematic framework" for National Historic Landmarks which outlines their interpretation of American History. Various categories in the framework relate to the history of work and working people, including "Agriculture," "Extractive or Mining Industries," "Manufacturing Organizations," "Construction and Housing," and "Labor Organizations." *The number of national historical landmarks listed under these categories is extremely small indicating that this important part of our history is not adequately represented or preserved* [emphasis added].[7]

The Senate report that appeared the next month indicates that only twelve properties relating to American labor history have been designated as National Historic Landmarks.[8] Even with support in the Senate and House, the elevation of labor sites to nationally sanctified landmarks will not happen immediately, if only by reason of cost. Few labor sites have been acquired by local and state governments, so the National Park Service would have to bear the entire price of acquiring, developing, and maintaining them from scratch. In time many of the sites of violent labor struggles probably will be canonized. Nonetheless it is unlikely that many will receive federal sanction until they have been developed further first by local and state governments, perhaps working in tandem with national labor organizations. One of the points of dissent raised in the House report was that labor unions are in a better financial position to begin the work of commemoration and that they should invest in these sites first before the federal government lends a hand.[9] This is an important point. By jumping from the local to national level, advocates of labor landmarks seem to be skipping a step that virtually all other nationally sanctified sites have had to take—the step in which a site's constituency is expanded through lobbying at the local, state, and regional level. National labor organizations, local and state historical agencies, and private individuals will have to share in this work before the labor movement gains the memorials it deserves in the American landscape.

America's Concentration Camps and Other Injustices

There are numerous other sites that, like the labor shrines, seem poised to receive national sanction but have not. The problem again is one of unresolved meaning. Among the most striking of these sites are those of the relocation centers used during World War II to confine Japanese American citizens.[10] In what is now recognized as one of the great miscarriages of American justice, all residents of Japanese extraction were stripped of their civil rights and evacuated from the West Coast under Executive Order 9066 of 19 February 1942. Without hearing or trial, these Japanese Americans were forced to give up their homes, businesses, and property, assembled in temporary detention centers, and then moved to one of ten relocation centers in inhospitable corners of Arkansas, Arizona, California, Colorado, Idaho, Utah, and Wyoming.[11] Altogether approximately 120,000 Japanese Americans were evacuated to these centers between March and November 1942. Some of the detainees were released and paroled before the end of the war, but the last of the camps did not close until 1946.

Even though internment was upheld as constitutional until 1944 by the Supreme Court, it was widely recognized at the time as an injustice stemming from wartime hysteria and racial prejudice. Defenders of the evacuation have always stressed its basis in military necessity, but no evidence was furnished during or after the war to justify the wholesale rescindment of civil rights. Laws of the time allowed for the prosecution of truly disloyal residents of all nationalities, citizen and alien alike; arrests under these laws began soon after the declaration of war. Even J. Edgar Hoover had argued against blanket detention of Japanese American citizens and residents as unwarranted and unnecessary since he and his FBI already had the situation under control. Others have dismissed the internment as being of little consequence because everyone suffers during wartime, and the Japanese Americans were asked only to do their part. This position ignores the irony and danger of a nation committed to—and willing to fight a world war for—freedom, liberty, and civil rights yet violating these values on the home front so readily and with so little reflection. Still fewer would be willing to see the obvious parallel between Executive Order 9066 and the Nuremberg Laws, through which the Nazis rescinded the citizenship and civil rights of Germany's Jews.

Here then is a lesson that should be inscribed on landscape as a way to remind us of the fragility of the civil rights taken for granted in American democracy, the lesson that the government can make terrible mistakes when it allows the hysteria of the many to violate the rights of the few. This sort of reflective self-criticism does not fit easily into traditions that celebrate America's past. There is no ready way to commemorate mistakes, to inscribe memorials with the message that a great injustice took place, one that should forever be remembered and never be repeated. In the absence of an interpretive scaffolding, the commemoration of such sites is problematic and can involve protracted negotiation. Nevertheless there is evidence that change is now taking place.

Until the 1970s little happened in terms of apology, redress, or the marking of the relocation centers. At the close of the war, both the federal government and the Japanese American internees seemed anxious to bring the entire episode to a rapid conclusion by simply closing the camps as quickly as possible. Many of the legal issues were swept under the carpet, and the relocation centers themselves were simply dismantled and abandoned. They had been built on large tracts of public land—parcels that could be requisitioned quickly in wartime—and the sites were returned to their original caretakers when closed, leaving scant evidence of their existence. The internees themselves did not all return to the West Coast. With their property gone and with little desire to face the same prejudices, many moved to different parts of the United States. Although the internees had lost their civil rights and over $400 million in property during the war, calls for an apology and restitution fell on deaf ears.[12]

It was only in July 1970 that the Japanese American Citizen League passed a resolution at its national convention to pursue redress as part of its work. Lobbying at the local and state levels began to succeed in at least marking some of the relocation center sites. The California Department of Parks and Recreation erected a historical landmark plaque at Manzanar in the Owens Valley in 1973 (Figure 9-6). The Topaz center in central Utah was designated in 1976 by the Utah American Bicentennial Commission (Figure 9-7). The markers formalized what some of the internees had been doing for years—making pilgrimages to the assembly camps and relocation centers to hold periodic reunions and to inscribe messages and tributes on the remaining fragments of the buildings. In November 1978 these chance gatherings were organized into the first Day of Remembrance, with 2,000 people traveling in caravan to Camp Harmony, the former assembly center in Puyallup, Washington. These events grew and spread to other camps and centers and helped to galvanize the Japanese American community into action. In her book *Righting a Wrong* Leslie Hatamiya does an excellent job of showing how these early efforts began to pay off.[13] President Ford finally rescinded Executive Order 9066 in February 1976, and over the next twelve years appeals were successful in righting the unjust court decisions of the 1940s. These and other actions led to passage of the Civil Liberties Act of 1988, which included both an apology and provision for compensation.

Hatamiya makes an important point when she notes the surprising success of these efforts. The Japanese American community is small and dispersed, and it was seeking compensation in a period of high federal budget deficits. The success of the efforts relied on effective and persuasive lobbying stressing the ethical and moral issues raised by the internment. In some respects the cause was helped by the fact that the redress movement coincided with two important national anniversaries—the bicentennials of independence and the Constitution. Much was gained by contrasting the treatment of the Japanese Americans with the values embodied in the Declaration of Independence and the Constitution. By rescinding Executive Order 9066 in 1976, President Ford made this connection explicit, as did the House of Representatives when it passed its version of the Civil Liberties Act on the bicentennial of the Constitution in September 1987.

How the relocation centers will develop in future years is an interesting question. Designation in the 1970s could lead to sanctification now that the Civil Liberties Act has been passed. It could be argued that some of these sites, such as Manzanar and Topaz, are already well on their way. At both sites the commemorative markers spell out exactly why the sites are significant: "May the injustices and humiliation suffered here as a result of hysteria, racism, and economic exploitation never emerge again," reads the inscription at Manzanar. At Topaz a longer inscription reads:

> In the never ending struggle for human dignity, there was enacted on this spot an event of historic significance for the nation and its people. During World War II this was the site of an internment camp, complete with barbed wire fence and armed sentries, for 8,000 of the 110,000 Americans of Japanese ancestry, who for no justifiable reason, were uprooted from their homes and interned by their own government. They were the victims of wartime hysteria, racial animosity, and a serious aberration of American jurisprudence. That a nation dedicated to the principle of individual freedom and justice through law would, under the stress of war, allow this to happen—and then recognized the injustice of this action, hastened to soften the effect of this action and make restitution. And that a whole generation of people, whose life and spirit was shattered and marred, would with courage and hope and perseverance, fight back to re-establish themselves in the American stream of life and were successful—are facts of sufficient historic importance to be remembered forever.

As early as 1974 a proposal was circulated within the California Department of Parks and Recreation to develop a portion of the Manzanar site into a state park.[14] No action was taken then, but the chance

Figure 9-6. The Manzanar Japanese American relocation center in California's Owens Valley between Lone Pine and Independence. The relocation centers were built quickly on public land at the start of the war and abandoned after they were closed near the end of the war. The traces of many of the camps can still be found, and many have been marked. The abandoned guard booth in the foreground carries a plaque placed by the California Department of Parks and Recreation, the Manzanar Committee, and the Japanese American Citizens League in 1973. Some of the camps served as rallying grounds for supporters of redress legislation.

of at least some of the centers being officially recognized and sanctified has increased significantly since 1988.

Even if the powerful messages already inscribed on the relocation centers are amplified in coming years, they will be exceptions to the rule that seems to consign such sites to invisibility; few other great miscarriages of American justice are marked in the landscape. Haymarket is perhaps one of the rare exceptions, but what of the cases of Dred Scott, Sacco and Vanzetti, the Scottsboro "Boys," or Leo Frank? One can search in vain for any sign that the famous Sacco and Vanzetti case began with a robbery in South Braintree, Massachusetts (Figure 9-8). It is not merely that Americans do not wish to be confronted by their mistakes—surely the case of the relocation centers offers evi-

Figure 9-7. The Topaz Mountain Japanese American relocation center just west of Delta, Utah. The memorial was
erected in 1976 as part of the national bicentennial. The
point stressed in commemorating this injustice is not just that
the internees suffered. More important is the fact that American citizens were imprisoned without charge, trial, or the establishment of guilt for any crime and that wartime hysteria
and racism were allowed to undermine constitutional freedoms and rights.

dence to the contrary. Perhaps it is more appropriate to view these cases
as wrongs that have been recognized and righted. Rectification—not
designation or sanctification—is the obvious outcome. Just like the sites
of accidental tragedies discussed in Chapter 5, the sites of these injustices are absolved of blame and returned to use.

In addition the meaning of many events remains difficult to resolve. These are isolated events, or perhaps incidents that simply do
not fit easily into any canon of interpretation. What, for example,
should be made of a small monument raised in Comfort, Texas, after
the Civil War (Figure 9-9), inscribed defiantly in German. Many of

Figure 9-8. The infamous Sacco and Vanzetti case began here in South Braintree, Massachusetts, on 15 April 1920. Nicola Sacco and Bartolomeo Vanzetti were charged with killing a guard and stealing the payroll of the Slater and Morrill Shoe Factory, then located along this road. Despite the attention focused on the trial and the executions of the defendants, the site of the robbery is all but invisible today.

the German settlers in this community had left Europe during the turmoil and war of the 1840s only to find themselves in a nation on the verge of war in the 1860s. The families tried to send their sons to Mexico to escape conscription into the Confederate Army, only to have them slaughtered shamefully by Southern troops on the Nueces River and at the Rio Grande.[15] The "Great Hanging" of alleged Union sympathizers at Gainesville, Texas, in 1862 was a dark episode of the period.[16] Perhaps such events will forever remain unmarked or will be marked only locally.

Sometimes it is possible to fit such events into a suitable frame, but only by a leap of interpretation. The site of the Andersonville Civil War prison camp will forever remain a scar on the landscape of Georgia (Figure 9-10). Andersonville was the most lethal of the hundreds of prisoner of war camps established by both South and North. Prisoners of both sides suffered and died in incredible numbers from malnutrition, disease, and exposure, but particularly so in the Southern camps toward the end of the war, as supplies of food and medicine

Figure 9-9. A memorial erected in 1866 in Comfort, Texas, to honor German-American settlers killed by Confederate troops on 10 August and 18 October 1862. These settlers had left Europe to escape the political turmoil in Germany only to find themselves trapped in the American Civil War just over a decade later. Fighting-age men of Comfort and the surrounding area sought to leave Texas via Mexico to join the Union army but were trapped and killed in the "Massacre of the Nueces River" and a later engagement on the Rio Grande.

Figure 9-10. Graves of Union soldiers at the National Cemetery in Andersonville, Georgia. Andersonville was the most notoriously lethal of all Civil War prisoner of war camps. After the war Union states erected major monuments to honor the almost 13,000 soldiers who died at the camp during the fourteen months of its existence in 1864–1865. The site, now administered by the National Park Service, is dedicated as a memorial to all Americans ever held as prisoners of war.

were exhausted. Andersonville was the worst of the Southern camps.[17] During the fourteen months it was open, it held more than 45,000 soldiers, almost 13,000 of whom died. The camp commandant was the only soldier executed for war crimes at the close of the conflict. Major memorials were erected by the Northern states in Andersonville's cemetery and prison compound around the turn of the century, when similar efforts were reaching a peak at the major Civil War battlefields. The monuments were dedicated to those who suffered and died at Andersonville but by their very presence were a slap in the face to the South. For many decades the site was held in this uneasy tension—to highlight the sacrifices of the Union prisoners was always to stress the brutality of the South. Andersonville held the potential to emerge as a very divisive symbol in a nation that was striving for re-unification on equal terms, North and South. I think this is partly why Andersonville was one of the last major Civil War sites to be passed to the National Park Service, which occurred only in 1971.

Like other Civil War sites, the Andersonville compound began to move toward national sanctification when it was purchased by Union veterans in 1890 and then passed to the War Department in 1910. Andersonville remained in limbo for the next sixty years, awaiting the sort of interpretive feat that would attenuate the camp's intensely dark symbolism of American brutality toward other Americans. This was accomplished in 1971 when Andersonville was transferred to the National Park Service and dedicated as a memorial to all Americans ever held as prisoners of war. As stated in the enabling legislation, the mission of the Andersonville park was to provide an understanding of the overall prisoner of war story of the Civil War, to help in interpreting the role of prisoner of war camps in history, to commemorate the sacrifice of Americans who lost their lives in such camps, and to preserve the monuments already in place at the camp. This was a remarkable transformation. In one broad interpretive stroke Andersonville's divisive meaning was overlaid with a patriotic message, one in harmony with the concerns of Vietnam-era America. Andersonville was dedicated at the very moment when the POW and MIA debate was being used as a rallying point to sustain support for the Vietnam War in the face of tremendous opposition and to slow negotiations with the North Vietnamese.[18] I do not think the message of Andersonville could have been so readily changed outside this context.

The Andersonville memorial is not the only site shaped, at least in part, by the Vietnam War. The 1960s and early 1970s were a period of tremendous turmoil resulting in some of the largest mass protests in American history. It is hard now to recapture the unsettling tenor of a time when every evening newscast and daily paper juxtaposed terrifying images of the war in Vietnam, campuses under siege, and cities on fire with stories reporting strident demands by students, African Americans, Native Americans, women, and gays. Even during the major periods of industrial and labor unrest, the United States had not experienced such mass domestic strife since the Civil War. Judging by the effects of this period on landscape, however, I maintain that the meaning of these events remains largely unresolved. Few of them have left a mark on landscape, and of those that have, the mark remains localized in the immediate context of a specific event.

Only one powerful monument—the Vietnam Veterans Memorial—has emerged from this period. Although I concede that this memorial is one of the most evocative shrines ever erected by Americans, it too speaks to the unresolved tensions of the Vietnam War era. Despite all that has been said and written about the memorial, one important fact remains—it occupies a site in Washington, D.C., unrelated to the violence and tragedy of the war itself. Debate over the meaning of the Vietnam War remains in such conflict that the only site on which compromise could be reached is one that was—in a sense—untouched by the war.[19] There are, of course, important symbolic meanings associated with the monument's site and design, and these were contentious issues during the memorial's construction. For instance, the original design would have listed the names of the war dead without any other inscription. A brief prologue and epilogue were eventually added to the list of names, but they steer clear of stating a cause for which the soldiers died. The fact remains that the Vietnam Veterans Memorial is very different from many of the monuments and shrines considered elsewhere in this book that were built at the site of violence. This is not to say that the memorial has not served an important cathartic, healing function for its hundreds of thousands of visitors or for the nation as a whole. My point is rather that the memorial represents an important compromise, one that leaves the ancillary meanings of the Vietnam War era unresolved. Not unlike that of the Pearl Harbor attack discussed in the previous chapter, the meaning of the Vietnam War is held in tension between competing inter-

Figure 9-11. The area at the epicenter of the massive bomb that destroyed the Army Mathematics Research Center at the University of Wisconsin in Madison in August 1970. The center was then headquartered in Sterling Hall, the building on the left. The bomb was a protest against university involvement in military research during the Vietnam War and killed one physics researcher. Sanctification or memorialization of the site was never considered. Instead the site was rectified.

pretations of the war's causes and consequences. So far Americans have been able to reach only a limited compromise in this one memorial. Other sites touched by the war and the antiwar movement remain in debate.

The treatment of other sites touched by the violence of the 1960s and 1970s has varied substantially from place to place. At the University of Wisconsin in Madison no memorial was ever considered to mark the site where a young research scientist was killed in August 1970 by a bomb intended to destroy the Army Mathematics Research Center.[20] The university quickly rectified the site so that hardly a trace of the damage remains (Figure 9-11). In New York City the townhouse destroyed by the famous Weatherman "bomb factory" explosion has been replaced by a home of gentrified appearance (Figure 9-12). Sites like Jackson State University in Jackson, Mississippi, and Kent State

Figure 9-12. The site of the Weatherman bomb factory on West 11th Street in New York City, which exploded in March 1970. The site is not designated and now has the appearance of a gentrified townhouse.

University in Kent, Ohio, are different. At both sites small markers were erected shortly after the killings of May 1970 (Figures 9-13 and 9-14). The Jackson State monument was funded by the class of 1971 and student government, whereas Kent State's first memorial was contributed by B'nai B'rith and the Hillel Foundation and replaced a few years later by one paid for by faculty. An abstract sculpture, *The Kent Four,* was also erected near the art school in the early 1970s, although in 1978 the administration rejected as inappropriate the donation of another sculpture, George Segal's *Abraham and Isaac.* But the Kent State efforts continued. Annual candlelight vigils have been held at the site of the Kent State Massacre since 1971 (Figure 9-15), and the university administration's plans to expand a gymnasium across the site in the late 1970s resulted in renewed campus unrest. Although proposals for a more substantial memorial surfaced early, none gained widespread support until the 1980s. The official May 4th Memorial was dedicated on 4 May 1990 (Figure 9-16). The slightly different outcomes at Jackson State and Kent State reflect, in part, the differing impact of the violence locally and nationally.

Figure 9-13. A small memorial at Kent State honoring the
students who died in the shootings of 4 May 1970. This was
sponsored by faculty and erected in 1975 at the site of the attack. This memorial replaced a metal plaque that was placed
at the site in 1971 by B'nai B'rith Hillel.

Figure 9-14. A memorial to the two victims of the shootings at Jackson State University on 14 May 1970. The memorial was erected within a year by the student government association and the class of 1971. The marker is sited where the riot began, just a short distance from where the students died.

Figure 9-15. The peace sign on the asphalt marks where a student died during the Kent State shootings. The faculty memorial is visible to the rear in the flowerbed around the tree. An all-night vigil is still observed each year on the anniversary of the shootings. Candles are lighted where the students fell. Some of the wax marks from the 1986 observance are visible in this photograph around the peace sign.

Figure 9-16. This memorial was erected at Kent State in time for the twentieth anniversary of the shootings. The memorial is close to the scene of the shootings, and its inscription reads: "Inquire. Learn. Reflect." Plans for the memorial met with considerable resistance, for some individuals saw it as marking a shameful event better left forgotten. Indeed the university administration sought to cover a portion of the shooting site with a gymnasium in the late 1970s but was stopped by additional student protests. Photograph by Gary Harwood, Kent State University.

Although the two shootings happened within ten days of each other, Kent State has always seemed to overshadow Jackson State—somewhat in the same way that the Alamo's heroic luster outshines Goliad's.[21] Certainly Kent State occurred first and claimed more victims. More important, Kent State presented the American public with far starker images of Americans killing other Americans over the Vietnam War than did Jackson State. In Kent, apart from role and uniform, little distinguished the young middle-class guardsmen on patrol from the young middle-class students on whom they fired. At Jackson State University, a historically African American campus, the message was perhaps not quite as clear because the killings involved differences of race as well. There had been other demonstrations at Jackson State during the 1960s inspired as much by the civil rights movement as by the Vietnam War. This was not the case at Kent State and may be one reason it became a far more potent emblem of antiwar sentiment, one that has come to be reflected in a larger landscape monument and sustained commemoration. It will be worth watching these sites in coming decades. As Americans continue to reassess and reinterpret the meaning of the 1960s and 1970s, it is likely that these few memorials will change as well. Their meaning remains perhaps as equivocal as Pearl Harbor's, and they could be used just as easily as political rallying points by both Right and Left.

There are a few other sites that will bear watching in coming years as Americans attempt to decide their meaning. Perhaps one of the most interesting will be the Stonewall Inn in New York City. The riot incited there in 1969 by a police raid on a gay bar had a galvanizing effect on the gay rights movement. Indeed, it is not unusual these days for the Stonewall Riot to be viewed as *the* starting point for contemporary gay activism, discounting all earlier efforts. In many ways the gay rights movement can be seen as developing a historical tradition, one largely rooted in Stonewall and the annual demonstrations and celebrations it inspired. Attempts have already been made to designate the Stonewall Inn as a historical site. These are likely to succeed, perhaps not immediately, given the current political climate, but soon. Already the street in front of the bar has been renamed and a statue has been erected across the street. Stonewall has become too important a rallying point to fade easily into oblivion.

Many contemporary social issues are just as capable of generating new rallying points and sacred places, some perhaps temporary but others permanent. The issue of abortion and the killings that this issue has already inspired have produced some small shrines, as have cases of child and spouse abuse. If tensions over these issues and others such as gun control, capital punishment, and illegal immigration ever reach a head, it may be over some expected tragedy that will leave a mark on landscape. These will be sites to watch in coming years.

CONFLICTING MEANING

Apart from sites of unresolved meaning, there are others where substantial barriers stand in the way of sanctification and tradition building. I am referring to sites subject to competing and contradictory interpretations that cannot easily be resolved. Conflict arises because it is nearly impossible to celebrate one side of the dispute without denigrating the other. This is the situation faced by almost all sites of the violence relating to Native American and African American history in the United States. It is the reason that so few of these events are marked in landscape, even though they are critically important to understanding the emergence of the nation economically, politically, and socially (Figure 9-17). To celebrate the heroism of Native Americans resisting the destruction of their cultures flies in the face of an entrenched frontier mythology that celebrates the perseverance of white settlers in driving these cultures to extinction. To mark the sites of African American resistance to slavery and racism is to call attention to glaring failures of the democratic institutions and egalitarian values in which the nation takes great pride.

America's white majority has had two centuries to develop and mark its myth of origins in the landscape. Its point of view has been etched into almost all historical memorials and markers at the local, state, regional, and national levels. If whites "won," the markers celebrate their heroism; if they "lost," tribute is paid to their pioneer spirit of fortitude and endurance. To question the noble sentiments expressed by these memorials is difficult. Just as problematic are attempts to sanctify sites that have not yet been marked by either side. The problem with these as yet unmarked sites—particularly sites of notorious lynchings, beatings, and shootings associated with African American history—is that they carry such shameful connotations. These sites would normally be obliterated or, at best, rectified. Sanctifying them as shrines can take tremendous effort both to overcome the

Figure 9-17. A roadside marker at Jamestown, Virginia, noting the arrival of the first African slaves in 1619—an unusually small sign for an institution that would touch millions of lives for centuries to come. Until quite recently it remained quite difficult to mark sites associated with African American history because they reflected so poorly on other, heroic interpretations of the national past.

power of shame and to position the sites in an interpretive scaffolding capable of challenging the one accepted by the ascendant majority.

Despite the barriers that will have to be overcome, the task of confronting these conflicting interpretations has already begun. Many sites significant to Native American and African American history are now in public debate.[22] Decades may have to pass before the meanings of these sites are resolved adequately, but at least the process of transformation has been set in motion. As the outlines of this debate take shape, they are assuming an unusual form. Rather than confront this legacy of racism and genocide head on, effective lobbying for change is taking place around the edges of these issues. Rather than try all at once to overturn two centuries of tradition building that has excluded blacks and Native Americans, stress is being placed instead on celebrating the heroism, fortitude, and sacrifice of the Native and African Americans themselves. This oblique means of confronting the past allows fresh and more encompassing interpretations to emerge that will make it easier—eventually—to question the central suppositions of the old myths.

What I mean is that few societies seem to have the moral courage needed to confront directly a legacy of genocide and racism unless they are forced to do so by unusual circumstances, as Germany was forced to confront the Holocaust by its defeat in World War II. In the absence of a powerful exogenous or endogenous force—a devastating defeat or the ascent of a new regime—change almost always occurs gradually. Finding neutral ground for reinterpretation is critical to this oblique approach. In the case of Native American and African American history, neutral ground for debate has emerged around three issues. First, lobbying to pay tribute to great black and Native American leaders and martyrs has the effect of enlarging the American pantheon to include heroes on both sides of these national conflicts. Second, efforts to re-mark some existing memorials have drawn attention to the heroism and sacrifice demonstrated by soldiers, warriors, and protesters on both sides of these conflicts. Third, the emergence of national memorials such as the Civil Rights Memorial in Montgomery, Alabama, and the Museum of the American Indian in New York City and Washington has allowed debate about controversial issues to take place at sites not directly tainted by specific acts of violence and tragedy.

All three techniques have attenuated conflict by downplaying divisive issues and instead stressing values and virtues held in common by parties on both sides of cultural conflicts. It may seem at first as if these efforts involve assimilating minority history into the framework of the dominant culture. Although this is true to a point, such conciliatory techniques are also an effective means of renegotiating meaning between competing groups. By canonizing heroes, drawing attention to common values, and creating shared monuments, the parties in conflict can be brought closer together, with each side offering certain concessions to the other. All three approaches have been employed to re-present African American and Native American history, but with differing results. It has proved difficult, for example, to canonize Native American leaders and martyrs and have them accepted as American heroes. Even the major shrine to Crazy Horse near Mount Rushmore has gained little attention, and no national historical sites have emerged for other Native American leaders. Expanding the pantheon of heroes has perhaps been more successfully employed in reinterpreting African American history. A number of black leaders are recognized by nationally sponsored monuments—George Washington Carver, Booker T. Washington, and Martin Luther King Jr.—and others are commemorated at the state and local levels.

I think the struggle to establish Martin Luther King's birthday as a national holiday was of more than symbolic significance. It helped to set a precedent that black Americans can be regarded as national heroes. This point has been reinforced in the American landscape in two places: King's tomb and assassination site. In the tradition of great edifices raised to presidents and national heroes, the Martin Luther King Jr. National Historical Site in Atlanta, the site of King's tomb, has emerged as perhaps the first true monument to the civil rights movement (Figure 9-18). King was the first black American to be commemorated in this fashion. After a long struggle the site of his assassination at the Lorraine Motel in Memphis has also been transformed into a civil rights educational center and memorial (see Figures 2-19 and 2-20).

Native Americans have had more success at recasting the meaning of the sites that have already been memorialized. Since many of the most significant battles and massacres are already marked—by whites—lobbying has been directed toward reinterpreting these existing memorials rather than toward the perhaps more difficult task of raising entirely new monuments. The sites of the Little Bighorn and Wounded Knee Massacres have received the most attention and have inspired a good deal of congressional debate.[23] The point of this debate is to reinterpret the sites to recognize the sacrifices made by Native Americans. The Little Bighorn Battlefield National Monument in southern Montana has always been an unusual site insofar as it is one of the few monuments in the United States to memorialize an unparalleled defeat by the armed forces, akin to the Alamo and Pearl Harbor.[24] The Little Bighorn battlefield never became the same sort of rallying point, however, except perhaps for the myths that emerged around George Armstrong Custer. The fact that it is marked at all owes much to the impulse to pay tribute to the fallen dead. In 1879, three years after the rout, a national cemetery was established on the battlefield to honor the soldiers Custer led to their deaths. When the

Figure 9-18. Martin Luther King Jr.'s tomb in Atlanta, Georgia. The tomb is the centerpiece of a large memorial complex adjacent to the church that King pastored. Nearby is King's childhood home, now a National Park Service site. This is the largest shrine to a black leader anywhere in America. Commemorating such heroes is in many ways easier than memorializing events relating to the brutalities of slavery and racial oppression and the struggles of the civil rights movement.

site became a monument in 1946, it was named for Custer. Just as the police and business community took charge of the Haymarket Riot site in Chicago after their "defeat" in 1886, the army and federal government assumed control of the maintenance—and meaning—of the Custer Battlefield National Monument. When the name of the battlefield was changed in 1992 to the Little Bighorn Battlefield National Monument, however, the issue of honoring fallen heroes arose again—only this time attention focused on the warriors who fought at the Little Bighorn, not the cavalry. As Ben Nighthorse Campbell noted at the ceremony, the point was "equal honor on the battlefield." [25]

New memorials have been authorized at both the Little Bighorn and Wounded Knee battlefields, the issue again being "equal honor." Gradually other sites of battles and massacres will no doubt be re-interpreted on the same terms. The point of conciliation will be that both Native Americans and whites died defending or fighting for their ways of life. This idea of equal honor is proving of little value in reinterpreting African American sites, perhaps because so little honor was involved in the beatings, lynchings, and massacres through which slavery and racism were enforced; the sense of honor was at best one-sided. Certainly African Americans can take pride in the sacrifices made willingly and unwillingly to end slavery and racism. The problem is that such events hold little honor for the white majority. The sites have been rectified and obliterated, and a tremendous one-sided effort would be required to retrieve them for designation or sanctification. Leaving aside individual acts of racial terrorism and murder, some of the largest events of racial conflict before the civil rights movement are particularly loathsome events that few would wish to revivify. The race riots that broke out in many cities after World War I represented the wholesale terrorization of urban African American populations by roving bands of whites. The Chicago riot of 1919 began with the slaying of a black youth who was said to have strayed through the water into a white swimming area along Lake Michigan (Figure 9-19).[26] When members of the African American community raised their voices in protest, the reply was almost a week of terror and random "drive-by" shootings by whites—and the black community was blamed for inciting the terror. The largest mutiny in army history occurred in Houston in 1917 when a battalion of black soldiers responded in violence to weeks of vicious bigotry on the part of Houston's citizens.[27] These were decorated and experienced troops who

Figure 9-19. Chicago's Lake Shore Drive now covers the beach where the race riot of 1919 began when white bathers killed an African American youth for straying toward a whites-only beach. Calls for justice by the local community resulted instead in bands of armed white vigilantes terrorizing the South Side and claiming additional African American lives. A shameful event such as this one is difficult to mark or commemorate.

had fought in the West and in the Spanish-American War. The army tended to station its African American soldiers away from cities, particularly in the South, to avoid racial tension. This one lapse of policy resulted in a riot that cost the lives of over a dozen Houston citizens and thirteen mutineers who were hung later in 1917 at Fort Sam Houston in San Antonio and buried in unmarked graves. The Rosewood, Florida, incident of 1923 gained attention only in the 1980s. In Rosewood an entire African American community was burned out of existence.[28] What of the killing of Black Panthers Fred Hampton and Mark Clark by Chicago police under the leadership of the FBI in December 1969?[29] The police claimed self-defense, but subsequent revelations proved the attack to have been cold-blooded assassination. There is little chance that the house will be converted into a shrine (Figure 9-20).

Such events are difficult to weave back into American history. Consequently, in the case of African American history, more progress

Figure 9-20. The house at 2337 West Monroe Street in Chicago, where Fred Hampton and Mark Clark were assassinated by police and FBI agents in the early hours of 4 December 1969. This is the sort of site that will always remain difficult to mark because of its strong negative connotations.

Figure 9-21. The Civil Rights Memorial, erected in 1989 on the grounds of the Southern Poverty Law Center in Montgomery, Alabama, close to the state capitol building. The upper face of the fountain is inscribed with the names of forty people who died between 1954 and 1968, caught in the violent resistance to the civil rights movement. The memorial is by Maya Y. Lin, the designer of the Vietnam Veterans Monument in Washington, D.C. Like the veterans monument, this one was erected on "neutral" ground unscarred by the violence of the events commemorated. Neutral sites can provide grounds for the debate of particularly controversial events and issues.

will be made by building memorials to individual heroes and martyrs such as King, Washington, Carver, Douglas, Tubman, or even Malcolm X. The one other option open to African Americans and Native Americans is to build memorials on neutral ground so that controversial issues can be addressed independently of the meaning of particular contested places. The Civil Rights Memorial in Montgomery, Alabama, and the Museum of the American Indian in New York City and Washington probably stem from this impulse. The memorial in Montgomery is on the grounds of the Southern Poverty Law Center, close to the state capitol (Figure 9-21). Although Montgomery played a role in the civil rights struggle, the site of the memorial was itself neither burnished by heroism nor tarnished by racism during this struggle.

Figure 9-22. The cemetery at Wounded Knee, South Dakota. The larger memorial is inscribed with the names of the warriors killed in the massacre of 1890 and stands atop their common grave. The two graves in the foreground are of men killed in the uprising of 1973. New public memorials are now envisioned for Wounded Knee and for the renamed Little Bighorn battlefield.

Certainly there is symbolic significance to the monument's position close to the Alabama capitol building, but the most important feature of the site is that it provides a neutral setting for a controversial subject. This project to commemorate the entire movement succeeded even though few sites directly associated with the violence of the 1950s and 1960s have ever been marked. The Museum of the American Indian may succeed in reshaping our view of the past for similar reasons. Controversy over this new museum is great, but less than if it had been established on contested ground such as Wounded Knee or the Little Bighorn battlefield (Figure 9-22). The interpretation of Native American cultures and legacies in the context of late-twentieth-century America is going to be a difficult task. Although New York City may at first be thought a fanciful arena for this debate, its distance from the West may make it an effective, neutral forum.

Of all the sites considered in this book, those relating to Native American and African American history may be the most important to monitor over the next several decades. In many ways Americans are just beginning to come to terms with the legacy of their colonial and frontier pasts. As attitudes change, so will the landscape. I expect many more significant Native American and African American sites to be canonized and sanctified in coming years as conflicting interpretations are resolved and as ways are found to accept the past in realistic terms rather than mythic ones. In the meantime other conflicts may arise to cast shadows over other places of meaning and memory (Figure 9-23).

THE SHADOW OF VIOLENCE

As these sites of unresolved and conflicting meaning change, they will offer insight into what geographers are fond of calling the social production of space and place. Nevertheless changes at each site are so closely bound to underlying social tensions and political competition over meaning that it is hardly possible to avoid asking one final question: how do these sites reflect attitudes toward violence and tragedy in society at large? The temptation is to look for a single, unequivocal answer, namely, that the sites somehow reflect either tolerance or intolerance of violence, acceptance or rejection, pride or shame. The answer is more involved, however, for attitudes are held in tension by a range of competing meanings. Tolerance, intolerance, pride, and shame are all mixed together. If anything, the message that comes through is one of deep ambivalence toward violence and tragedy— pride in some events, shame in others, and a desire all around not to confront the issue too directly. In exploring this ambivalence, it is useful to consider landscapes both visible and invisible because, in this context, sites that have been effaced are just as informative as those that have been sanctified.

There can be no doubt that Americans find virtue in many instances of violence and tragedy. This pride is visible in the hundreds of shrines that have been raised at the national, state, and local levels to battles, massacres, martyrs, uprisings, accidents, and disasters. The sanctification of such sites and events is a key to understanding the national past. In this light, violence and tragedy are viewed as fundamental to the settlement and conquest of the continent and the crea-

Figure 9-23. A follower of Louis Farrakhan in the plaza of the United States Holocaust Memorial Museum in Washington, D.C., protesting the memorial. His point is that the "black Holocaust" has never been acknowledged by the national government, even though it claimed more lives and lasted much longer. He is objecting to the attention devoted to the Holocaust museum when the victims of events far closer to home remain unmemorialized. Protests by other groups at the Holocaust museum are not unusual and underscore the conflicts of memory and meaning that can cast shadows over place.

tion of the nation. Writers such as Richard Slotkin make the point that the celebration, or at least acceptance, of such violence has much to do also with national character.[30] Given the tasks at hand, and the violence that followed inevitably from pushing the nation westward and destroying entire cultures, Americans had to cast violence in a positive light or be crushed by it. Violence should be seen in this way as a regenerative force, one capable of refining and forging a new society. Violence thus becomes tightly interwoven with the myth of the frontier and with the celebration of the national past.

This is not merely an issue of using a mythologized, romantic notion of violence to rationalize American history. Rallying around violence has been of practical value to Americans. As I argue in the previous chapter, celebrating hardship and accomplishment—of developing among citizens a common body of traditions and values— is critical to the emergence of a civil, secular society such as the United States. Civil religion is not merely an abstraction but a means by which people rally around common goals and a way to mobilize and focus social action when "enlightened self-interest" and the pursuit of life, liberty, and happiness lead in other directions. At issue is how American society has balanced communitarian goals against libertarian values—the ways in which individuals acting in their own self-interest have been persuaded occasionally to work together toward common community goals that are, at best, of limited or abstract self-interest. Positive appeals to patriotism and the conquest of new frontiers can be as effective as negative appeals to fear and insecurity. Americans have rallied around issues at both extremes and many in between.

The key point is that violence and tragedy have come to be intimately interwoven with both strategies. Whether people were reaching out along a new frontier or responding to perceived threats from within and without, violence has provided crucial rallying points throughout American history. Time and again cries such as "Remember the Alamo!" "Remember the Maine!" and "Remember Pearl Harbor!" have served to rally Americans around common goals. The inescapable fact is that violence has played a critical, instrumental role in helping Americans to build a sense of state and nation. Places that have been touched by this violence and tragedy are celebrated in the American landscape as visible emblems of identity and tradition.

Even though Americans have not hesitated to use violence and tragedy to reach common goals, they do not appear to be altogether comfortable with this embrace. Celebrated sites are relatively few and far between, and uncelebrated—invisible—sites predominate. These are the homicides, accidents, and other acts of violence and instances of tragedy that are never marked in the landscape. This widespread invisibility can be traced to a certain discomfort in accepting violence as a prominent characteristic of American life. This discomfort reflects deep ambivalence. On the one hand, Americans have been quick to rally around violence and weave it into a sense of the national past. On the other, they resist acknowledging its pervasiveness by seeking to ignore or explain it away. The basic problem is that, once accepted as a motive force in society, violence is difficult to bring under reign. In a nation created from revolution, it can be difficult to rationalize the suppression of protest and insurrection. In a society that came to rely on rugged individualism and violence to push back its frontiers, it is hard to reject interpersonal violence as a means now of resolving dispute. Much of what is visible and invisible in the American landscape today reflects this ambivalence.

Indeed invisibility may simply be an easy way to come to terms with this ambivalence. By tolerating so much violence and tragedy but ignoring its ramifications or treating it as so common as to be unremarkable, Americans do not have to confront their ambivalence directly. They can ascribe violence to other causes—criminal elements or foreign agitation—rather than view it as a fundamental part of American life. This dual tendency—to celebrate and to ignore—speaks to the highly equivocal nature of violence and tragedy in American society. Violence and tragedy are essential elements of the traditions and common values that bind Americans as a nation. Continued reliance on these traditions and values can just as easily fracture social bonds and divide society into winners and losers, victors and victims. This irony—that violence and tragedy can both unify and divide—rests like a shadow across the American dream.

Denial may be the easiest way of facing this paradox, but it is not necessarily the only way to come to terms with the creative and destructive power of violence in American life. Acceptance of the underlying paradox may be a more effective way of confronting violence and tragedy as they have played out in American society. Acknowledging the paradox makes it possible to confront the past more fairly and to look to the future more realistically. The clock cannot be turned back on the American past, nor should it be. The fact that Americans have resorted to violence and drawn strength from tragedy does not mean that these forces should be allowed to cast a shadow over all American history and over the future as well. At present the American landscape seems excessively shaped by the belief that acknowledging the darker side of violence will detract from society's positive and often heroic accomplishments. Sites that do not fit an idealized, patriotic vision are ignored or hidden in the landscape. Yet hiding these sites makes it more difficult to come to terms with the full range of events that have shaped American life. Perhaps the point is that many more events could and should be openly acknowledged in landscape as a step toward a more encompassing view of the roles played by violence and tragedy in American society. Casting light on many of the forgotten sites may be one way of pushing back the shadow that violence and tragedy have cast over the American past.

Notes

Chapter 1

1. Sidney Perley, *Where the Salem "Witches" Were Hanged* (Salem, Mass.: Essex Institute, 1921).

2. Paul Boyer and Stephen Nissenbaum, *Salem Possessed: The Social Origins of Witchcraft* (Cambridge, Mass.: Harvard University Press, 1974).

3. David Lowenthal, "Past Time, Present Place: Landscape and Memory," *Geographical Review* 65 (1975): 31.

4. Geoffrey H. Hartman, ed., *Holocaust Remembrance: The Shapes of Memory* (Oxford: Blackwell, 1994); Reinhard Rürup, ed., *Topographie des Terrors: Gestapo, SS und Reichssicherheitshauptamt auf dem "Prinz-Albrecht-Gelände"* (Topography of terror: The Gestapo, the SS, and the headquarters of the Office of State Security at the "Prinz-Albrecht-Terrain") (Berlin: Verlag Willmuth Arenhövel, 1987); James E. Young, *The Texture of Memory: Holocaust Memorials and Meaning* (New Haven, Conn.: Yale University Press, 1993). An excellent account of the controversy surrounding the creation of a Holocaust memorial in the United States is provided in Edward T. Linenthal, *Preserving Memory: The Struggle to Create America's Holocaust Museum* (New York: Viking, 1995).

5. Lowenthal, "Past Time, Present Place."

6. Philip B. Kunhardt Jr., *A New Birth of Freedom: Lincoln at Gettysburg* (Boston: Little, Brown, 1983), 214–215.

7. U.S. Congress, House, Committee on Interior and Insular Affairs, Subcommittee on National Parks and Public Lands, *Custer Battlefield National Monument Indian Memorial: Hearing before the Subcommittee on National Parks and Public Lands of the Committee on Interior and Insular Affairs on H.R. 4660 to Authorize the Establishment of a Memorial at Custer Battlefield National Monument to Honor the Indians Who Fought in the Battle of the Little Bighorn, and for Other Purposes,* 101st Cong., 2d sess., 4 September 1990 (serial no. 101-48); U.S. Congress, Senate, Select Committee on Indian Affairs, *Wounded Knee Memorial and Historic Site, Little Big Horn National Monument Battlefield: Hearing before the Select Committee on Indian Affairs to Establish Wounded Knee Memorial and Historic Site and Proposal to Establish Monument Commemorating Indian Participants of Little Big Horn and to Redesignate Name of Monument from Custer Battlefield to Little Big Horn National Monument Battlefield,* 101 Cong., 2d sess., 25 September 1990 (Senate hearing 101-1184); U.S. Congress, Senate, Select Committee on Indian Affairs, *Proposed Wounded Knee Park and Memorial: Hearing before the Select Committee on Indian Affairs to Establish a National Park and Memorial at Wounded Knee,* 102d Cong., 1st. sess., 30 April 1991, Pine Ridge Indian Reservation, South Dakota (Senate hearing 102-193). The name of the Custer Battlefield Na-

tional Monument was changed to the Little Big Horn National Monument on 11 November 1992.

8. For an assessment of how Lincoln's reputation changed, see Lloyd Lewis, *Myths after Lincoln* (New York: Harcourt, Brace, 1929); and especially Merrill D. Peterson, *Lincoln in American Memory* (New York: Oxford University Press, 1994).

9. John Bodnar, *Remaking America: Public Memory, Commemoration, and Patriotism in the Twentieth Century* (Princeton, N.J.: Princeton University Press, 1992), 13.

10. Kenneth E. Foote, "Stigmata of National Identity: Exploring the Cosmography of America's Civil Religion," in *Person, Place and Thing: Interpretive and Empirical Essays in Cultural Geography*, ed. Shue Tuck Wong, 379–402, *Geoscience and Man* 31 (Baton Rouge: Louisiana State University, Department of Geography and Anthropology, 1992).

11. Hiller B. Zobel, *The Boston Massacre* (New York: Norton, 1970), 180–205.

12. Franklin J. Moses, "Mob or Martyrs? Crispus Attucks and the Boston Massacre," *The Bostonian* 1 (1895): 640–650.

13. The Texas Revolution began in the fall of 1835 and was over by the spring of 1836. The siege of the Alamo began on 23 February 1836 and ended on 6 March 1836 with the loss of all troops fighting for the Texans. The massacre at Goliad occurred on 27 March 1836 following the surrender of Colonel James Fannin and his troops at the Coleto Creek battlefield on 19 March. Texas finally won its independence at the Battle of San Jacinto on 21 April 1836. The Alamo passed into public ownership between 1883 and 1905, gradually to be transformed into a shrine administered by the Daughters of the Republic of Texas. No marker was placed at the Goliad massacre site until 1936, although the Coleto Creek battlefield was marked in the 1880s. At San Jacinto the cemetery and battlefield were marked by veterans between 1883 and 1897. The park passed into public ownership in 1907, and markers were added in 1910. The major monument at San Jacinto was built between 1936 and 1939.

14. Eric Hobsbawm and Terence Ranger, *The Invention of Tradition* (Cambridge: Cambridge University Press, 1983).

15. George Allan, *The Importances of the Past: A Meditation on the Authority of Tradition* (Albany: State University of New York Press, 1986); Richard Johnson, Gregor McLennan, Bill Schwarz, and David Sutton, eds., *Making Histories: Studies in History-Writing and Politics* (London: Hutchinson, 1982); Michael Kammen, *Selvages and Biases: The Fabric of American Culture* (Ithaca, N.Y.: Cornell University Press, 1987); idem, *Mystic Chords of Memory: The Transformation of Tradition in American Culture* (New York: Knopf, 1991); Bernard Lewis, *History: Remembered, Recovered, Invented* (Princeton, N.J.: Princeton University Press, 1975); John Lukacs, *Historical Consciousness, or, the Remembered Past* (New York: Harper and Row, 1968).

16. Gaines Foster, *Ghosts of the Confederacy: Defeat, the Lost Cause, and the Emergence of the New South, 1865–1913* (New York: Oxford University Press, 1987).

17. Kenneth E. Foote, "To Remember and Forget: Archives, Memory, and Culture," *American Archivist* 53 (1990): 378–392. See also James Fentress and Chris Wickham, *Social Memory* (Oxford: Blackwell, 1992).

18. Kenneth E. Foote, "Object as Memory: The Material Foundations of Human Semiosis," *Semiotica* 69 (1988): 259–63; David Lowenthal, *The Past Is a Foreign Country* (New York: Cambridge University Press, 1985), 185–259.

Chapter 2

1. For information about Garfield's life, times, and assassination, see Robert G. Caldwell, *James A. Garfield: Party Chieftain* (New York: Dodd, Mead, 1931); Allan Peskin, *Garfield* (Kent, Ohio: Kent State University Press, 1978); and Theodore C. Smith, *The Life and Letters of James Abram Garfield* (New Haven, Conn.: Yale University Press, 1925).

2. Stewart M. Brooks, *Our Murdered Presidents: The Medical Story* (New York: Frederick Fell, 1966), 101–122; James W. Clarke, *American Assassins: The Darker Side of Politics* (Princeton, N.J.: Princeton University Press, 1982), 214.

3. Thomas Wolfe, *From Death to Morning* (New York: Scribner's, 1932), 121.

4. Peskin, *Garfield*, 612.

5. Eighty-sixth Congress, 1st session, H.R. 5148, March 2, 1959.

6. For information about McKinley and his assassination, see H. Wayne Morgan, *William McKinley and His America* (Syracuse, N.Y.: Syracuse University Press, 1963), 519.

7. "McKinley Park As a Memorial: Exposition Directors and Creditors Favor This Means of Perpetuating Memory of Assassinated President. Government Will Be Asked for Money," *Buffalo Courier*, 15 November 1901, Buffalo and Erie County Public Library, Clippings File, "The McKinley Monument, Buffalo, New York, 1901–," 1.

8. Almont Lindsey, *The Pullman Strike* (Chicago: University of Chicago Press, 1942), 359.

9. Emma Goldman, *Living My Life* (Garden City, N.Y.: Garden City, 1931), 306, 324–325.

10. "Working for Monument: Meeting of the Mayor's McKinley Memorial Committee Yesterday," *Buffalo News*, 6 February 1902, Buffalo and Erie County Public Library, Clippings File, "The McKinley Monument, Buffalo, New York, 1901–," 8.

11. Ibid., 8–9.

12. Ed Scanlan, "How the McKinley Monument Came to Be," *Buffalo News*, 11 October 1930, Buffalo and Erie County Public Library, Clippings File, "The McKinley Monument, Buffalo, New York, 1901–," 124–125.

13. "Niagara Square Site Is Opposed: Locating McKinley Monument There May Be Stopped by Injunction," *Buffalo Commercial*, 2 May 1904, Buffalo and Erie County Public Library, Clippings File, "The McKinley Monument, Buffalo, New York, 1901–," 55–56; "McKinley Monument Case Was Heard," *Buffalo Commercial*, 24 September 1904, 67 (all subsequent page numbers in this note refer to this clippings file); *Buffalo Express*, "Nothing to Stop It: Work on McKinley Monument Will Go on, Pending Further Legal Action," *Buffalo Express*, 24 August 1904, 66; "Is This a New Scheme to Delay Work on Monument?" *Buffalo Express*, 27 August 1904, 66; "City Wins First Bout: Justice Childs Flatly Refuses to Give Mr. Locke a Temporary Injunction Stopping the Proposed Improvement of Niagara Square," *Buffalo Express*, 28 August 1904, 65–66; "Busy Trying to Block the Monument to McKinley," *Buffalo Express*, 3 September 1904, 66; "Attorneys Seek Early Trial of McKinley Monument Case," *Buffalo Express*, 11 September 1904, 67; "Mr. Locke Continues His Fight against Monument," *Buffalo Express*, 12 October 1904, 68; "Monument Case Will Be Argued Out on Tuesday," *Buffalo Express*, 16 October 1904, 69; "City Wins Monu-

ment Case," *Buffalo Express*, 22 October 1904, 70; "Bradley Claim Preposterous," *Buffalo Express*, 6 November 1904, 70; *Buffalo News*, "Monument Site Complaint Is Dismissed," 8 October 1904, 68.

14. "Our Monument Is Unveiled," *Buffalo Express*, 6 September 1907, Buffalo and Erie County Public Library, Clippings File, "The McKinley Monument, Buffalo, New York, 1901–," 111–114.

15. Frank H. Severance, "The McKinley Marker," *Publications of the Buffalo Historical Society* 25 (1921): 356–361.

16. William Hanchett, *The Lincoln Murder Conspiracies* (Urbana: University of Illinois Press, 1983)

17. For an examination of the delay and controversy surrounding the creation of the Washington Monument in the District of Columbia, see Kirk Savage, "The Self-made Monument: George Washington and the Fight to Erect a National Memorial," in *Critical Issues in Public Art: Content, Context, and Controversy*, ed. Harriet F. Senie and Sally Webster, 5–32 (New York: HarperCollins, 1992).

18. Bess Martin, *The Tomb of Abraham Lincoln* (Springfield, Ill.: Lincoln Souvenir and Gift Shop, 1941).

19. Roy P. Basler, *The Lincoln Legend: A Study of Changing Conceptions* (Boston: Houghton Mifflin, 1935); Lloyd Lewis, *Myths after Lincoln* (New York: Harcourt, Brace, 1929); Merrill D. Peterson, *Lincoln in American Memory* (New York: Oxford University Press, 1994). The changing image of Lincoln is the subject of part 3 of Don E. Fehrenbacher's *Lincoln in Text and Context: Collected Essays* (Stanford, Calif.: Stanford University Press, 1987), 181–286. See also Waldo W. Braden, ed., *Building the Myth: Selected Speeches Memorializing Abraham Lincoln* (Urbana: University of Illinois Press, 1991); Gabor S. Boritt, ed., *The Historian's Lincoln: Pseudohistory, Psychohistory, and History* (Urbana: University of Illinois Press, 1988); and Harold Holzer, Gabor S. Boritt, and Mark E. Neely Jr., *The Lincoln Image: Abraham Lincoln and the Popular Print* (New York: Scribner's, 1984).

20. Edward F. Concklin, *The Lincoln Memorial in Washington* (Washington: Government Printing Office, 1927); William H. Taft, *Lincoln Memorial Commission Report*, 62d Congress, 3d session, Senate document 965 (Washington: Government Printing Office, 1913); F. Lauriston Bullard, *Lincoln in Marble and Bronze* (New Brunswick, N.J.: Rutgers University Press), 332–344.

21. Concklin, *The Lincoln Memorial*, 16.

22. The most thorough record of the transformation of Ford's Theatre is George J. Olszewski, *Restoration of Ford's Theatre* (Washington, D.C.: National Park Service, 1963). Other sources include Stanley W. McClure, *Ford's Theatre National Historic Site* (Washington, D.C.: U.S. Department of the Interior, National Park Service, 1984); and James T. Mathews, *The Lincoln Museum: A Memorial to the Human Qualities of Abraham Lincoln* (Washington, D.C.: National Park Service, 1935). For information about the Petersen House, see George J. Olszewski, *The House Where Lincoln Died* (Washington, D.C.: National Park Service, 1967); and Matthew Virta, "Archeology at the Petersen House: Unearthing an Alternative History" (Washington, D.C.: Regional Archeology Program, National Park Service, 1991).

23. Quoted in Olszewski, *Ford's Theatre*, 62.

24. James O. Hall, *John Wilkes Booth's Escape Route* (Clinton, Md.: Surratt Society, 1984); and Edward Steers Jr., *The Escape and Capture of John Wilkes Booth* (N.p: Marker Tours, 1985).

25. Conspiracy theories aside, the best source for details about Kennedy's trip to Texas and the events on the day of the assassination remains William Manchester, *The Death of a President: November 20–November 25, 1963* (New York: Harper and Row, 1967).

26. J. M. Shea Jr., "Memo from a Dallas Citizen," *Look Magazine*, 24 March 1964, p. 88.

27. "Sterrett Calls for Kennedy Memorial," *Dallas Times Herald*, 24 November 1963, p. A2.

28. "Two Leaders to Suggest Monument," *Dallas Morning News*, 1 December 1963, p. 1:9.

29. "Thornton Says He Wants No Reminder," *Dallas Morning News*, 4 December 1963, p. 4:5.

30. "Monuments," *Dallas Times Herald*, 5 December 1963.

31. Shea, "Memo from a Dallas Citizen."

32. William L. McDonald, *Dallas Rediscovered: A Photographic Chronicle of Urban Expansion 1870–1925* (Dallas: Dallas Historical Society, 1978), 15, 17.

33. "New Park Planned As JFK Memorial," *Dallas Times Herald*, 19 April 1964.

34. "Kennedy Memorial Dedicated in Plaza," *Dallas Times Herald*, 25 June 1970.

35. Candace Floyd, "Too Close for Comfort," *History News*, September 1985, pp. 9–14.

36. Attempted assassinations have occurred in Washington (Andrew Jackson, 1835), Milwaukee (former president and presidential candidate Theodore Roosevelt, 1912), Miami (President-elect Franklin D. Roosevelt, 1933), Washington (Harry S. Truman, 1950), Baltimore-Washington (Richard M. Nixon, 1974), Sacramento (Gerald R. Ford, 1975), San Francisco (Gerald R. Ford, 1975), and Washington (Ronald Reagan, 1981).

37. For information about Robert F. Kennedy's assassination, see Robert B. Kaiser, *"RFK Must Die!": A History of the Robert Kennedy Assassination and Its Aftermath* (New York: Dutton, 1970); Godfrey Jansen, *Why Robert Kennedy Was Killed* (New York: Third, 1970), 199–207; Jack Newfield, *Robert F. Kennedy: A Memoir* (New York: Berkeley, 1969), 319–337; Arthur M. Schlesinger Jr., *Robert Kennedy and His Times* (Boston: Houghton Mifflin, 1978), 903–916; and Francine Klagsbrun and David C. Whitney, eds., *Assassination: Robert F. Kennedy—1925–1968* (New York: Cowles Education, 1968).

38. For information about Huey Long's assassination, see Hermann B. Dautsch, *The Huey Long Murder Case* (Garden City, N.Y.: Doubleday, 1963); and David H. Zinman, *The Day Huey Long Was Shot* (New York: Ivan Obolensky, 1963).

39. For information about Martin Luther King Jr.'s assassination, see William B. Huie, *He Slew the Dreamer* (New York: Delacorte, 1970); and George McMillan, *The Making of an Assassin* (Boston: Little, Brown, 1976). One of the best accounts of the civil rights movement under King, although it does not touch on the assassination, is Taylor Branch, *Parting the Waters: America in the King Years, 1954–63* (New York: Simon and Schuster, 1988).

40. "Funds Sought for Rights Museum," *Memphis Commercial Appeal*, 12 February 1985, p. B1.

41. Benjamin Lawless, "A National Civil Rights Center: Technical Proposal," manuscript proposal submitted to the Lorraine Civil Rights Museum Foundation, 23 April 1986.

42. Center City Commission, *Strategic Plan 1985–2000: Report of the Long Range Planning Task Force* (Memphis: Center City Commission, 1985), 23, 34.

43. "A Question of Spirit," *Memphis Commercial Appeal*, 9 June 1986, p. A6.

44. Harry Miller quoted in Gregg Gordon, "Lorraine Museum Proposal Stirs Rumblings of Emotion: Race Seen As Theme of Public Reactions, *Memphis Commercial Appeal*, 6 May 1986, pp. A1, A18.

45. "A Question of Spirit."

Chapter 3

1. Duncan McDonald and Seymour Stedman, *The Cherry Mine Disaster* (Chicago: Campbell, 1910); F. P. Buck, *The Cherry Mine Disaster*, 3d ed. (Chicago: M. A. Donohue, 1910); Ernest P. Bicknell, *The Story of Cherry: Its Mine, its Disaster, the Relief of its People* (Washington, D.C.: American Red Cross, 1911).

2. James Mullenbach, *Report of the Cherry Relief Commission for the Period from June 15, 1910, to December 31, 1914* (Chicago: Cherry Relief Commission, 1915), 5; State of Illinois, Bureau of Labor, State Board of Commissioners of Labor, *Report on the Cherry Mine Disaster* (Springfield, Ill.: State Printers, 1910), 65–90.

3. Arthur F. McEvoy, *The Triangle Shirtwaist Factory Fire of 1911: Social Change, Industrial Accidents, and the Evolution of Common-Sense Causality*, American Bar Foundation Working Paper No. 9315 (Chicago: American Bar Foundation, 1994), 27.

4. Anton Demichelis, *Memorial of the Fiftieth Anniversary of the Cherry Mine Disaster, 1909—November 13—1959* (Peru, Ill.: St. Bede Abbey, 1959).

5. Lorine Z. Bright, *New London 1937: The New London School Explosion, 1937* (Wichita Falls, Tex.: Nortex, 1977).

6. R. L. Bunting quoted in Steve Blow, "New London School Blast Survivors Deal with Deaths of 300," *Dallas Morning News*, 1 March 1987, pp. 1A, 26A.

7. Mollie Ward quoted in ibid.

8. Bill Thompson quoted in ibid.

9. Other major school disasters have included fires at the Cleveland Rural Graded School in Camden, South Carolina, on 17 May 1923 and at the Babb Switch School in Hobart, Oklahoma, on Christmas Day 1924. The Our Lady of the Angels fire in Chicago in 1958 is discussed below.

10. Ron Stone, *Disaster at Texas City* (Fredericksburg, Tex.: Shearer, 1987).

11. The most accessible history of the disaster is David G. McCullough, *The Johnstown Flood: The Incredible Story behind One of the Most Devastating "Natural" Disasters America Has Ever Known* (New York: Simon and Schuster, 1968). Other sources include J. J. McLaurin, *The Story of Johnstown* (Harrisburg, Pa.: James M. Place, 1890); David J. Beale, *Through the Johnstown Flood: By a Survivor* (Philadelphia: Hubbard Brothers, 1890); George T. Ferris, *The Complete History of the Johnstown and Conemaugh Valley Flood* (New York: H. S. Goodspeed, 1889); James H. Walker, *The Johnstown Horror* (Chicago:

L. P. Miller, 1889); Richard O'Connor, *Johnstown: The Day the Dam Broke* (Philadelphia: Lippincott, 1957); Harold H. Strayer and Irving London, *A Photographic Story of the 1889 Johnstown Flood* (Johnstown, Pa.: Camera Shop, 1964); Nathan D. Shappee, *A History of Johnstown and the Great Flood of 1889: A Study of Disaster and Rehabilitation* (unpublished Ph.D. diss., University of Pittsburgh, 1940); and Paula Degen and Carl Degen, *The Johnstown Flood of 1889: The Tragedy of the Conemaugh* (Philadelphia: Eastern National Park and Monument Association, 1984).

12. Beverley Raphael, *When Disaster Strikes: How Individuals and Communities Cope with Catastrophe* (New York: Basic, 1986), 55–148.

13. Robert Pattison quoted in McCullough, *The Johnstown Flood*, 268.

14. Quoted in Degen and Degen, *The Johnstown Flood*, 64.

15. George Swank, *Johnstown Tribune*, 31 May 1890; quoted in Degen and Degen, *The Johnstown Flood*, 64.

16. John Wesley Powell, "The Lesson of Conemaugh," *North American Review* 149, no. 393 (Aug. 1889): 150–156; quotation on 156.

17. Robert W. Wells, *Fire at Peshtigo* (Englewood Cliffs, N.J.: Prentice-Hall, 1968).

18. Peter Pernin, "The Great Peshtigo Fire: An Eyewitness Account," *Wisconsin Magazine of History* 54 (1971): 246–272.

19. Thomas H. Baker, "Yellowjack: The Yellow Fever Epidemic of 1878 in Memphis, Tennessee," *Bulletin of the History of Medicine* 42 (3) (1968): 241–264; Gerald M. Capers Jr., *The Biography of a River Town, Memphis: Its Heroic Age* (New Orleans: author, 1966); J. M. Keating, *History of the City of Memphis and Shelby County, Tennessee,* 2 vols. (Syracuse, N.Y.: D. Mason, 1888), 1:656–684; S. Rulin Bruesch, "Yellow Fever in Tennessee in 1878" (in three parts), *Journal of the Tennessee Medical Association* 71 (Dec. 1978): 889–896, 72 (Feb. 1979): 91–104, 72 (Mar. 1979): 193–205.

20. Khaled J. Bloom, *The Mississippi Valley's Great Yellow Fever Epidemic of 1878* (Baton Rouge: Louisiana State University Press, 1993).

21. Capers, *Biography of a River Town*, 189.

22. Carolyn White, "Ground Is Broken in Park for Yellow Fever Memorial," *Memphis Commercial Appeal*, 20 December 1969.

23. For an account of the disaster, see Polk Laffoon IV, *Tornado* (New York: Harper and Row, 1975).

24. Harry C. Koenig, ed., *A History of the Parishes of the Archdiocese of Chicago* (Chicago: Archdiocese of Chicago, 1980), 672.

25. Michele McBride, *The Fire That Will Not Die.* (Palm Springs, Calif.: ETC, 1979), viii–x.

26. Ibid., ix.

27. Ibid.

Chapter 4

1. James M. Mayo, *War Memorials as Political Landscape* (New York: Praeger, 1988). A collection of essays on the debate over such memorials is contained in Harriet F. Senie and Sally Webster, eds., *Critical Issues in Public Art: Content, Context, and Con-*

troversy (New York: HarperCollins, 1992). A good overview of the history and design of such memorials in Western culture is provided by Alan Borg in *War Memorials: From Antiquity to the Present* (London: Cooper, 1991). The general issue of how Americans have commemorated war is the subject of G. Kurt Piehler's *Remembering War the American Way* (Washington, D.C.: Smithsonian Institution Press, 1995).

2. Edward T. Linenthal, *Sacred Ground: Americans and Their Battlefields* (Urbana: University of Illinois Press, 1991); and Emory M. Thomas, *Travels to Hallowed Ground: A Historian's Journey to the American Civil War* (Columbia: University of South Carolina Press, 1987).

3. For an overview of these events, see Robert Middlekauff, *The Glorious Cause: The American Revolution, 1763–1789* (New York: Oxford University Press, 1982).

4. Linenthal, *Sacred Ground*, 9–51; Richard Frothingham, *History of the Siege of Boston and of the Battles of Lexington, Concord, and Bunker Hill. Also, An Account of the Bunker Hill Monument*, 6th ed. (Boston: Little, Brown, 1903), 82–83.

5. Frothingham, *History of the Siege of Boston*, 344–345.

6. Fred N. Scott, ed., *Webster's Bunker Hill Oration and Washington's Farewell Address* (New York: Longmans, Green, 1905), 2.

7. Ibid., 4.

8. Ibid., 5.

9. Ibid., 32–33.

10. The Gettysburg battlefield monuments are well documented. Some of the major popular and scholarly sources include Wayne Craven, *The Sculptures at Gettysburg* (Philadelphia: Eastern National Park and Monument Association, 1982); William C. Davis, *Civil War Parks: The Story behind the Scenery* (Las Vegas, Nev.: KC, 1984); idem, *Gettysburg: The Story behind the Scenery* (Las Vegas, Nev.: KC, 1983); Kathleen R. Georg, comp., *The Location of the Monuments, Markers, and Tablets on Gettysburg Battlefield* (Philadelphia: Eastern National Park and Monument Association, 1982); David G. Martin, *Confederate Monuments at Gettysburg*, vol. 1 of *The Gettysburg Battle Monuments* (Hightstown, N.J.: Longstreet, 1986); and John M. Vanderslice, *Gettysburg: Then and Now* (Philadelphia: Lippincott, 1897; repr., Dayton, Ohio: Morningside Bookshop, 1983). The transformation of the battlefield is the subject of Linenthal, *Sacred Ground*, 87–126.

11. Philip B. Kunhardt Jr., *A New Birth of Freedom: Lincoln at Gettysburg* (Boston: Little, Brown, 1983), 214–215.

12. Garry Wills, *Lincoln at Gettysburg: The Words That Remade America* (New York: Simon and Schuster, 1992); Kunhardt, *New Birth of Freedom*; Frank L. Klement, *The Gettysburg Soldier's Cemetery and Lincoln's Address: Aspects and Angles* (Shippensburg, Pa.: White Mane, 1993).

13. Oscar Handlin, "The Civil War as Symbol and as Actuality," *Massachusetts Review* 3 (Autumn 1961): 135.

14. Ibid., 135.

15. Ibid., 143.

16. Lewis E. Beitler, ed., *Fiftieth Anniversary of the Battle of Gettysburg: Report of the Pennsylvania Commission* (Harrisburg, Pa.: Wm. Stanley Ray, State Printer, 1913), 6–7, 10, 15–16, 165–168, 173.

17. Henry L. Rice quoted in Paul Avrich, *The Haymarket Tragedy* (Princeton, N.J.: Princeton University Press, 1984), 264.

18. Julius S. Grinnell quoted in William J. Adelman, *Haymarket Revisited* (Chicago: Illinois Labor History Society, 1976), 21.

19. William Black quoted in Averich, *The Haymarket Tragedy*, 396–397.

20. Albert Currlin quoted in ibid., 397.

21. Lyman Trumball quoted in Adelman, *Haymarket Revisited*, 24.

22. Ernst Schmidt quoted in Avrich, *The Haymarket Tragedy*, 413–414.

23. Quoted in William J. Adelman, "The True Story behind the Haymarket Police Statue," in *Haymarket Scrapbook*, ed. Dave Roediger and Franklin Rosemont (Chicago: Charles H. Kerr, 1986), 167.

24. Ibid., 167–168.

Chapter 5

1. Marshall Everett, *The Great Chicago Theater Disaster* (Chicago: Publishers Union of America, 1904); Louis Guenzel, *Retrospects: "The Iroquois Theater Fire"* (Chicago: Champlin-Shealy, 1945); H. D. Northrop, *World's Greatest Calamities: The Baltimore Fire and Chicago Theater Horror* (N.p: D. Z. Howell, 1904); Julia Westerberg, "Looking Backward: The Iroquois Theatre Fire of 1903," *Chicago History* 7 (1978): 238–244.

2. "Iroquois Company Debts Clear: Discharge in Bankruptcy Ends Damage Suits," *Chicago Tribune*, 13 November 1906.

3. "Continue Fight on the Iroquois: Memorial Association Stirred by Granting of License for Reopening Ask Aid of the Public, Say Owners of Vaudeville House Count on Patrons' Morbid Curiosity," *Chicago Tribune*, 18 September 1904, p. 6.

4. "City Is Given Hospital: Institution Honoring 600 or More Dead in Iroquois Blaze Is Dedicated," *Chicago Daily News*, 30 December 1910.

5. "Iroquois Victims' Memory Honored: Lorado Taft's Tablet Unveiled at Hospital by Mrs. Maud M. Jackson to Be Recast in Bronze, Mayor Formally Accepts Institution and Memorial on Behalf of the City," *Chicago Tribune*, 31 December 1911.

6. George W. Hilton, *Eastland: Legacy of the Titanic* (Stanford, Calif.: Stanford University Press, 1995).

7. Ibid., 1–2.

8. Kelly Shaver, *The Attribution of Blame: Causality, Responsibility, and Blameworthiness* (New York: Springer-Verlag, 1985).

9. "Hartford Firemen Pay Tribute," *The White Tops*, July/August 1994, p. 48.

10. Arthur F. McEvoy, *The Triangle Shirtwaist Factory Fire of 1911: Social Change, Industrial Accidents, and the Evolution of Common-Sense Causality*, American Bar Foundation Working Paper no. 9315 (Chicago: American Bar Foundation, 1994), 27.

11. Harry Stainer, "Nineteen Deaths Here in '08 Sparked Fireworks Ban," *Cleveland Plain Dealer*, 4 July 1975, p. B1.

Chapter 6

1. Robert Gollmar, *Edward Gein: America's Most Bizarre Murderer* (Delavan, Wisc.: Chas. Hallberg, 1981).

2. Hannah Arendt addresses this issue in an indirect way in the epilogue to her book on Eichmann's trial: "They knew, of course, that it would have been comforting indeed to believe that Eichmann was a monster. . . . The trouble with Eichmann was precisely that so many were like him, and that the many were neither perverted nor sadistic, that they were, and still are, terribly and terrifyingly normal. From the viewpoint of our legal institutions and of our moral standards of judgment, this normality was much more terrifying than all the atrocities put together, for it implied . . . that this new type of criminal, who is in actual fact *hostis generis humani*, commits his crimes under circumstances that make it well-nigh impossible for him to know or to feel that he is doing wrong" (*Eichmann in Jerusalem: A Report on the Banality of Evil* [New York: Viking, 1963], 253). Arendt is, of course, commenting on the perpetrators of the Holocaust who claimed again and again that they were simply "following orders." Nevertheless the point applies more broadly to mass murders as well. Often the shock of such events lies partly in the recognition that "normal" members of a community can commit terrible and terrifying acts of violence.

3. Richard L. Johannesen, "The Functions of Silence: A Plea for Communication Research," *Western Speech* 38 (1974): 25–35; Bernard P. Dauenhauer, *Silence: The Phenomenon and Its Ontological Significance* (Bloomington: Indiana University Press, 1980).

4. Thomas J. Bruneau, "Communicative Silence: Forms and Functions," *The Journal of Communication* 23 (1973): 33.

5. Ibid., 37.

6. Ibid., 41. Peter Ehrenhaus's study of the Vietnam Veterans Memorial in Washington, D.C., is also interesting in this context. It stresses how the memorial itself frames silence to establish the context for the visitors' experience. See Peter Ehrenhaus, "Silence and Symbolic Expression," *Communication Monographs* 55 (1988): 41–57.

7. Clifford Linedecker, *The Man Who Killed Boys: A True Story of Mass Murder in a Chicago Suburb* (New York: St. Martin's, 1980); Terry Sullivan, *Killer Clown* (New York: Grosset and Dunlap, 1983).

8. Don Davis, *The Milwaukee Murders: Nightmare in Apartment 213: The True Story* (New York: St. Martin's, 1991).

9. Edward Keyes, *Cocoanut Grove* (New York: Atheneum, 1984).

10. Robert G. Lawson, *Beverly Hills: The Anatomy of a Nightclub Fire* (Athens: Ohio University Press, 1984).

11. Paul Boyer and Stephen Nissenbaum, *Salem Possessed: The Social Origins of Witchcraft* (Cambridge, Mass.: Harvard University Press, 1974).

12. Gordon Melton, *Magic, Witchcraft, and Paganism in America: A Bibliography* (New York: Garland, 1982), 89, 92.

13. David Lowenthal, "Past Time, Present Place: Landscape and Memory," *Geographical Review* 65 (1975): 31.

14. Charles W. Upham, *Salem Witchcraft, with an Account of Salem Village and a History of Opinions on Witchcraft and Kindred Subjects*, 2 vols. (New York: Ungar, 1959 [1867]), 2:376–382.

15. Sidney Perley, *Where the Salem "Witches" Were Hanged* (Salem, Mass.: Essex Institute, 1921).

16. Christopher Burns, "Morbid Silliness," letter to the editor, *Salem Evening News*, 6 June 1986, p. 4.

17. "Tercentenary Chance to Set Record Straight," *Salem Evening News*, 25 April 1986, p. 4.

18. John K. Gurwell, *Mass Murder in Houston* (Houston: Cordovan, 1974); Jack Olsen, *The Man with the Candy: The Story of the Houston Mass Murders* (New York: Simon and Schuster, 1974).

19. Herbert Asbury, *Gem of the Prairie: An Informal History of the Chicago Underworld* (New York: Knopf, 1940), 177–196; Robert L. Corbitt, *The Holmes Castle* (Chicago: Corbitt and Morrison, 1895); David Franke, *The Torture Doctor* (New York: Hawthorn, 1975); James D. Horan and Howard Swiggett, *The Pinkerton Story* (New York: Putnam's, 1951), 278–288; Richard Wilmer, *The Pinkertons: A Dectective Dynasty* (Boston: Little, Brown, 1931), 313–324; Sewell P. Wright, *Chicago Murders* (New York: Duell, Sloan and Pearce, 1945), 70–84; Harold Schechter, *Depraved: The Shocking True Story of America's First Serial Killer* (New York: Pocket, 1994).

20. Jack Altman and Marvin Ziporyn, *Born to Raise Hell: The Untold Story of Richard Speck* (New York: Grove, 1967); George Carpozi, *The Chicago Nurse Murders* (New York: Banner, 1967).

21. Afterward officials of the University of Texas were guarded in their response to the tragedy. Few public statements were made apart from those offering condolences to the survivors and the families of the victims. The tower was reopened without fanfare. Unfortunately over the years the tower also attracted suicides and was eventually closed to prevent further deaths. Efforts remain alive to reopen the tower employing appropriate safety measures, but none has yet succeeded.

22. Jack Levin and James Fox, *Mass Murder: America's Growing Menace* (New York: Plenum, 1985), 99–105. Other sources of information on mass murder include Ronald M. Holmes and James De Burger, *Serial Murder* (Newbury Park, Calif.: Sage, 1988); and Donald Lunde, *Murder and Madness* (New York: Norton, 1979).

23. Walter N. Burns, *The One-Way Ride: The Red Trail of Chicago Gangland from Prohibition to Jake Lingle* (Garden City, N.Y.: Doubleday, Doran, 1931), 258; Allen Churchill, *A Pictorial History of American Crime, 1849–1929* (New York: Holt, Rinehart and Winston, 1964), 173–176.

24. Merle Clayton, *Union Station Massacre: The Shootout That Started the FBI's War on Crime* (Indianapolis: Bobbs-Merrill, 1975).

25. Hal Higdon, *The Crime of the Century: The Leopold and Loeb Case* (New York: Putnam's, 1975), 9–10.

26. Vincent Bugliosi, *Helter Skelter: The True Story of the Manson Murders* (New York: Norton, 1974).

27. I have heard that this property has been redeveloped recently, but I have not been able to revisit the site to confirm these reports.

28. John Gold and Jacquelin Burgess, eds. *Valued Environments* (London: Allen and Unwin, 1982); Edmund C. Penning-Rowsell and David Lowenthal, eds., *Landscape Meaning and Values* (London: Allen and Unwin, 1986).

29. Edward Relph, *Place and Placelessness* (London: Pion, 1976); Yi-Fu Tuan, *Landscapes of Fear* (Minneapolis: University of Minnesota Press, 1979).

30. George W. Arndt, "Gein Humor," appendix to Gollmar, *Edward Gein*, 209–217; Antonin J. Obrdlik, "'Gallow's Humor'—a Sociological Phenomenon,"

American Journal of Sociology 47 (1942): 709–716; Sigmund Freud, *Jokes and Their Relation to the Unconscious* (New York: Penguin, 1976).

31. I am able to mention only a few examples in the text, but over the last thirty years mass murder has gained tremendous attention in literature and film. Truman Capote's *In Cold Blood: A True Account of Multiple Murder and Its Consequences* (New York: Random House, 1966) is attributed with beginning a wave of nonfiction bestsellers with mass murder or murder as their themes. *In Cold Blood* was, of course, produced as an award-winning film in 1967. Since 1966 various individuals have written books about virtually every major American mass murderer, perhaps in the hope of duplicating Capote's success. Norman Mailer has come closest to matching Capote with his account of the crimes of Gary Gilmore in *The Executioner's Song* (Boston: Little, Brown, 1979). Ted Bundy's crimes are the subject of Stephen G. Michaud and Hugh Aynesworth's *Only Living Witness* (New York: Simon and Schuster, 1983), Ann Rule's *Stranger beside Me* (New York: Norton, 1980), Richard W. Larsen's *Bundy: The Deliberate Stranger* (Englewood Cliffs, N.J.: Prentice-Hall, 1980), and Stephen Winn and David Merrill's *Ted Bundy: The Killer Next Door* (New York: Bantam, 1980). Juan Corona is the subject of Ed Cray's *Burden of Proof: The Case of Juan Corona* (New York: Macmillan Publishing, 1973), Tracy Kidder's *Juan Corona Murders: A Personal Journey* (Garden City, N.Y.: Doubleday, 1974), and Victor Vallasenor's *Jury: The People vs. Juan Corona* (Boston: Little, Brown, 1977). The Boston Strangler was covered by Gerold Frank in *The Boston Strangler* (New York: New American Library, 1966), and the Hillside Strangler case was the subject of Ted Schwarz's *Hillside Strangler: A Murderer's Mind* (Garden City, N.Y.: Doubleday, 1981). David Berkowitz is the subject of Lawrence D. Klausner's *Son of Sam* (New York: McGraw Hill, 1981) and David Abrahamson's *Confessions of Son of Sam* (New York: Columbia University Press, 1985). For a short period in the early 1970s, Santa Cruz, California, was victimized by three mass murderers almost simultaneously; see Donald Lunde and Jefferson Morgan, *The Die Song: A Journey into the Mind of a Mass Murderer* (New York: Norton, 1980).

32. Jan H. Brunvand, *The Vanishing Hitchhiker* (New York: Norton, 1981); idem, *The Choking Doberman* (New York: Norton, 1984); idem, *The Mexican Pet* (New York: Norton, 1986); idem, *Curses! Broiled Again!* (New York: Norton, 1986).

33. "Scene of Death Made a Bazaar!" *Chicago Herald Examiner* 24 July 1934, pp. 1, 5. For more information on the killing, see John Toland, *The Dillinger Days* (New York: Random House, 1963), 314–321.

34. Howard F. Stein, *Developmental Time, Cultural Space: Studies in Psychogeography* (Norman: University of Oklahoma Press, 1987); Howard F. Stein and William G. Neiderland, eds., *Maps from the Mind: Readings in Psychogeography* (Norman: University of Oklahoma Press, 1989). On the issue of shame in everyday life, see Agnes Heller, *The Power of Shame: A Rational Perspective* (London: Routledge and Kegan Paul, 1985); and Sissela Bok, *Secrets: On the Ethics of Concealment and Revelation* (New York: Pantheon, 1982).

Chapter 7

1. Eric Hobsbawm and Terence Ranger, eds., *The Invention of Tradition* (Cambridge: Cambridge University Press, 1983).

2. Richard Johnson, Gregor McLennan, Bill Schwarz, and David Sutton, eds., *Making Histories: Studies in History-Writing and Politics* (London: Hutchinson. 1982). This and related themes are the subject of George Allan, *The Importances of the Past: A Meditation on the Authority of Tradition* (Albany: State University of New York Press, 1986); Michael Kammen, *Mystic Chords of Memory: The Transformation of Tradition in American Culture* (New York: Knopf, 1991); idem, *Selvages and Biases: The Fabric of History in American Culture* (Ithaca, N.Y.: Cornell University Press, 1987); Bernard Lewis, *History: Remembered, Recovered, Invented* (Princeton, N.J.: Princeton University Press, 1975); Patricia N. Limerick, *The Legacy of Conquest: The Unbroken Past of the American West* (New York: Norton, 1987); and John Lukacs, *Historical Consciousness, or, The Remembered Past* (New York: Harper and Row, 1968).

3. For information about the Texas Revolution, see Stephen L. Hardin, *Texian Iliad: A Military History of the Texas Revolution, 1835–1836* (Austin: University of Texas Press, 1994); and T. R. Fehrenbach, *Lone Star: A History of Texas and the Texans* (New York: Collier, 1968), 152–233.

4. Fehrenbach, *Lone Star,* 166.

5. A more detailed study of the transformation of the Alamo is provided by Edward T. Linenthal in *Sacred Ground: Americans and Their Battlefields* (Urbana: University of Illinois Press, 1991), 53–86. See also Holly B. Brear, *Inherit the Alamo: Myth and Ritual at an American Shrine* (Austin: University of Texas Press, 1995).

6. Texas Centennial Commission, *Commemorating a Hundred Years of Texas History* (Austin: Texas Centennial Commission, 1936), 1.

7. Ibid.

8. Ibid., 26.

9. For more information about the rise of a wide range of Texas myths, see Robert F. O'Connor, ed., *Texas Myths* (College Station: Texas A&M University Press, 1986).

10. Harold Schoen, ed., *Monuments Erected by the State of Texas to Commemorate the Centenary of Texas Independence* (Austin: Commission of Control for Texas Centennial Celebrations, 1938).

11. Kathryn S. O'Connor, *The Presidio La Bahia del Espiritu Santo de Zuniga, 1721–1846,* 2d ed. (Victoria, Tex.: Armstrong, 1984).

12. Texas Centennial Commission, *Commemorating a Hundred Years,* 1.

13. "Marker to Honor African Americans," *Austin American-Statesman,* 16 July 1994, pp. B1, B4.

14. "Battle for Alamo Will Continue," *Austin American-Statesman,* 17 November 1994, p. B7.

15. "Osbourne Pays Dues for Alamo," *Austin American-Statesman,* 12 September 1992, p. B2.

16. Ross Miller, *American Apocalypse: The Great Fire and the Myth of Chicago* (Chicago: University of Chicago Press, 1990).

17. Alfred T. Andreas, *From 1857 until the Fire of 1871,* vol. 2 of *History of Chicago from the Earliest Period to the Present Time,* 2 vols. (Chicago: A. T. Andreas, 1885; repr., New York: Arno, 1975), 701–780.

18. Christine M. Rosen, *The Limits of Power: Great Fires and the Process of City Growth in America* (Cambridge: Cambridge University Press, 1986).

19. Alfred T. Andreas, *Ending with the Year 1857*, vol. 1 of *History of Chicago from the Earliest Period to the Present Time*, 2 vols. (Chicago: A. T. Andreas, 1885; repr., New York: Arno, 1975), 81–83; Juliette M. Kinzie, *Wau-Bun: The "Early Day" in the North-west* (Cincinnati: H. W. Derby, 1856; repr. Portage, Wisc.: National Society of Colonial Dames in Wisconsin, 1975), 157–193.

20. Pullman quoted in Chicago Historical Society, *Ceremonies at the Unveiling of the Bronze Memorial Group of the Chicago Massacre of 1812* (Chicago: Chicago Historical Society, 1893), 6.

21. For a general overview of Mormon history, see Leonard J. Arrington and Davis Bitton, *The Mormon Experience* (New York: Knopf, 1979); or Jan Shipps, *Mormonism: The Story of a New Religious Tradition* (Urbana: University of Illinois Press, 1985).

22. For a detailed account of events at Nauvoo, see Robert B. Flanders, *Nauvoo: Kingdom on the Mississippi* (Urbana: University of Illinois Press, 1965).

23. Davis Bitton and Leonard J. Arrington, *Mormons and Their Historians* (Salt Lake City: University of Utah Press, 1988), 7.

24. James B. Allen, "Since 1950: Creators and Creations of Mormon History," in *New Views of Mormon History: A Collection of Essays in Honor of Leonard J. Arrington*, ed. Davis Bitton and Maureen U. Beecher, 407–438 (Salt Lake City: University of Utah Press, 1987), 409.

25. For examples, see works such as Edward W. Tullidge, *Life of Brigham Young* (New York: n.p., 1876); idem, *Life of Joseph the Prophet* (New York: n.p., 1878); idem, *History of Salt Lake City and Its Founders* (N.p.: n.p., 1886); Orson F. Whitney, *History of Utah*, 4 vols. (N.p.: n.p., 1892–1904); Hubert H. Bancroft, *History of Utah, 1540–1886* (San Francisco: n.p., 1889). For discussions of the main currents of Mormon history, see Bitton and Arrington, *Mormons and Their Historians*.

26. A good sampling of contemporary Mormon history is found in Bitton and Beecher, *New Views of Mormon History*. See also Bitton and Arrington, *Mormons and Their Historians*, 126–169.

27. Stanley B. Kimball, *Historic Sites and Markers along the Mormon and Other Great Western Trails* (Urbana: University of Illinois Press, 1988).

28. Juanita Brooks, *The Mountain Meadows Massacre*, 2d ed. (Norman: University of Oklahoma Press, 1962), vii–viii. See also William Wise, *Massacre at Mountain Meadows: An American Legend and a Monumental Crime* (New York: Crowell, 1976).

Chapter 8

1. Portions of this argument are drawn with permission from my article "Stigmata of National Identity: Exploring the Cosmography of America's Civil Religion," in *Person, Place and Thing: Interpretive and Empirical Essays in Cultural Geography*, ed. Shue Tuck Wong, *Geoscience and Man* 31 (Baton Rouge: Louisiana State University, Department of Geography and Anthropology, 1992), 379–402.

2. Paul Wheatley, *The Pivot of the Four Quarters: A Preliminary Enquiry into the Origins and Character of the Ancient Chinese City* (Chicago: Aldine, 1971), 411–76.

3. Donald Horne, *The Great Museum: The Re-Presentation of History* (London: Pluto, 1984).

4. Lois A. Craig, *The Federal Presence: Architecture, Politics, and Symbols in U.S. Government Buildings* (Cambridge: MIT Press, 1978); Richard A. Etlin, ed., *Nationalism in the Visual Arts* (Washington, D.C.: National Gallery of Art, 1991); Bates Lowry, *Building a National Image: Architectural Drawings for the American Democracy, 1789–1912* (Washington, D.C.: National Building Museum, 1985); Ron Robin, *Enclaves of America: The Rhetoric of American Political Architecture Abroad, 1900–1965* (Princeton, N.J.: Princeton University Press, 1992); Lawrence J. Vale, *Architecture, Power, and National Identity* (New Haven, Conn.: Yale University Press, 1992). The symbolic expression of totalitarian and fascist ideologies in particular has attracted much attention, including Igor Golomstock, *Totalitarian Art in the Soviet Union, the Third Reich, Fascist Italy, and the People's Republic of China* (New York: HarperCollins, 1990); Hugh D. Hudson, *Blueprints and Blood: The Stalinization of Soviet Architecture, 1917–1937* (Princeton, N.J.: Princeton University Press, 1994); Barbara M. Lane, *Architecture and Politics in Germany, 1918–1945* (Cambridge, Mass.: Harvard University Press, 1968); Robert R. Taylor, *The Word in Stone: The Role of Architecture in the National Socialist Ideology* (Berkeley: University of California Press, 1974); and Nina Tumarkin, *Lenin Lives! The Lenin Cult in Soviet Russia* (Cambridge, Mass.: Harvard University Press, 1983).

5. Emile Durkheim, *The Division of Labor in Society*, trans. George Simpson (New York: Free Press, 1964), 70–132.

6. Peter Bondanella, *The Eternal City: Roman Images in the Modern World* (Chapel Hill: University of North Carolina Press, 1987); George Hersey, *The Lost Meaning of Classical Architecture: Speculations on Ornament from Vitruvius to Venturi* (Cambridge, Mass.: MIT Press, 1988); Otto von Simson, *The Gothic Cathedral: Origins of Gothic Architecture and the Medieval Concept of Order*, expanded ed. (Princeton, N.J.: Princeton University Press, 1988).

7. Catherine L. Albanese, *Sons of the Fathers: The Civil Religion of the American Revolution* (Philadelphia: Temple University Press, 1976); Robert N. Bellah, "Civil Religion in America," *Daedalus* 96 (1967): 1–19.

8. Albanese, *Sons of the Fathers*, 8.

9. Joseph Galloway, *Historical and Political Reflections on the Rise and Progress of the American Rebellion* (London: G. Wilkie, 1780), 45–46.

10. Albanese, *Sons of the Fathers*, 8.

11. George Allan, *The Importances of the Past: A Meditation on the Authority of Tradition* (Albany: State University of New York Press, 1986); Eric Hobsbawm and Terence Ranger, eds., *The Invention of Tradition* (Cambridge: Cambridge University Press, 1983); Richard Johnson, Gregor McLennan, Bill Schwarz, and David Sutton, eds., *Making Histories: Studies in History-Writing and Politics* (London: Hutchinson, 1982); Bernard Lewis, *History: Remembered, Recovered, Invented* (Princeton, N.J.: Princeton University Press, 1975).

12. John Lukacs, *Historical Consciousness, or, The Remembered Past* (New York: Harper and Row, 1968).

13. Michael Kammen, *Mystic Chords of Memory: The Transformation of Tradition in American Culture* (New York: Knopf, 1991); idem, *Selvages and Biases: The Fabric of History*

in *American Culture* (Ithaca, N.Y.: Cornell University Press, 1987); idem, *Meadows of Memory: Images of Time and Tradition in American Art and Culture* (Austin: University of Texas Press, 1992); Patricia N. Limerick, *The Legacy of Conquest: The Unbroken Past of the American West* (New York: Norton, 1987); Richard Slotkin, *Regeneration through Violence: The Mythology of the American Frontier, 1600–1860* (Middletown, Conn.: Wesleyan University Press, 1973); idem, *The Fatal Environment: The Myth of the Frontier in the Age of Industrialization, 1800–1890* (New York: Atheneum, 1985).

14. David Lowenthal, "Past Time, Present Place: Landscape and Memory," *The Geographical Review* 65 (1975): 1–36; idem, *The Past Is a Foreign Country* (New York: Cambridge University Press, 1985); Denis Cosgrove, *Social Formation and Symbolic Landscape* (London: Croom Helm, 1984); Denis Cosgrove and Stephen Daniels, eds., *The Iconography of Landscape: Essays on the Symbolic Representation, Design, and Use of Past Environments* (Cambridge: Cambridge University Press, 1988).

15. Hiller Zobel, *The Boston Massacre* (New York: Norton, 1970); Robert Middlekauff, *The Glorious Cause: The American Revolution, 1763–1789* (New York: Oxford University Press, 1982), 203–207.

16. Franklin J. Moses, "Mob or Martyrs? Crispus Attucks and the Boston Massacre," *The Bostonian* 1 (1895): 640–650.

17. Charlotte J. Fairbairn, "John Brown's Fort, 1848–1961," (unpublished report, Harpers Ferry National Historical Park, Harpers Ferry, W.Va., 1961).

18. Joseph Barry, *The Strange Story of Harper's Ferry* (Martinsburg, W.Va.: Thompson Brothers, 1903; repr., Shepherdstown, W.Va.: Woman's Club of Harpers Ferry District, 1984), 96–144.

19. William C. Davis, *Civil War Parks: The Story behind the Scenery* (Las Vegas, Nev.: KC, 1984); James M. Mayo, *War Memorials as Political Landscape* (New York: Praeger, 1988); Emory M. Thomas, *Travels to Hallowed Ground: A Historian's Journey to the American Civil War* (Columbia: University of South Carolina Press, 1987).

20. John M. Vanderslice, *Gettysburg: Then and Now* (Philadelphia: Lippincott, 1897; repr., Dayton, Ohio: Morningside Bookshop, 1983).

21. David G. Martin, *Confederate Monuments at Gettysburg*, vol. 1 of *The Gettysburg Battle Monuments* (Hightstown, N.J.: Longstreet House, 1986).

22. Horace M. Albright, *The Birth of the National Park Service: The Founding Years, 1913–1933* (Salt Lake City, Utah: Howe Brothers, 1985). For more information about the changing role of the park service in the New Deal, see Hal Rothman, *Preserving Different Pasts: The American National Monuments* (Urbana: University of Illinois Press, 1989), 162–86.

23. A detailed examination of the Pearl Harbor memorial is also provided by Edward T. Linenthal in *Sacred Ground: Americans and Their Battlefields* (Urbana: University of Illinois Press, 1991), 173–212.

24. Michael Slackman, *Remembering Pearl Harbor: The Story of the USS Arizona Memorial* (Honolulu, Hawaii: Arizona Memorial Museum Association, 1984), 44–86.

25. Ibid., 65–66.

26. Roger Dingman, "Reflections on Pearl Harbor Anniversaries Past," *Journal of American-East Asian Relations* 3 (Fall 1994): 279–293.

27. The coupling of Washington and Lincoln in the nation's vision of the past is

the subject of Marcus Cunliffe's book *The Doubled Images of Lincoln and Washington* (Gettysburg, Pa.: Gettysburg College, 1988).

28. Maurice Agulhon, *Marianne into Battle: Republican Imagery and Symbolism in France, 1789–1850*, trans. Janet Lloyd (Cambridge: Cambridge University Press, 1981); James A. Leith, *Space and Revolution: Projects for Monuments, Squares, and Public Buildings in France, 1789–1799* (Montreal: McGill-Queen's University Press, 1991); Pierre Nora, ed., *Les lieux de memoire* (The places of memory), 2 vols. (Paris: Gallimard, 1984); and Paul Trouillas, *Le complexe de Marianne* (The Marianne complex) (Paris: Editions du Seuil, 1988).

29. Carol M. Highsmith and Ted Landphair, *Forgotten No More: The Korean War Veterans Memorial Story* (Washington, D.C.: Chelsea, 1995).

30. For information about the debate and controversies surrounding the Holocaust Memorial Museum, see Edward T. Linenthal, *Preserving Memory: The Struggle to Create America's Holocaust Museum* (New York: Viking, 1995).

Chapter 9

1. Leo Stein, *The Triangle Fire* (Philadelphia: Lippincott, 1962).

2. John R. Commons, et al., *History of Labour in the United States*, 2 vols. (New York: Macmillan, 1918); Richard B. Morris, *Government and Labor in Early America* (New York: Columbia University Press, 1946); Philip Taft, *Organized Labor in American History* (New York: Harper and Row, 1964).

3. Chatland Parker, *The Herrin Massacre: The Trial, Evidence, Verdict* (N.p.: Chatland Parker, 1923; repr., Marion, Ill.: Williamson County Historical Society, 1979); Paul M. Angle, *Bloody Williamson* (Urbana: University of Illinois Press, 1992).

4. Craig Storti, *Incident at Bitter Creek: The Story of the Rock Springs Chinese Massacre* (Ames: Iowa State University Press, 1991).

5. Michael Goldfield, *The Decline of Organized Labor in the United States* (Chicago: University of Chicago Press, 1987).

6. Perhaps the best study of Homestead's rise and demise is William Serrin, *Homestead: The Glory and Tragedy of an American Steel Town* (New York: Vintage, 1993). The strike and its legacy are the subject of Richard M. Brown, "Violence in American History: The Homestead Ethic and 'No Duty to Retreat,'" in *The Rights of Memory: Essays on History, Science, and American Culture*, ed. Taylor Littleton, 97–124 (University: University of Alabama Press, 1986); Arthur G. Burgoyne, *Homestead* (Pittsburgh: Rawsthorne Engraving and Printing, 1893); Paul Krause, *The Battle for Homestead, 1880–1892: Politics, Culture, and Steel* (Pittsburgh: University of Pittsburgh Press, 1992); and Leon Wolff, *Lockout: The Story of the Homestead Strike of 1892* (New York: Harper and Row, 1965).

7. U.S. Congress, House of Representatives, *Authorizing a Study of Nationally Significant Places in American Labor History*, 102d Cong., 1st sess., 1991, report 102-50, 1–2.

8. U.S. Congress, Senate, *Authorizing a Study of Nationally Significant Places in American Labor History*, 102d Cong., 1st sess., 1991, report 102-91.

9. U.S. Congress, House of Representatives, *Authorizing a Study of Nationally Significant Places in American Labor History*, 101st Cong., 1st sess., 1989, report 101–295, 8. See also U.S. Congress, Senate, *Authorizing a Study of Nationally Significant Places in American Labor History*, 101st Cong., 2d sess., 1990, report 101–495.

10. Not all the evacuees were American citizens. Under the immigration laws of the time, first-generation Japanese-American immigrants (Issei) were not allowed citizenship. Their children and grandchildren born in the United States (Nisei and Sansei) were citizens automatically, however.

11. For more information about the internment, see Jeanne W. Houston and James D. Houston, *Farewell to Manzanar: A True Story of Japanese American Experience during and after the World War II Internment* (Boston: Houghton Mifflin, 1973); Roger Daniels, *Concentration Camps USA: Japanese Americans and World War II* (New York: Holt, Rinehart and Winston, 1972); and Deborah Gesensway and Mindy Roseman, *Beyond Words: Images from America's Concentration Camps* (Ithaca, N.Y.: Cornell University Press, 1987). For information about individual camps, see John Armor and Peter Wright, *Manzanar* (New York: Vintage, 1989); and Leonard J. Arrington, *The Price of Prejudice: The Japanese-American Relocation Center in Utah during World War II* (Logan: Utah State University Faculty Association, 1962). In addition to the relocation *centers*, ten relocation *camps* were established for enemy aliens interned during the war. These camps have gained less attention than have the centers, but some of these remained in operation until the 1950s.

12. It should be noted that Congress passed the Japanese American Evacuation Claims Act in 1948. The act was intended to cover the loss of property caused by the evacuation but was not completely effective. As Leslie T. Hatamiya notes: "This law did not allow claims for lost income or physical hardship and mental suffering, only loss of physical property. Because proof of loss was required and few internees had managed to gather and pack detailed records in the rush before departing for camp, only 26,568 claims totaling $148 million were filed under the act, with the government distributing a total of $37 million. Although there exist no accurate estimates of the extent of property loss, it seems reasonable to conclude that $37 million could not have fairly compensated the internees' economic losses." See Leslie T. Hatamiya, *Righting a Wrong: Japanese Americans and the Passage of the Civil Liberties Act of 1988* (Stanford, Calif.: Stanford University Press, 1993), 31.

13. See also Roger Daniels, Sandra C. Taylor, and Harry H. L. Kitano, ed., *From Relocation to Redress* (Salt Lake City: University of Utah Press, 1986).

14. California, Department of Parks and Recreation, *Manzanar Feasibility Study*, September 1974.

15. Guido E. Ransleben, *A Hundred Years of Comfort in Texas: A Centennial History* (San Antonio: Naylor, 1954), 79–126; R. H. Williams and John W. Sansom, *The Massacre on the Nueces River: The Story of a Civil War Tragedy* (Grand Prairie, Tex.: Frontier Times, n.d.); *Diamond Jubilee Souvenir Book of Comfort, Texas Commemorating Its 75th Anniversary, 18 August 1929* (San Antonio: Standard, 1929), 36–48.

16. Richard B. McCaslin, *Tainted Breeze: The Great Hanging at Gainesville, Texas 1862* (Baton Rouge: Louisiana State University Press, 1994).

17. N. P. Chipman, *The Tragedy of Andersonville: The Trial of Captain Henry Wirz, the*

Prison Keeper (San Francisco: N. P. Chipman, 1911); Ovid L. Futch, *History of Andersonville Prison* (Gainsville: University of Florida Press, 1968).

18. H. Bruce Franklin, *M.I.A. or Mythmaking in America* (Brooklyn, N.Y.: Lawrence Hill, 1992); Susan Katz Keating, *Prisoners of Hope: Exploiting the POW/MIA Myth in America* (New York: Random House, 1994).

19. Jan C. Scruggs and Joel L. Swerdlow, *To Heal a Nation: The Vietnam Veterans Memorial* (New York: Harper and Row, 1985). See also Charles L. Griswold, "The Vietnam Veterans Memorial and the Washington Mall: Philosophical Thoughts on Political Iconography," in *Critical Issues in Public Art: Content, Context, and Controversy*, ed. Harriet F. Senie and Sally Webster, 71–100 (New York: HarperCollins, 1992).

20. Tom Bates, *Rads: The 1970 Bombing of the Army Math Research Center at the University of Wisconsin and Its Aftermath* (New York: HarperCollins, 1992).

21. Among the sources concerned with the shootings and their aftermath are Scott L. Bills, ed., *Kent State/May 4: Echoes through a Decade* (Kent, Ohio: Kent State University Press, 1982); Thomas R. Hensley, *The Kent State Incident: Impact of Judicial Process on Public Attitudes* (Westport, Conn.: Greenwood, 1981); Thomas R. Hensley and Jerry M. Lewis, *Kent State and May 4th: A Social Science Perspective* (Dubuque, Iowa: Kendall/Hunt, 1978); James A. Michener, *Kent State: What Happened and Why* (New York: Random House, 1971); and Robert M. O'Neil, John P. Morris, and Raymond Mack, *No Heroes, No Villains: New Perspectives on Kent State and Jackson State* (San Francisco: Jossey-Bass, 1972). For information about both Kent State and Jackson State, see the special reports contained in President's Commission on Campus Unrest, *The Report of the President's Commission on Campus Unrest* (Washington, D.C.: Government Printing Office, 1970).

22. Debate at the national level concerning African-American monuments is reflected in U.S. Congress, House of Representatives, Committee on Interior and Insular Affairs, *Report Directing the Secretary of the Interior to Prepare a National Historic Landmark Theme Study on African American History*, 102d Cong., 1st sess., 6 May 1991, report 102-49, 1991; and U.S. Congress, Senate, Committee on Energy and Natural Resources, *Report on African American History Landmark Theme Study Act*, 102d Cong., 1st sess., 11 June 1991, report 102-90, 1991. Documents related to congressional debate on Native-American monuments are cited in note 23 to this chapter.

23. U.S. Congress, House of Representatives, Committee on Interior and Insular Affairs, Subcommittee on National Parks and Public Lands, *Custer Battlefield National Monument Indian Memorial: Hearing on H.R. 4660 to Authorize the Establishment of a Memorial at Custer Battlefield National Monument to Honor the Indians Who Fought in the Battle of the Little Bighorn, and for Other Purposes*, 101st Cong., 2d sess., 4 September 1990, serial no. 101-48, 1991; U.S. Congress, Senate, Select Committee on Indian Affairs, *Wounded Knee Memorial and Historic Site and Little Big Horn National Battlefield: Hearing to Establish Wounded Knee Memorial and Historic Site and Proposal to Establish Monument Commemorating Indian Participants of Little Big Horn and to Redesignate Name of Monument from Custer Battlefield to Little Big Horn National Monument Battlefield*, 101st. Cong., 2d sess., 25 September 1990, Senate hearing 101-1184, 1991; and U.S. Congress, Senate, Select Committee on Indian Affairs, *Proposed Wounded Knee Park and Memorial: Hearing to Establish a National Park and Memorial at Wounded Knee*, 102d Cong., 1st sess., 30 April 1991 at Pine Ridge Indian Reservation, South Dakota, Senate hearing 102-193, 1991.

24. An excellent study of the controversy over this site is provided by Edward T. Linenthal, *Sacred Ground: Americans and Their Battlefields* (Urbana: University of Illinois Press, 1991), 127–71.

25. Ben Nighthorse Campbell quoted in "Custer Redux," *The Economist*, 21 November 1992, p. 28. The issue of the memorial remains highly controversial to the point that the superintendent of the national monument, Gerard Baker, a Mandan Hidatsa Indian, has received death threats; see "Little Bighorn Again Inspires Passion," *New York Times*, 23 June 1996, p. 14.

26. Chicago Commission on Race Relations, *The Negro in Chicago: A Study of Race Relations and a Race Riot* (Chicago: University of Chicago Press, 1922; repr., New York: Arno and the *New York Times*, 1968), 1–52; Carl Sandburg, *The Chicago Race Riots, July 1919* (New York: Harcourt, Brace and Howe, 1919); William M. Tuttle Jr., *Race Riot: Chicago in the Red Summer of 1919* (New York: Atheneum, 1970); Lee E. Williams, *Anatomy of Four Race Riots: Racial Conflict in Knoxville, Elaine (Arkansas), Tulsa, and Chicago, 1919–1921* (Hattiesburg: University and College Press of Mississippi, 1972), 74–96.

27. Robert V. Haynes, *A Night of Violence: The Houston Riot of 1917* (Baton Rouge: Louisiana State University Press, 1976).

28. Michael D'Orso, *Like Judgment Day: The Ruin and Redemption of a Town Called Rosewood* (New York: Putnam's, 1996).

29. Roy Wilkins and Ramsey Clark, *Search and Destroy: A Report by the Commission of Inquiry into the Black Panthers and the Police* (New York: Metropolitan Applied Research Center, 1973).

30. Richard Slotkin, *Regeneration through Violence: The Mythology of the American Frontier, 1600–1860* (Middletown, Conn.: Wesleyan University Press, 1973).

Index

the Rebellion Monument, 51, 123,
129–130, *130*, 278; Lincoln's address
at, 8–10, 126–127; memorials, 51,
112, 113, 122–123, 127–133, *127*,
140, 142; National military cemetery,
8, *9*, 123–125, *124*, 133; reunions at,
51, 128, 131
Goldman, Emma, 36, 42–43
Goliad, Tex.: and battle of Coleto
Creek, 218–220, *222*, 225–226, 230;
massacre during Texas Revolution,
28–29, 217–220, 224–225, 232,
321; mass grave, 219–220, 225, *229;*
memorial, 86, *229*, 230. *See also* Fannin, James
Gonzales, Tex., 218, 226
Grand Army of the Republic (GAR),
128
Great Hanging (Gainesville, Tex.),
310
Great Railroad Strike of 1877, 134
grief and grieving, 15, 25, 59, 80–81,
92, 101, 148, 177, 179–180, 208,
213, 292; hidden, 106–110
graffiti, 25, 209. *See also* vandalism
Guiteau, Charles, 37–38

Handlin, Oscar, 128–129
Hampton, Fred, 328–329, *329*
Harpers Ferry, W.V.: John Brown's raid
and aftermath, 268, 273–279, *275,
276*, 283–284
Harrison, Carter, 134, 148
Harrison, William, 38
Hartford, Conn.: circus fire, 167
Hatamiya, Leslie, 306
Haymarket riot (Chicago), 7, 11, 12, 13,
133–140, *137, 139, 141*, 142, 296,
301–302, 308, 327
Hayes, Rutherford B., 38
Henley, Elmer, 191–192, *192*
heroes and heroism: veneration and
commemoration of, 2, 7–8, 10, 14,
18, 24–25, 29, 35–79, 100,
103–105, 109, 111–144, 212,

214–215, 218, 224, 236–237, 240,
243, 254, 263–264, 271, 277, 279,
284, 289, 291–294, 299, 322,
324–325, 327, 330, 336
Herrin, Ill.: strike and massacre, 301
hierarchy of sanctified sites, 284–287
Hill Cumorah (N.Y.), 248, 253, 256
Hilton, George, 153
Hindenburg, 20
Hitchcock, Alfred, 209
Hobsbawm, Eric, 29, 214
Holocaust, 324; black, 333; memorials
in Europe, 3, *4;* U.S. Holocaust
Memorial Museum, 291, *333*
Holmes, H. H., 192–193, *193*, 209
Homestead, Pa., 302, *303;* strike, 7, 134,
295, 301–302
homicide, 24, 167, 192, 200, 207, 335.
See also mass murder
Horne, Donald, 266
Houston, Sam, 218
Houston, Tex.: army mutiny, 327–328;
Corll mass murder, 182, 191–192,
192
Huberty, James, 197–198
humor. *See* jokes
hurricane, 169
Hyatt Regency (Kansas City), 161

I Don't Like Mondays, 209
Independence, Mo.: and early Mormon
Church, 250, 252–253, 256
Indianapolis, Ind.: war memorials and
civic space, 285
Indianola, Tex., 170
industrialists: and philanthropy, 242,
300; struggle with labor, 134, 138,
295, 296, 300
invention of tradition, 27, 29, 31, 100,
142, 214–215, 267–268, 293
Iroquois Theater fire (Chicago):
145–151, *146, 150*, 156–157, 161,
164, 167, 168
Iwo Jima memorial (Arlington, Va.),
291

Jackson State University (Jackson, Miss.): 1970 shooting and commemoration, 14, 315–316, *318*, 321

Jamestown, Va.: slavery marker, *323*

Japan: and Pearl Harbor, 268, 279; and relationships with U.S., 281–282

Japanese American(s), 14, 18, 284, 304–308; Manzanar relocation center (California), *34*, 35, 306–308, *308*; redress legislation, 34, 305–307; relocation centers, 35, 142–143, *143*, 304–308, *309;* Topaz relocation center (Utah), 142, 306–307, *309;* Tule Lake relocation center (Cal.), 142–143, *143*

Jefferson, Thomas, 36, 50

Johnson, Philip: design and explanation of Kennedy cenotaph, 64–65, *66*, *67*

Johnstown, Pa.: floods and commemoration, 16, *17*, 92–101, *95*, *97*, *100*, 105, 169; as labor heritage site, 302

jokes: about tragic events, 25, 209, 212

Kammen, Michael, 268

Kansas City, Mo.: and early Mormonism, 250; fireworks ban, 170; Hyatt Regency disaster, 161; Union Station massacre, 204

Kennedy, John F.: assassination and commemoration in Dallas, 15, 37–38, 58–59, 62–70, *66*, *67*, *68*, *69;* funeral and grave, 287, *288*, 289

Kennedy, Robert F.: assassination in Los Angeles, 70

Kent State University (Kent, Ohio): shooting of 1970 and commemoration, 14, 32, 142, 315–317, *317*, *319*, *320*, 321

Killeen, Tex., mass murder and aftermath, 166, 200, *203*, 291

King, Martin Luther, Jr.: assassination and its commemoration, 18, *19*, 31, 75–79, *76*, *77*, 143–144, 325; death of, and memorializing civil rights movements, 18, 31, 37, 75–79,

143–144, 330; national holiday, 325; tomb in Atlanta, 31, 76–77, 325, *326*

King Street, battle of. *See* Boston, massacre of 1770

Kirtland, Ohio: and early Mormon Church, 250, 256

Klement, Frank, 126

Knickerbocker Theater collapse, 164, *164*

Korean War, 291; veterans memorial in Washington, 291

Kunhardt, Philip, 126

LaBianca, Leno and Rosemary, 206–207

labor movement, 20, 31–32, 133–134, 140, 142, 295–304; monuments to, 11–14, 136–137, *137*, 284, 295–304, *296*, *297;* problems of interpretation, 140, 296–302. *See also* Haymarket riot

Ladd, Ill., 83

Lakeview School. *See* Collinwood, Ohio

landscape: and American national past, 265, 267, 277, 284, 292, 298, 299–300, 304–305, 308, 314; 321, 322, 334–335; and commemoration of heroes, 36; and conflicting meaning, 322–332; as cosmographical representation, 265–268, 278, 292; as evidence of attitudes toward violence, 5, 7, 33–35, 174, 294, 332–336; and hierarchy of shrines, 285–287; and debate about historical events and traditions, 7, 27–33, 100, 142, 215, 218, 226, 231, 236–237, 248, 253, 255, 257, 262, 264–265, 267–268, 277, 284, 292–293, 299, 302–303, 325, 332; as memory, 33; pathological, 180, 207–213; political, 111; and projection of sacral myth, 268, 276, 292; reliquary, 273, 278; remedial, 168–173; shaped or inscribed by tragedy and violence, 1, 3–4, 7–27, 110, 112, 113, 122–123, 133, 140,

commemoration, 15, 37–38, 42–47, *46, 48, 49,* 53, 58–59, 78

Meade, George G.: at Gettysburg, *112,* 125

Memorial Day massacre (Chicago), *299*

memory, 26, 35, 48, 51, 168, 206; of heroes and victims, 43–44, 47, 52, *73,* 83, 105, 122, 137, 151, 167, 188, 190, 240, 252; and landscape, 5, 8, 27–28, 31, 33, 35, 95, 174, 214, 293, 332, *333*

Memphis, Tenn.: and assassination of Martin Luther King Jr., 18, *19,* 31, 75–79, *76, 77;* Martyr's Park, 103, *104,* 105, 167; National Civil Rights Museum, 18, 75–79, *76, 77,* 143–144, 325; yellow fever epidemics, 103–105, 167. *See also* King, Martin Luther, Jr.

Mexican-American War, 231, 291

Mexico: and Texas revolution, 215–219, 230–232, 236

Miller, Harry, 78

Milwaukee, Wis.: Dahmer mass murder, 183; attempted presidential assassination, 70

Missing in action (MIA). *See* prisoners of war

Mississippi River and valley: *Sultana* disaster, 152; and yellow fever epidemics, 103

Missouri Compromise, 273

Montgomery, Ala.: civil rights memorial, 31, 324, 330, *330*

monument building: practice in, 284, 287, 289

Moran, "Bugs," 204

Mormons and Mormonism, 246–262; histories and historians, 254–255; marking of historical sites, 32, 215, 253, 255–258, *257, 258;* movement west to Utah and strength in, 32, 215, 247–248, 250, 252–256, 259, 262; and Joseph Smith, 246–252, 256–258; sense of history, 253–255, 264; trail, 257, 265, 285; and vio-

lence, 248–251, 259–261. *See also* Mountain Meadows massacre (Utah)

Mountain Meadows massacre (Utah), aftermath and memorial, 259–261, *262, 263*

movies: dealing with shameful events, 209

Murrah Federal Building bombing (Oklahoma City): 161–163, 166, 213, 292

murder. *See* homicide; mass murder

Museum of the American Indian (New York and Washington, D.C.), 324, 330–331

music: dealing with shameful events, 209

mutiny: by army in Houston, 327–328

myth(s) and mythmaking: frontier, 322, 334; and labor movement, 295; national, 231, 264, 266–267, 283, 285, 322, 332, 334; of origins, 215, 230, 266–268, 283, 285, 322; in respect to history and tradition, 29, 142, 214–215, 231, 267, 334; sacral, 268, 276, 292; and stigmatized places, 210, 212; surrounding George Custer, 325; surrounding Lincoln, 50–51; and Texas, 215, 219, 225, 226, 230, 231

nation (term): versus "union" in Gettysburg address, 126–127

National Civil Rights Museum (Memphis), 18, 75–79, *76, 77,* 143–144, 325

National Park Service: at Andersonville, 312–313, *312;* and Boston's Freedom Trail, 271, 273; and Bunker Hill, 20; creation of, and changing mission, 133, 273, 278, 284, 285, 292; and Ford's Theatre, *55,* 56, 58; at Fort Sumter, 277; at Gettysburg, 133; at Harpers Ferry, 273–274, 276–278; and Johnstown Flood National Memorial, 99; and Lowell, Mass., 298; and marking of labor movement, 298–299, 303–304; and Mormon

Trail, 257, 285; at Pearl Harbor, 282; and Petersen House, 56–58, *57;* and Texas shrines, 285

Native American(s): conflict with and suppression by whites, 6, 32, 35, 113, 284, 293, 314, 322; debate over commemoration, 14, 32, 322–325, 327, 330–332; and Fort Dearborn massacre, 237, 240, 242–243; monuments and memorials, 18, 32, 293, 322–325, 327, 330–332, *331;* and Mountain Meadows massacre, 259–261; Museum of the American Indian, 324, 330–331; rallying points, 32. *See also* genocide; Little Bighorn Battlefield; Wounded Knee massacre

natural disasters, 7, 15–16, 92, 169. *See also* floods; hurricane; tornado

Nauvoo, Ill.: and early Mormon Church, 250–252; restoration and visitors' centers, 253, 256–257, *257, 260*

Navy, U.S.: and Pearl Harbor memorial, 279–280, 282, *283*

negligence, 149, 155–156, 184, 186, 200

Nelson, Donald, 86

Nueces, Massacre of the, 309–310, *311*

New London, Tex., 16, 85–86, *87, 88,* 89, 107, 108, 164–165

New York City: B-25 crash into Empire State Building, 161; fire at film distribution center, 170; *General Slocum* disaster, 152, 163–164, 168; memorial to John Lennon, 15, *73,* 75; Stonewall Inn riot, 321; Triangle Shirtwaist factory fire, 82, 170, 295, *297;* urban fire, 169; Wall Street bombing, 24, 162–163, *163;* Weatherman Faction explosion, 315, *316;* World Trade Center bombing, 161–163

Nissenbaum, Stephen, 187–188

Northwest Airlines flight 255, 166

obliteration, 79, 163, 167, 184, 186, 195, 198, 204, 214, 219, 263, 293,

295, 327; compared to designation, 18, 20; compared to rectification, 23, 180, 191, *192, 196;* compared to sanctification, 179; definition and process, 7–8, 24–27; incompleteness of, 207–208, 213; of Mountain Meadows massacre site, 261; passive, 187, 190, 193; and shame, 109, 161, 174–181, 190–191, 200, 205, 322

Oklahoma City: bombing of Murrah Federal Building, 161–163, 166, 213, 292

Oldroyd, Osborn, 56, 242

Osbourne, Ozzy, 235

Oswald, Lee Harvey, 69, 212

Our Lady of the Angels School (Chicago): fire and aftermath, 16, 106–110, *107*

Owens Valley, California. *See* Manzanar

Palmyra, N.Y.: and early Mormon Church, 248

Pan-American Exposition: and McKinley assassination, 42, 44–45, 47, *48, 49,* 59

Parker, Bonnie. *See also* Bonnie and Clyde

Pearl Harbor: attack and commemoration, 268, 278–284, *283,* 314, 321, 325, 334

patriot(s) and patriotism, 27, 29, 31, 42, 114, 121–122, 214, 223–224, 231–232, 236, 265, 267–269, 284, 289, 291–292, 313, 334, 336

patriotic organizations, 52, 56, 119, 221

Pendleton Act, 38

Perley, Sidney, 189–190

Peshtigo, Wis.: forest fire and memorial, 101, *102,* 105, 167

Petersburg, Va., 128

Petersen House (Washington, D.C.), as Lincoln deathsite, 49, 53–54, 56, *57,* 58–59, 68, 242

Petersen, Anna and William, 54